The Arts in Higher Education

Series editor
Nancy Kindelan
Department of Theatre
Northeastern University
Boston, MA, USA

The role the arts play in higher education continues to be a complex and highly debated topic, especially in the changing climate of North American education. Showcasing cutting-edge research, this series illuminates and examines how engagement in the arts helps students meet the challenges and opportunities of a twenty-first century life and workplace by encompassing a wide range of issues from both scholars and practitioners in the arts. Key topics the series will cover include: evolving interdisciplinary degrees that include the arts; creating innovative experiential/pedagogical practices in the arts; discovering new methods of teaching and learning that involve the arts and technology; developing inventive narrative forms that explore social issues through play making; exploring non-traditional sites for creative art making; demystifying the process of creative thinking (especially as creativity relates to business practices, scientific thought, inter-active media, and entrepreneurial activities); engaging the arts in understanding global perspectives; and illustrating how the arts create life-long skills that help students manage a challenging job market. While the scope of the series is focused on the arts in higher education in North America, the series may also include scholarship that considers the total educational spectrum from K through 16, since there is now interest in creating a seamless educational progression from kindergarten through the baccalaureate degree.

More information about this series at
http://www.palgrave.com/gp/series/14452

Nancy H. Hensel
Editor

Exploring, Experiencing, and Envisioning Integration in US Arts Education

palgrave
macmillan

Editor
Nancy H. Hensel
The New American Colleges and University
Los Angeles, CA, USA

The Arts in Higher Education
ISBN 978-3-319-71050-1   ISBN 978-3-319-71051-8   (eBook)
https://doi.org/10.1007/978-3-319-71051-8

Library of Congress Control Number: 2017964612

Cover illustration: © D.T. Shane Cynewski, Design Corps, University of Maine at Farmington

Printed on acid-free paper

This Palgrave Macmillan imprint is published by Springer Nature
The registered company is Springer International Publishing AG
The registered company address is: Gewerbestrasse 11, 6330 Cham, Switzerland

CONTENTS

LIST OF CONTRIBUTORS

Jennifer Blackmer Ball State University, Muncie, IN, USA

Margaret Cullen Ohio Northern University, Ada, OH, USA

Don Cusic Belmont University, Nashville, TN, USA

Sean Dillon University of La Verne, La Verne, CA, USA

Linda Ferguson Valparaiso University, Independence, MO, USA

Placido Gomez University of La Verne, La Verne, CA, USA

Nancy H. Hensel New American Colleges and Universities, Laguna Woods, CA, USA

Heidi Laudien Manhattan College, Riverdale, NY, USA

Ilene Lieberman Widener University, Chester, PA, USA

Kevin S. Marshall University of La Verne, La Verne, CA, USA

Michael O'Connor University of La Verne, La Verne, CA, USA

Steven Pane University of Maine Farmington, Farmington, ME, USA

Mara Parker Widener University, Chester, PA, USA

Mary Rist St Edward's University, Austin, TX, USA

Beverly Schneller Belmont University, Nashville, TN, USA

Sarah J. Scott Wagner College, Staten Island, NY, USA

Samantha Siegel Wagner College, Staten Island, NY, USA

Traci Sooter Drury University, Springfield, MO, USA

Adriane Thompson-Bradshaw Ohio Northern University, Ada, OH, USA

Timothy J. Tomasik Valparaiso University, Valparaiso, IN, USA

Sasha West St. Edward's University, Austin, TX, USA

Gregory Young Montana State University, Bozeman, MY, USA

LIST OF FIGURES

CHAPTER 1

Introduction and Overview

Nancy H. Hensel

The arts and liberal arts are at a crossroad. Many people question the value of the arts and liberal arts in preparing young people for their future careers. "What kind of career is possible with a history or English literature degree?" skeptics ask. Such questions entered the political arena in 2013 when Patrick McCrory, newly elected Governor of North Carolina, said that he wanted to base funding for public universities on post-graduation employment rather than enrollment. Kentucky's governor, Matt Bevin, also made similar statements in 2015.[1] Rick Scott, Governor of Florida, suggested in 2015 that taxpayers should not foot the education bill for majors that have limited job prospects. Students, the governor said, should be encouraged to study science, technology, engineering, or math.[2] President Obama once commented, while promoting job training, that "a lot of young people no longer see the trades and skilled manufacturing as a viable career. But I promise you, folks can make a lot more, potentially, with skilled manufacturing or the trades than they might with an art history degree."[3] And the arts fare no better. When a funding crisis hits public elementary and secondary schools, the arts are typically the first programs to be eliminated. Colleges and universities may soon follow the same path.

N. H. Hensel (✉)
New American Colleges and Universities, Laguna Woods, CA, USA

© The Author(s) 2018
N. H. Hensel (ed.), *Exploring, Experiencing, and Envisioning Integration in US Arts Education*, The Arts in Higher Education,
https://doi.org/10.1007/978-3-319-71051-8_1

Declining enrollments in some arts and humanities courses mean administrators are under pressure to either close or down-size departments, causing institutions to review and rank programs for possible closure.[4] A recent Hechinger Report said that Indiana State University, as part of a comprehensive review, eliminated or suspended 48 academic programs.[5] Art and history were two of those programs. In a major budget cut, the University of Southern Maine cut French, despite a significant Franco-American population in the state, and combined its English, philosophy, and history departments. Music, art, and theater were also combined. The University of Alaska Anchorage has considered either reducing or eliminating music instruction.

Why is there so little economic, cultural, and intellectual value placed on the arts in the United States? Perhaps it is because they are so little understood. The perception is that graduates find it difficult, as President Obama suggested, to earn a good living with a liberal arts or arts degree. A recent report from the Association of American Colleges & Universities and the National Center for Higher Education Management Systems found, however, that liberal arts majors close the earnings gap by the time they reach the peak earnings ages, have low unemployment rates that decline over time, and disproportionately pursue social services professions.[6] The Strategic National Arts Alumni Project (SNAAP) reports that for "arts graduates 92% of those who wish to work currently are, with most (81%) finding employment soon after graduating. Two-thirds said their first job was a close match for the kind of work they wanted." The report quotes Steven Tepper, formerly associate director of the Curb Center at Vanderbilt University and senior SNAAP scholar, as saying, "Artistic careers exemplify new ways of working in the growing contingent economy, and the experiences of artists might increasingly become the norm for many 21st century workers."[7] He further indicates that arts alumni have high rates of self-employment.

We can demonstrate statistically that students majoring in the liberal arts and arts can develop successful and remunerative careers; however, questions still arise about what role the arts and liberal arts should play in a student's education. Do the liberal arts and arts contribute to professional development? What do students learn from the liberal arts and the arts that will prepare them for a future career? Do the liberal arts and arts benefit students regardless of the career path they choose?

The Impact of Arts on Intellectual Development

Cognitive psychologists have described the ways in which the arts contribute to the education of young children and to the intellectual development of college students and adults. Business leaders and scientists have also commented on the importance of the arts in the development of human potential and professional skills.[8]

The National Endowment for the Arts published a white paper in March 2011 that examined the role of the arts in early childhood, adolescent, and adult older development.[9] The report said that many studies had found that arts participation and arts education are associated with improved cognitive, social, and behavioral outcomes in individuals across their lifespan—in early childhood, in adolescence and young adulthood, and in later years.

Developmental psychologist Howard Gardner is noted for his early study, published in 1973, on the artistic development of young children as a means to understand their cognitive development.[10] He discovered that young children display significant aesthetic development as well as cognitive development and suggested that the concepts of making, perceiving, and feeling are of great importance in the developmental process. As Gardner continued to study cognitive development, he came to believe that there are different kinds of intelligences and different ways in which children learn. Initially, in 1983, he described five kinds of intelligence: linguistic, musical, logical-mathematical, bodily kinesthetic, and personal.[11] It should be noted that three of the five intelligences relate directly to the arts—writing, music, and dance. More recently Gardner has thought about what kind of minds or mindsets people will need in the future. In his 2008 book, *Five Minds for the Future*, Gardner talks about disciplined, synthesizing, creative, respectful, and ethical minds.[12] Gardner believes that it will be important for people to develop at least one way of thinking that relates to a specific discipline, skill, or profession.

Best-selling author Malcolm Gladwell has summarized the research concerning the amount of time it takes to become an expert in a given area, finding that it may take about 10,000 hours or ten years to achieve mastery.[13] Thus a disciplined mind is one that can focus on a subject over an extended period of time. Our information age requires that people take information from an increasingly wide array of sources, objectively evaluate the sources, and then synthesize the information. Gladwell himself is a master at synthesizing, bringing together large amounts of information and developing a new interpretation or describing a previously unobserved trend. Creativity builds on discipline and synthesis to develop new and innovative ideas, solutions, or products. Creativity is necessary to maintain a vibrant economy as well as a responsive and stimulating cultural environment. In a fast changing and increasingly diverse environment, a respectful mind is also critical. Many educators and business people talk about the need for cultural understanding and appreciation of the diversity of our society. Respect is the foundation for understanding the beliefs and mores of cultures different from our own. Howard Gardner suggests that the ethical mind asks, "What is my role as a responsible citizen, worker, or friend?" The person with an ethical mindset looks beyond self-interest and seeks to take into consideration the impact of his or her actions on others.

Daniel Pink, in 2005, conceptualized the successful mind of the future somewhat differently than does Gardner. In *A Whole New Mind* he suggests that in the future the right brain that is associated with emotion, creativity, and intuitiveness will be increasingly more important.[14] He further suggests that we are moving from an information age to a conceptual age. Many professionals, including lawyers, engineers, and accountants, rely on specific knowledge, while artists, counselors, and inventors rely on creativity and sensitivity to be successful. We need both ways of thinking for a healthy society and economy. We are tilting toward, if not relying more on, conceptual approaches to engendering progress, at least recognizing the need for both conceptual thinking and specific knowledge. The new economy that Pink envisions relies on six senses or attributes: design, story, symphony, empathy, play, and meaning. As the American economy has become more able to meet basic human needs, Pink suggests we will think more about design rather than basic functioning.

The emphasis that Steve Jobs placed on all aspects of design, from the computer or phone to its packaging, is a good example of the significance of design. "Style" sections of many newspapers often showcase functional items such as toasters or mixing bowls with designs that go beyond mere functionality. In the conceptual age, stories will become increasingly important. While we have a great deal of information that can be used to try to persuade people to adopt our ideas, we also need stories that help people understand problems and their possible solutions. Stories appeal to the emotions and can assist people in remembering the key points of a new approach. Knowledge has become increasingly specialized; solving our most pressing problems requires collaboration across disciplines. The ability to synthesize and also to collaborate are essential skills, and that is what Pink calls symphony. Problems cannot be solved by only looking at data; problem solving also requires the ability to see different perspectives and to understand feelings. Pink calls this ability empathy. Children and adults develop empathy, problem-solving skills, and creativity through play. Innovators in Silicon Valley understand the role of play in developing new technologies, and play is also important in other areas of innovation. Finally, Pink suggests that as people have attained material comforts, many now seek a meaningful life through purposeful work, volunteer activity, or spiritual fulfillment. It is important to acknowledge the impact the arts play in intellectual and social development as we think about how undergraduate education contributes to social, cultural, and economic development.

Psychologists, educators, and business leaders continue to think about the kinds of minds that will be needed for the future. A recent report by the Brookings Institute, *Skills for a Changing World: Advancing Quality Learning for Vibrant Societies*, suggests that mastering content knowledge will no longer ensure professional success.[15] The report suggests that in addition to the academic skills of literacy, numeracy and sciences the skills of teamwork, critical thinking, communication, persistence, and creativity are also needed.[16] Geoff Colvin, senior editor-at-large for *Fortune* and author of *Humans are Underrated: What High Achievers Know that Brilliant Machines Never Will*, suggests that the skills of empathy, collaborating, and creating are essential skills for the future.[17] Data literacy, technology literacy, and human literacy are the new literacies that Joseph E. Aoun, President of Northeastern University, sees as important for jobs of the future.[18] Aoun elaborates on cognitive capacities to include systems thinking, entrepreneurship, cultural agility, and critical thinking. Systems thinking is the ability to look at things in a holistic, connected, and integrated way. Entrepreneurship involves a creative mindset that is manifested though economic activities. Cultural agility is a necessary skill for living and working in a complex and diverse world. The work of these thought leaders provides additional support for the kinds of skills needed for the future that can be developed through engagement in the arts.

The Impact of Arts and Liberal Arts on Professional Development

In Defense of Liberal Education, Fareed Zakaria, editor-at-large of *Time* magazine and host of a CNN Sunday news program, discusses how the liberal arts teach students to write clearly and to think analytically and creatively. Zakaria's views of what contributes to professional development closely match the list of "Top Ten Things Employers Look for in New

College Graduates" that resulted from AAC&U's collaborative survey with Peter D. Hart Research Associates.[19] The Hart survey found that employers want college graduates who can work in teams, write and speak well, apply creativity and innovation in solving problems, apply knowledge and skills to new settings, think clearly about complex problems, and analyze a problem to develop workable solutions. These are some of the same skills that Louis E. Catron, the late professor of theater at William and Mary College, described when he wrote about the benefits of a theater major. He describes a discussion with business leaders in which a CEO told the group that "she liked to hire theater majors because they are energetic, enthusiastic, and able to work under pressure."[20]

Students who major in theater and the other arts combine the broad intellectual aspects of a liberal arts degree with hands-on learning. The theater student, for example, needs to study history to understand the context of a particular play. Costume designers need to know what people were wearing during the period of the play and what their clothes might indicate about the character's status. Set designers need to know about the architecture and interior design of the period. Theater and other arts majors and professionals involve many disciplines in their work. Music and theater majors learn to work collaboratively and to value the contribution of each individual to the completed project. Successful managers in any field understand the importance of collaboration and recognition of individual contributions. Students who study any of the arts also develop the ability to work independently. Actors need to memorize and practice their lines. Visual artists and writers typically work on their own without supervision, an important ability in any profession. All artists learn to deal with disappointment and how to bounce back when a short story is not published or a role goes to someone else. Artists also understand that every performance, painting, or story carries with it the risk of rejection. Understanding the possibility of rejection means that arts students must have a high level of commitment and motivation to the project. Employers will value the traits of commitment and motivation. In an age of constant distraction, employers will also value the ability of actors, who must imagine themselves to be someone else, to maintain the intense concentration and focus needed to stay in character. Concentration and focus are valuable skills in any career.

The workplace of the future and the new economy will need people with the mindsets described earlier by Pink and Gardner. A competitive global economy needs people who are intellectually nimble, can integrate ideas from more than one discipline, are attuned to seeing patterns and relationships, use these skills to make meaning of what they know, and are able to apply their knowledge to solve the challenges of the day. The arts develop these skills beginning in early childhood education and extending through professional development.

THE IMPACT OF THE ARTS ON SOCIETY

What would our society be like without the arts? It is difficult to imagine that because the arts influence our lives in so many ways. Music is, perhaps, the art that has played the most prominent role in our daily lives and has had the most powerful impact on our society. Nations use song to celebrate pride in their country. Weddings, funerals, graduations, and church services use music to celebrate the occasions and inspire the attendees. Even our national pastime, baseball, includes music as a traditional part of the game when fans sing "Take Me Out To the Ballgame" at the seventh inning stretch. Music brings people together to share joy, provide comfort, and challenge the inequities in society. "Amazing Grace," written in 1773 by a former English slave trader, has become a powerful African American spiritual calling for forgiveness and reconciliation. When Barack Obama sang "Amazing Grace" during the eulogy for Rev. Clementa Pinckney, who was killed in a shooting at a Charleston church, he provided comfort and hope not only for the congregation at the memorial service but also for many across the country.

American history can be documented through song starting with "Yankee Doodle" during the Revolutionary War. "Over There" was an inspirational World War I song, and Irving Berlin's "God Bless America" celebrated pride in our country during World War II (WWII). "I'll Be Seeing You" and "I'll Be Home for Christmas," also WWII songs, suggested hope that soldiers would return home from the war. Both are still popular today. War protesters used music to convey their message and to rally people to the cause. Pete Seeger's "Where Have All the Flowers Gone" and Bob Dylan's "With God on Our Side" were part of the protests against the Vietnam War, and John Lennon urged the world to "Give Peace a Chance" in his 1969 song.

Slave songs like "Wade in the Water" had hidden codes to guide slaves to freedom. Other songs helped them endure hard work in the fields and their harsh living conditions. Music also played an important role in the labor and civil rights movements. People still sing today "Take This Hammer" and "John Henry," songs that were symbols of the labor movement and union organization. "We Shall Overcome," the anthem of the civil rights movement, continues to stir people to action in their fight for justice.

Theater and film provide a mirror to society that can help us understand others, our times, and ourselves. The film "Philadelphia" for example, changed the national conversation about HIV/AIDS. It provided not only knowledge about AIDS but also helped people to see the human side of the disease with more compassion. Arthur Miller's play, *Death of a Salesman,* is a critique of the American capitalist system and its failure for many Americans. Unemployed or underemployed workers can identify with the economic insecurity and hopelessness that Willy Loman experienced. Indeed, on seeing the play many people see themselves in Willy Loman, and the play touched an emotional chord in everyone who saw it. Henrik Ibsen's play, *A Doll's House,* which he called a "humanist" play, nevertheless, shed light on the circumscribed role of women and their desire for individual freedom and the right to live a full life.

Explicit protest has always had a place in theater. During the 1960's several protest theater groups developed, and at least two continue to perform. Today El Teatro Campesino, founded around the same time that Cesar Chavez was organizing farm workers in California, has a mission of presenting a "more just and accurate account of human history." The San Francisco Mime Troupe, in a commedia dell'arte style, produces socially relevant theater on contemporary issues. Sometimes theater can serve as a healing process for painful events. This was the case of the *Laramie Project,* a play that was based on interviews with residents of Laramie, Wyoming, where a young gay man, Andrew Shepherd, had been brutally murdered. Theater can also serve as an agent of communication and healing in small groups. Role playing in contentious situations can develop mutual understanding and help to resolve conflicts.

The visual arts also make significant social contributions. The creation of community arts projects, such as murals on freeway walls or other outdoor structures, can be a way of helping communities to share their visions, ideals, and hopes for the future. Community art can also build cohesiveness. Many non-profit groups, such as the Iraqi American Reconciliation Project, share art from the communities they serve or are advocating for as a way of building understanding across groups and cultures. Art can also communicate to a world audience various common emotions and thoughts. Picasso's *Guernica,* a 1937 painting that responded to the deliberate targeting of civilians by a military force, is one example. *Guernica* was a powerful political statement of the destruction and tragedies of war. Tapping into the anxieties that many people feel, Edvard Munch portrayed his inner feelings of anxiety in *The Scream*. The painting has become an iconic symbol of such feelings for the whole world. The visual and performing arts have sometimes changed the course of history, brought people together through shared experiences to increase understanding and compassion for social issues and events. In all these ways, the arts are important to our society and need to be included in the undergraduate college experience.

Exploring the Arts: Interdisciplinarity, Professional Skills, and Community

This collection of essays suggests that the combination of liberal arts and arts provides the type of education needed for success, in work and life, for today's students. Our purpose is to provide practical examples of how the arts can be integrated into the undergraduate curriculum and list the benefits this integration can provide to student development. We have divided the essays into three thematic sections: interdisciplinarity, professional skills, and community. Nearly every essay describes programs that are interdisciplinary to some degree; however, the essays by Young, Sooter, Pane, Tomasik, and Laudien specifically address interdisciplinarity. Gregory Young provides examples of interdisciplinary courses he taught with a colleague that integrated music and architecture, music and the economy, and music and the brain.

Drury University Professor Traci Sooter engaged students from multiple disciplines in a creative project that addressed a significant community issue. Students from architecture, art history, nursing, communications, and 18 other disciplines collaborated to build a solar-energy home that was designed to withstand the debris cloud and wind pressure of a tornado. The project is an excellent example of how campuses can integrate the liberal arts, arts, professional studies, and civic engagement to address a compelling community issue.

Steven Pane discusses how learning from music can deepen the reading and writing experience for non-majors. At Valparaiso University film students study the critical and production sides of film, an art form that utilizes images and sounds. Timothy Tomasik suggests that the approach encourages experiential learning through practical application, engaging students in topical discussions about the modern world using traditional liberal arts critical inquiry. At Manhattan College students have opportunities to study children's literature, thought and motion through dance, religion and performance art in Italy, theater and the city, and music and culture.

The liberal arts develop many of the skills that employers look for, such as the ability to think clearly about complex problems; to write and speak well; analyze a problem to develop solutions; apply knowledge in new settings; understand numbers, statistics, technology and science; and a sense of ethics and integrity. These are all important skills for success in work; however, they leave out other important skills such as the ability to see the perspective of the other, compassion, and comfort with risk and critical evaluation. These latter skills are more likely to be developed through the arts. The authors in this volume believe that the development of professional skills in combination with the theoretical aspects of a liberal arts curriculum, which traditionally includes music, theater, art and creative writing, provides a high-quality undergraduate educational experience that uniquely prepares students for adaptability in their careers and engaged citizenship grounded in their abilities to think creatively, critically, and ethically.

Ilene Lieberman and Mara Parker expand on how the arts can prepare students for the workplace. They suggest that when students take arts courses they develop new ways of thinking, communicating, and evaluating. They also may develop a more compassionate understanding of human nature; this is especially important in contemporary society, as we must develop comfort with the unknown, whether it is a different culture, religion, or unfamiliar idea. The arts open up new ways of taking in information, analyzing it, and finally communicating it.

Kevin Marshal, Michael O'Connor, Placido Gomez and Sean Dillon collaborate on theater studies and law because they see a commonality between the theater and the drama in a courtroom. The authors examine theatrical theories and practices that are relevant to communicating facts and influencing perceptions, analyze the parts of a jury trial that relate to theater arts, and demonstrate the value of the cross-disciplinary study. They propose an integrated course model that involves theater and law. The authors conclude that the integration of theater and law, for graduate and undergraduate students, prepares students for success in their careers as well as engaged citizenship.

Mary Rist and Sasha West describe a collaborative writing program that includes creative-writing students and professional-writing students. Rist and West suggest that creative-writing students learn editing, digital media skills, and rhetorical history, while professional-writing students learn creative approaches to their writing and benefit from the critique in a writing workshop.

Jennifer Blackmer discusses how the arts contribute to entrepreneurial learning and thinking as a way of developing the "soft skills" necessary for a successful career in any field. She argues that entrepreneurship is inherent in the arts as artists think creatively, work collaboratively, embrace risk, and connect to the broader world. She offers examples of how student-driven experiences can be designed to develop the abilities to adapt, integrate knowledge, act with ethical responsibility, and communicate effectively. The soft skills mentioned by Blackmer are developed when the arts and the community interact around local culture and significant local or national events. Linda Ferguson suggests that music serves as a community transaction and has often provided inspiration and solace in times of national crisis. Adriane Thompson-Bradshaw describes how participation in a gospel choir brought African American and white students together at Ohio Northern University. The Gospel Ensemble offered opportunities for cross-cultural dialogue that eventually developed a deeper appreciation for others. Wagner College has a long and successful history of community engagement, particularly in a community university arts program. Sara Scott and Samantha Siegel present two case studies based on their community work in the arts. The first case study was the development of a community mural, and the second study involved students and the community in theater projects about the history and culture of the local area. The authors suggest that both projects had a positive impact on the campus and community climate.

The development of a person's fullest capacity is most likely to occur through the integration of liberal arts and the arts in an undergraduate education. This is the case we hope to make in this series of chapters.

NOTES

1. Kevin Kiley, "Another Liberal Arts Critic," *Inside Higher Education*. Jan. 30, 2013, accessed October 28, 2015. Adam Beame, "Kentucky Gov. Matt Bevin Wants State Colleges and Universities to Produce More Electrical Engineers and Less French Literature Scholars," *US News and World Reports*, January 29, 2016, accessed December 29, 2016.
2. Daniel Lende, PLOS Blog. blogs.plos.org, October 11, 2015, accessed October 28, 2015.
3. Scott Jaschik, "Obama vs. Art History," *Inside Higher Education*, January 31, 2014, accessed October 28, 2015.
4. Humanities Indicators, "Bachelor's Degrees in the Humanities," *American Academy of Arts and Sciences*, March 2016, and Richard E. Goodstein,

Eric Lapin, and Ronald C. McCurdy, "The New Performing Arts Curriculum," *Chronicle of Higher Education*. October 23, 2016.

5. Matt Krupnick, "Academics Forced to Prove Their Worth," *The Hechinger Report*, January 28, 2015, accessed February 8, 2017.
6. Debra Humphreys and Patrick Kelly, "How Liberal Arts and Sciences Majors Fare in Employment: A Report on Earnings and Long-Term Career Paths," Association of American Colleges & Universities, Washington, D.C., 2014.
7. Strategic National Arts Alumni Project (SNAAP), "Forks in the Road: The Many Paths of Arts Alumni," Indiana University Center for Postsecondary Research, Bloomington, Indiana, 2011, and SNAAP press release, accessed October 28, 2015.
8. Elizabeth Segran, "Why Top Tech CEOs Want Employees with Liberal Arts Degrees," *Fast Company,* August 28, 2014, accessed February 8, 2017. David H. Bailey, "Why Science Needs the Humanities," *Huffington Post.* November 18, 2016. Steven Lynn Bernasek, "Science is a Key Part of a Good Liberal Arts Education," *Times Higher Education,* October 28, 2016. David J. Skorton, "Why Scientists Should Embrace the Liberal Arts," *Scientific American,* January 16, 2014, accessed October 28, 2015.
9. National Endowment for the Arts, "The Arts and Human Development: Framing A National Research Agenda for the Arts, Lifelong Learning, and Individual Well-Being," white paper, Washington, D.C., 2011, 13.
10. Howard Gardner, *The Arts and Human Development: A Psychological Study of the Artistic Process* (New York: John Wiley & Sons, 1973).
11. Howard Gardner, *Frames of Mind: The Theory of Multiple Intelligence* (New York: Basic Books, 1983).
12. Howard Gardner, *Five Minds for the Future* (Boston: Harvard Business School Publishing, 2008).
13. Malcolm Gladwell, *Outliers: The Story of Success* (New York: Little Brown and Company, 2008).
14. Daniel H. Pink, *A Whole New Mind: Why Right-Brainers Will Rule the Future* (New York: Riverhead Books, 2005).
15. Rebecca Winthrop and Eileen McGivney, "Skills for a changing World: Advancing Quality Learning for Advancing Societies," Brookings Institution. Washington, D. C, 2016, accessed October 6, 2017.
16. Geoff Colvin, *Humans are Underrated: What High Achievers Know that Brilliant Machines Never Will* (New York: Random House, 2015).
17. Joseph E. Aoun, *Robot-Proof: Higher Education in the Age of Artificial Intelligence* (Cambridge, Massachusetts: MIT Press, 2017).
18. Fareed Zakaria, *In Defense of a Liberal Education* (New York: W. W. Norton & Company, Inc., 2015).

19. Peter D. Hart, "How Should Colleges Prepare Students to Succeed in Today's Global Economy" Peter D. Hart Research Associates, Washington, D. C. 2007.
20. Louis E. Catron, *What Majors Learn: The Advantages Majors have for all Jobs* accessed August 27, 2016, http://lecatr.people.wm.edu/majorslearn.html.

CHAPTER 2

Creative Interdisciplinarity in the Arts

Gregory Young

Over the past 25 years, there has been increasing emphasis on interdisciplinary research and teaching at Montana State University (MSU), as well as a transformation of the general education program to include four inquiry courses and a research/creativity course for all students. In addition, some of the senior capstone courses are now interdisciplinary by design, which helps students integrate professional skills with analysis, creativity, and collaboration. Why is MSU placing such importance on creativity and interdisciplinarity? As the result of a thorough strategic planning process, the integration of learning, discovery, and engagement across disciplinary boundaries became a stated goal of the university.

THE BENEFITS OF CREATIVE INTERDISCIPLINARITY

"One need only think of the artist-scientist Leonardo, or the poet-printmaker-mystic William Blake, or the poet-painter-designer-socialist William Morris to find examples of venerated artists of the past whose interests spanned various modes of thought and expression," notes the introduction to Eckerd College's web page describing its interdisciplinary

G. Young (✉)
Montana State University, Bozeman, MT, USA

© The Author(s) 2018
N. H. Hensel (ed.), *Exploring, Experiencing, and Envisioning Integration in US Arts Education*, The Arts in Higher Education, https://doi.org/10.1007/978-3-319-71051-8_2

arts program.[1] Some of the most exciting discoveries are made at the intersection of traditional disciplines, and some of these intersections are so synergistic that they have become accepted disciplines in their own right. Biochemistry is an older example from the early nineteenth century, and astrobiology is a newer one, which has attracted significant funding from NASA. Indeed, the twenty-first century is becoming the era of global interconnection. Solutions to our current and future problems require the integration of far more diverse inputs—technological, economic, political, cultural, social, and environmental—than we have seen in the past. In order for us to manage these complexities we need to reconsider our approach, creating teams that are interdisciplinary and integrated, both in the academy and in the workplace. Educated people prepared to work at the frontiers of knowledge recognize that interdisciplinary teamwork is essential. Discovery and innovation occur particularly well when existing ideas are projected onto the unknown from different perspectives and with unanticipated, serendipitous cross-pollination.[2]

Given this, the most recent strategic plan at MSU focuses on the integration of learning, discovery, and engagement, to provide the basis for productive pedagogies that are interesting to students. Team-taught seminars such as Musi-Tecture: Seeking Useful Correlations Between Music & Architecture, London and the Lakes: Music and Economics from Handel to McCartney, and Music and the Brain allow students to design their own projects, conduct original interdisciplinary research, present the work in class, and write summative essays. Student work has been published in peer-reviewed journals and presented at national conferences. Not only are students motivated by the possibilities inherent in these connections among the disciplines, but they also present them with a less-trodden path so that students can spend less time wading through the literature and more time pondering potential areas of discovery.

TEACHING CREATIVITY

How we teach creativity in higher education, the way students learn, and the economic imperative for both are important for many reasons. At this point in history, the need for increasing creativity in US undergraduate and graduate curricula has never been greater. Given an economic disadvantage with other countries in many types of manufacturing, creativity offers the best hope for American competitiveness. This fits in well with the teaching transformation that is happening now as we shift toward more interactive learning, collaboration, and teamwork, and away from traditional lectures. These changes are being driven by three major forces: (1) employers want employees who can adapt quickly to change, work well in teams, and solve problems; (2) the big problems facing the world today, such as global warming, drought, poverty, and sustainable energy needs, are interdisciplinary in nature and require creativity and cooperation to solve; and (3) students desire learning and projects that are more active, more social, and more applicable to the real world. Creativity is defined as the tendency to generate or recognize ideas, alternatives, or possibilities that may be useful in solving problems, communicating with others, and entertaining ourselves and others.[3]

> The next phase of the competitiveness debate must look inside the black box and attempt to understand how our colleges and universities can better promote innovation. If innovation were simply a numbers game, our future would indeed be bleak, but the strength of U.S. higher education has always been more than sheer numbers of graduates. America's phenomenal economic success has rested in large part on the dynamism of our economy, driven by the creativity, innovativeness, and entrepreneurialism of our students and faculty. That is our competitive advantage and it is our greatest hope in a world of more nearly equal competitors.[4] (David Attis, Educause)

In Daniel Pink's *A Whole New Mind* he predicts that the need for right-brained creativity (R-Directed) will become more important as automation and outsourcing will pick up much of the left-brained activity (L-Directed):

> Asia is now performing large amounts of routine, white-collar, L-Directed work at significantly lower costs, thereby forcing knowledge workers in the advanced world to master abilities that can't be shipped overseas. And automation has begun to affect this generation's white-collar workers in much the same way it did last generation's blue-collar workers, requiring L-Directed professionals to develop aptitudes that computers can't do better, faster or cheaper.[5]

The word education comes from two Latin roots: *educare and educere.* The first means to cultivate, rear, or bring up. This refers to the passing down of knowledge from teacher to student, helping the student to understand facts about the world. It is internalizing the external. In our education system, this has become a common approach because it is easy to prepare for and quantitatively test. *Educere,* on the other hand, means to evoke, lead forth, or draw out.

This is externalizing the internal. Thinking critically and creatively is often subjective, and therefore much harder for faculty to encourage in terms of lesson preparation and grading. There is no standard for conveying these skills to students, and yet this is the type of education that results in the much-needed creative and innovative solutions to our problems.

An undergraduate researcher at Montana State, Madison Gabig, interviewed students and faculty a few years ago on the creative process and the need for creativity in education. When faculty members were asked how they encourage creativity in their classrooms, they often paused to reflect. It is not something that comes instantly to mind, and the question is often hard for them to answer. The inability to supply an immediate answer to this question may be the result of professors' focus on covering specific content and achieving specific learning outcomes in their classes. However, if faculty members do not have the opportunity to be creative in their teaching, how will their students have the opportunity to understand the creative process?

Perspectives from Students

Gabig's interviews indicated that the most influential classes seem to be those in which the students have considerable freedom to actively participate in projects, papers, and discussions in which they receive support and guidance for their ideas. This builds trust between the student and the professor, resulting in student empowerment.

Regular lectures and labs as a rule do not induce creativity. According to one student interviewed, "creativity is important because it takes students out of the routine and makes life more interesting." Examples include debates; improvisation, whether in jazz, art, or poetry; research; service learning; interdisciplinary study; case studies; and so on. These interactive and exploratory experiences enhance creativity and prepare students for almost any situation, empowering them to solve problems and generate new ideas.

We now have the technology to instantly access information on a wide variety of topics. As the world presents us with ever-more-challenging problems, we will need an interdisciplinary perspective to discover solutions. Fortunately, Millennials have grown up with this technology, and as a result, they have become accustomed to interacting across the disciplines. These students also want components of their degree programs that differentiate them from their competition in the work force. They desire an interesting academic niche centered on something about which they are passionate and to which they feel they can contribute. Having taught several interdisciplinary undergraduate research seminars, I have found that creativity in students is fostered by examining a given discipline from the perspective of a different discipline.

PERSPECTIVES FROM PROFESSORS

David Sands, a plant pathologist at Montana State, has taught and written about a course based on Linus Pauling's premise that in order to generate good ideas, one has to generate lots of ideas and throw the bad ones away. One major assignment is to generate 17 original ideas with no limits regarding the topic. They must be generated by students and each explained in one page or less, including the problem each idea is intended to solve. In his biotechnology class, in which he brings in colleagues from a variety of other disciplines as guest lecturers, Sands tapes a $5 bill to the podium at the beginning of class, which will be awarded at the end to the student asking the best question. By mid-semester, even when he does not display the cash, students are well accustomed to asking insightful questions.

In Gabig's interview with architecture professor David Fortin, he said, "I don't think in a creative endeavor you can push anyone anywhere. ... For me, the key is if you can find out what that student wants to do, what makes them tick, and what makes them passionate, they fill their palette." Composer, conductor, and jazz pianist Eric Funk said that when ideas start coming, a composition sometimes starts to flow and takes on a life of its own. He realized at one point he wanted to compose a cello concerto because "I just hadn't heard the one I wanted yet. I thought ... nobody is writing it." He began to write what he wanted to hear. Many composition students find that their best work takes less time than their worst work; that is, when a composition begins to flow, it is usually worth writing down.

In keeping with the concept of creative flow, *Architectural Record* magazine has a "Cocktail Napkin Sketch Contest" in which registered architects, including professors, of course, sketch their ideas on a white cocktail napkin and send it in. There is also a non-professional category that students and interns can enter. In 2011 the contest received 1200 entries. The winners' drawings are featured annually in the September issue of *Architectural Record* and in its Online Cocktail Napkin Sketch Gallery.[6]

New approaches to education, some of which have been exemplified above, are imperative to the success of our students and, indeed, the future of humanity. Of course, given that this premise is based on the need for creativity, there will be countless other innovative approaches to education that have yet to be imagined. Statistics show that a majority of the jobs that our current students will have in 20 years do not exist yet.[7] Therefore, preparing students to be adaptable, creative, innovative, and thoughtful are essential learning outcomes for any university degree.

A Sequence of Interdisciplinary Events

In 1991 when I was a young music professor, an architecture professor approached me and asked, "Have you heard the quote, 'Architecture is frozen music'?" I had, and we both thought it was by Frank Lloyd Wright, only to later find out that Goethe had said it centuries earlier. What followed was a series of discussions over coffee and a realization that many of the technical terms and sources of inspiration we thought were discipline-specific had common applications in both music and architecture. To further our research and share our findings, we designed a senior research seminar for 16 students, 8 from music and 8 from architecture. After getting up to speed with the comparative research study, the students delved deeper and found more examples illustrating similar terms and sources of inspiration between the two disciplines. For their final project, the architecture students designed buildings inspired and guided by musical selections, and the music students composed music inspired and guided by existing architecture. Judging by the speed at which the students completed their projects, we concluded that the students were both inspired and motivated. Their work was published in the MIT journal *Leonardo*.[8] My colleague and I presented this research at national conferences and at two universities in Milan, Italy, by invitation.

Shortly after that experience, Mark Emmert, then MSU's provost, hired me as the founding director of the Undergraduate Scholars Program, one of the first campus-wide undergraduate research programs at a public university in the United States. As director, I continued to foster interdisciplinarity and incorporated this style of research seminar within the framework of the University Honors Program (now an Honors College). Teaming up with a professor of economics, I taught "London and the Lakes: Music and Economics from Handel to McCartney" for 20 honors students from a variety of disciplines. The students assisted the faculty members in their research on the influence of money on music and then chose topics for their own final projects that pertained to the trip abroad. The trip was the culminating part of this "Great Expeditions" course. While abroad, individual students planned and led short side trips for the group to explore the areas upon which their projects focused. For example, one student had researched the music composed specifically to be played in St. Paul's Cathedral, including commissions and other benefits paid. On the trip, he organized a tour of that cathedral for the group and explained his project along the way.[9]

Interdisciplinary seminars such as these represent one way in which faculty members in the arts and humanities can deliver undergraduate research as a mainstream pedagogy to more than one student at a time, while working toward their own scholarly products.

National data indicate that the undergraduate research movement is spreading rapidly across all disciplines, promoting inquiry and creativity in labs, studios, advanced tutorials, and small seminars. Membership in the Council on Undergraduate Research (CUR) has risen dramatically over the last few years, with 687 institutional members at the time of this publication, as has the demand for faculty workshops across the nation on how to institutionalize undergraduate research.

UPGRADING GENERAL EDUCATION

In 2001, the William and Flora Hewlett Foundation funded a revision of MSU's general education curriculum. The result, entitled "Core 2.0," includes inquiry courses in arts, humanities, social sciences and natural sciences; a freshman seminar; and foundational courses in diversity, quantitative reasoning, and writing. The most significant revision was the addition of a requirement that all students complete a research/creativity course (known as Research & Creative Experience courses), which placed MSU on the leading edge of general education reform. The following describes the criteria for research/creativity courses to be accepted as part of Core 2.0:

1. Students experience the process of research and creative experience as a unique intellectual activity and generate a scholarly product.
2. Students have the autonomy to direct the research and creative experience, while faculty and staff provide the framing concepts and contexts.

3. Research and Creative Experience courses provide frequent and early benchmarks for student progress to encourage early engagement in the research and creative process.
4. The research and creative experience component done individually or in small groups constitutes at least one-third of the course. The remaining part of the course should provide sufficient information about the subject to enable the student to formulate a project as well as provide the student with the tools to do a research and creative project.
5. Courses geared toward sophomore-level students are particularly encouraged, but Research & Creative Experience courses can be offered at any level and may have prerequisites.
6. Courses must address the responsible conduct of research.

Through the Research and Creative Experience course students will:

1. improve their ability to put concepts and facts into practice;
2. increase their understanding of the processes and dynamic nature of knowledge;
3. strengthen their habits of critical and creative thinking while seeking and synthesizing information from broad and diverse sources;
4. deepen their understanding of the importance of teamwork and collaboration;
5. develop responsibility, competency, and confidence; and
6. expand intellectual curiosity and interest in the subject area.[10]

In response to the campus-wide introduction of Core 2.0, many departments redesigned their senior capstone courses to fit the criteria for acceptance as undergraduate research/creativity courses. This not only revitalized the departmental degree requirements but also benefited the students by allowing them to finish core and departmental requirements with this course. An example of such a curriculum revision was the senior capstone course in the School of Music, which was retitled, MUSI 499R—Undergraduate Research in Music. This served several important purposes. It fit into Core 2.0; it included several of the required learning outcomes contained in the National Association of Schools of Music Handbook; it allowed a high degree of freedom for students to choose topics that really interested them; it enabled faculty members to get course credit for mentoring undergraduate researchers; and, in many instances, it allowed students to work alongside professors on research projects. For the most part, the students come up with their own projects, which may contribute to a larger faculty research project, and the class only meets once a week as a group. The rest of the time is made up of short individual student meetings with their mentors or the course's instructor. A sample project is Nicole Jerominski Krause's design and construction of a small marimba from recycled materials with a goal of zero cost, not counting the cost of the tools she used in the wood shop in the School of Architecture. She presented her project, including a video that documented the design and construction process, at the National Conference on Undergraduate Research.

Another possible outcome of interdisciplinary course offerings is the potential for new programs, based on demonstrated student interest and the capacity to tap into current resources. For example, when the School of Music was considering a new music therapy degree, faculty members offered an honors seminar entitled Music and the Brain, which I co-taught with neuroscience professor John Miller and Shane Colvin, a licensed music therapist and teaching assistant. It drew great interest from students across campus, and we had to turn away several students after reaching our cap of 22 students. This successful seminar resulted in students presenting high-quality individual and small-group research projects. The School of Music is currently considering offering a new music therapy degree program.

In another example, in 2015 the College of Arts & Architecture sponsored a course taught by Elizabeth Croy, The Art of Mental Healing. Students from a variety of disciplines researched how the fine arts could be used to promote mental health and wellness, culminating in a mental and emotional wellness fair, Headspace: The Art of Mental Healing. At this fair, students displayed interactive exhibits that promoted better understanding of mental health issues through creative group projects.

MSU Honors College Interdisciplinary Offerings

MSU's Honors College offers advanced interdisciplinary seminars in courses that emphasize class discussion, development of analytic thinking, and writing skills as well as encouraging independent creativity/research.[11] These seminars satisfy the Core 2.0 requirement. Three examples in 2016 included Origins, which was co-taught by a physicist, a paleontologist, and a former Catholic priest, The Art and Science of Medicine, and The Science of Happiness.[12]

The senior honors thesis is an independent research/creativity project of graduate-level caliber and, ideally, meriting publication, which enables honors students to synthesize what they have learned. In their thesis proposal, students outline the groundwork necessary to do the projects, describe the project itself, and indicate what results are expected. On the completion of the thesis, the students must present the work publicly on campus, and many have also presented at the National Collegiate Honors Council conference, the National Conference on Undergraduate Research, and professional disciplinary conferences.

DEVOTING RESOURCES TO INTERDISCIPLINARITY

MSU's commitment to an interdisciplinary culture in the arts is further reflected by a recent call for internal grant proposals. The Office of the Vice President of Research and Economic Development requested proposals for interdisciplinary, collaborative projects in the arts, humanities, and social sciences. The collaborative grants are intended to be planning grants that could lead to building new programs, initiatives, or centers that will enhance the national and international reputation of Montana State.

Proposals are reviewed according to the following criteria:

1. intellectual creativity, originality, and novelty;
2. interdisciplinary collaboration and ability to form a coherent program, initiative, or center that will lead to novel research and enhance the national and international reputation of MSU;
3. plans for public exhibitions or performances and books leading to releases for continued scholarship or creative work related to the award;
4. appropriateness of the budget; and
5. experiential learning opportunities for students (undergraduate and/or graduate) who are associated with the project.[13]

Earlier I mentioned astrobiology, a discipline that was created from the intersection of two traditional disciplines. The Astrobiology Research Center (ABRC) at MSU, which was founded in 1998, could be used as a model for creative interdisciplinarity in the arts, as its research mission focuses on the integration of multiple disciplines. The center provides a unique niche within the NASA Astrobiology Institute (NAI) as a multidisciplinary umbrella for conducting research on the origin and evolution of life, work that is intimately linked to sustainable energy and global climate change. The center focuses on interdisciplinary research and teaching as well as on communicating and educating the public about this science while inspiring the next generation of scientists. The nearby natural laboratory of Yellowstone National Park provides ABRC with unique field research opportunities because the park's abundant and unique thermal features give researchers insights into the origin, evolution, and future of life.[14] A film entitled "Search for the Origin of Life" has aired on Montana PBS multiple times since 2013. MSU students studying art and film played a significant role in the production of this film.[15]

The culture of creative interdisciplinarity in the arts that has developed over the past two decades at MSU has proven exciting and motivating for students, who are learning in new ways that will help them adapt to and be successful in a changing economy. As educators, we have much more to do, but these changes are a solid beginning toward preparing students to be important contributors in an era of global interconnection.

NOTES

1. "Interdisciplinary Arts," Eckerd College Interdisciplinary Arts website, accessed December 6, 2016, https://www.eckerd.edu/interdisciplinary-arts/about/.
2. "Interdisciplinary Activities at MSU: A Rationale and Some Opportunities," Montana State University website, accessed January 25, 2016, http://www.montana.edu/facultysenate/documents/White%20Paper%20Interdisciplinary%20Activities%20at%20MSU%202-5-15.pdf.
3. Robert E. Franken, Introduction. *Human Motivation. 3rd ed.* (Pacific Grove, CA: Brooks/Cole, 1993), 396.
4. David Attis, "Higher Education and the Future of U.S. Competitiveness," Educause website, accessed May 2012, http://www.educause.edu/research-and-publications/books/tower-and-cloud/higher-education-and-future-us-competitiveness.
5. Daniel H. Pink, *A Whole New Mind: Why Right-brainers Will Rule the Future* (New York: Riverhead, 2006) 46–47.
6. *Architectural Record* Cocktail Napkin Sketch Contest, *Architectural Record* website, accessed May 2013, http://www.architecturalrecord.com/ext/resources/archives/call4entries/pdf/2015-napkin-Sketch-Entry-Form.pdf.
7. Jessica Lyons, "How Can Colleges Prepare Students for Jobs That Don't Exist Yet?" Study.com website, accessed December 6, 2016, http://study.com/articles/How_Can_Colleges_Prepare_Students_for_Jobs_That_Dont_Exist_Yet.html.

8. Jerry Bancroft, Gregory Young, Mark Sanderson, "Musi-Tecture: Seeking Useful Correlations between Music & Architecture," *Leonardo*, MIT Press, Dec. 1993.
9. Gregory Young, "Interdisciplinary Undergraduate Research in the Arts & Humanities at Montana State University" *CUR Quarterly*, Winter 2008.
10. "Core 2.0 Inquiry," Montana State University website, accessed May 2016, http://www.montana.edu/core2/inquiry.html.
11. "Course Descriptions—Honors College," Montana State University website, accessed December 6, 2016, http://catalog.montana.edu/coursedescriptions/honr/.
12. "Honors College—Honors Seminars," Montana State University website, accessed December 6, 2016, http://www.montana.edu/honors/seminars.html.
13. "Office of Research and Economic Development," Montana State University website, accessed May 1, 2016, http://www.montana.edu/research/funding-opportunities/.
14. "Astrobiology Biogeocatalysis Center," Montana State University website, accessed December 1, 2016, http://abrc.montana.edu/.
15. "Search for the Origin of Life" video on Montana PBS website, accessed June 2016, http://www.montanapbs.org/SearchfortheOriginofLife/.

CHAPTER 3

Architecture and the Liberal Arts: A Whole-School Approach to Community Engagement

Traci Sooter

A COMMUNITY IN TURMOIL

At 5:17 p.m. on Sunday, May 22, 2011, tornado sirens sounded, but the sirens could not lift the veil of the rain-wrapped, multiple-vortex tornado bearing down on Joplin, Missouri. As the storm made its way across the city, it ripped a path of destruction nearly a mile wide. A slow-moving (at times no more than 10 mph) and therefore a more destructive storm, it stalled for several minutes as it gained wind speeds of more than 200 miles per hour over St. John's Hospital and Cunningham Park. When the storm finally passed, the five-story, concrete hospital was completely destroyed and the park, once filled with 100-year-old trees, was unrecognizable (Fig. 3.1).

The storm and the deadly debris cloud that began on the western edge of Joplin was slow to dissipate and continued on to the town of Duquesne and into Jasper and Newton counties, a total of 22.1 miles over 38 horrific minutes.

T. Sooter (✉)
Drury University, Springfield, MO, USA

© The Author(s) 2018
N. H. Hensel (ed.), *Exploring, Experiencing, and Envisioning Integration in US Arts Education*, The Arts in Higher Education,
https://doi.org/10.1007/978-3-319-71051-8_3

27

Fig. 3.1   St. Johns Hospital following 2011 tornado. Photo courtesy of the City of Joplin

The impact was devastating: 161 lives were lost, and more than 7500 homes and 3000 commercial buildings were damaged or destroyed. It was the deadliest tornado in US history since 1953 (Fig. 3.2).[1]

What happened immediately after the storm was best described by the then City Manager Mark Rohr as "the miracle of the human spirit."[2] The tornado had passed, but rain continued to pour as the people of Joplin pulled themselves out of the rubble and began helping their neighbors. Community members from outside of the storm zone raced in to help, along with people from neighboring towns and cities. Local, state, and federal government agencies and first responders also raced to the scene. From across town to across the world, volunteers were pouring in. By mid-April, nearly two years after the storm, the count for registered volunteers from reporting agencies/organizations stood at 176,869 individuals who completed 1,146,083 hours of volunteer service. This amounted to nearly 110 years' worth of service, at a 24/7 pace (Fig. 3.3).[3]

Drury University, a small liberal arts university in Springfield, Missouri, 70 miles from Joplin, immediately organized groups to help and contributed many volunteers. Athletic teams collected and distributed vans full of food and supplies. Faculty and staff went both in small groups and independently to assist with search and rescue, serve meals, collect and distribute clothing and supplies, and provide counseling. One staff member even donned his clown costume to cheer up children in shelters. While doing so, he also noticed that women in the shelters did not have purses or any

Fig. 3.2 Tornado's path. Photo courtesy of the City of Joplin

Fig. 3.3 A message of thanks to volunteers from Tennessee. Photo by Mike Gullett, Joplin Globe

of the things they would normally carry in them, and children did not have books. He soon organized a drive on campus for donations of books and new purses and asked faculty and staff to fill them for the women and children in the shelters. The campus community contributed 200 filled purses and 1100 books. From moments after the storm lifted in May 2011 through spring 2014, Drury University faculty, staff, and students contributed more than 12,000 hours of volunteer service in aid of Joplin.

In July 2011, the Drury Design-Build Program partnered with the ABC television show *Extreme Makeover: Home Edition* to help create a second wave of awareness and volunteerism for Joplin. It was the fourth time *Extreme Makeover* and Drury Design-Build would partner, each time designing and building a special project for families or a community. In the Joplin project, Drury Design-Build was asked to design and construct a tribute in Cunningham Park to thank the 170,000 volunteers who came to the aid of Joplin after the devastating storm. The result was the Volunteer Tribute with a monument entitled "Miracle of the Human Spirit" (Fig. 3.4).

Fig. 3.4 Joplin Volunteer Tribute. Photo by Evan Melgren, communications major, Drury University

THE DESIGN-BUILD MODEL

Tell me and I'll forget. Teach me and I'll remember. Involve me and I'll learn.
(Benjamin Franklin)

Drury Design-Build, housed in the Hammons School of Architecture at Drury University, is an engaged-learning opportunity for students to design and construct projects for charities and communities in need. A small number of schools of architecture across the country offer design-build programs, all of which are top-notch programs creating admirable design projects for worthy causes. Traditionally, design-build in an academic setting means that architecture students are engaged in the entire process from conceiving the design to constructing a building or some sort of built space for individuals. What sets the Drury model apart from other such programs is its "whole-school" approach. Whereas a traditional design-build program is set in a school of architecture and is open exclusively to architecture students, the whole-school model opens participation on projects to the entire student body at the institution and encourages students in all majors to participate in all phases of design, construction, and overall aspects of the project.

The theory is that students from varied majors will bring diverse approaches to critical thinking and problem-solving using the perspective of their disciplines in the design and implementation process. Students in liberal arts and professional programs, including fine arts, philosophy, physics, biology, music, communications, business administration, and marketing are commonly involved in our projects. Everyone is encouraged to participate in design discussions and have input and impact on design. The whole-school method benefits students from all disciplines as they take lessons learned from the experiences and apply them to their course work in their respective majors.

Today's architect is expected to understand the perspectives and needs of a broad, never-ending range of clients. The problem is that architecture students have minimal opportunities to be challenged by external points of view. Leaders of the Hammons School of Architecture, rooted in the liberal arts at Drury University, have always believed in and celebrated the liberal arts education that our architecture students receive. However, collaboration on an architecture project with a history, literature, theater, or environmental biology major will further expand the education and perspectives of architecture students. While most academic design-build programs provide wonderful interaction between clients and students, the whole-school approach challenges students to think through the visions and perspectives of others. Partnering with disciplines across campus allows this important interaction.[4]

This whole-school method also gives liberal arts and other students not majoring in architecture an opportunity to put their ideas, knowledge, and skill sets to the test in a way very different than the typical experience engaged-learning provides, enriching students' preparation for their particular careers.

A student in a professional school of management and a theater student in the liberal arts will be trained to think critically and creatively in many different ways; their perspectives differ yet again from those of an architecture student. In their professional careers, non-architecture students may later become the clients of architects, collaborating at some level with an architect on the design of a building. In our academic setting, business, theater, and architecture students are all equally responsible for the design-build outcomes.

The influence and effects on design of such diverse groups of students can be rich and rigorous. Working with transdisciplinary teams has steadily increased the rigor of our work and improved design outcomes. New friendships have formed and long-term professional connections have begun for students. This inclusive strategy of cross-pollination of liberal arts and professional students has had overwhelmingly rewarding results for students, professors, stakeholders, and recipients of the projects.

Development of the Whole-School Model

Drury Design-Build has provided architecturally based engaged-learning experiences for students for nearly 19 years. Early collaborations on these projects were interdisciplinary but there were clear separations of assignments, divided along the lines of the disciplines. One example was the C-Street Farmers Market pavilion, which offers fresh produce and accepts WIC (Women, Infants, and Children) coupons and food stamps in an underserved area of Springfield, Missouri. In this project, architecture students executed all of the design work on the pavilion while advertising/public relations students developed a marketing campaign for the grand opening of the market in a separate course. While the two groups of students had an ongoing dialogue, only the architecture students developed the design of the pavilion, although on crucial build days, the advertising and public relations students did lend a hand in the construction (Fig. 3.5).

The whole-school approach grew from the C-Street Market collaboration and developed over several years, but it was greatly influenced by our participation in the *Extreme Makeover: Home Edition* builds. At our first makeover at Camp Barnabus, more than 4000 volunteers from all walks of life came together to construct three buildings, a quarter mile of new road, and a camp site for recreational vehicles and campers. Also noteworthy was the fact that this project was completed in less than seven days while the camp was in full swing with children attending the camp. While the three buildings at Camp Barnabus were designed by a local architect, the collaboration of the community in executing the design, solving problems as they developed, and supporting one another while benefitting the young campers was described by many team members as life-changing.

The enormous number of volunteers, united by the common goal of helping an identified family or community in need, made the *Makeover*

Fig. 3.5   C-Street Farmers Market, 2015. Photo by Angie Woodcock

projects the most positive group experiences most of us had ever witnessed. The buzz of goodwill and compassion flowing from the large number of human beings working in unison was almost impossible not to feel physically.

Thousands of diverse individuals from every industry imaginable worked alongside our students behind-the-scenes on each episode of *Extreme Makeover* projects. When each episode of the television show aired, it portrayed the story as the celebrities doing most of the work. While the celebrities and the production company are most certainly the catalyst, create the enthusiasm, and play a critical role in the project, the untold story is that it is the members of the local community who step up en masse, donate all the funds and materials, and execute the almost unachievable goals set for each episode. The cultivation of large-scale community enthusiasm and engagement was influential in the development of the inclusive nature of the whole-school approach (Fig. 3.6).

After the inspiring first experience with *Extreme Makeover*, our program purposely invited every faculty and staff member and the entire student

Fig. 3.6 Freshman class prefabricates walls of home for Habitat for Humanity International, 2007. Photo by Mark Schiefelbein

body to participate in constructing the first LEED (Leadership in Energy and Environmental Design) platinum-level home for Habitat for Humanity International. More than 300 freshmen prefabricated the frame walls of the house in a single 90-minute session as a service-learning component of a freshman common-core class, and 16 separate faculty members took their classes to the job site to volunteer for the construction process. Each volunteer group heard a short talk on sustainability that included topics such as why the home was considered to be sustainable and how they, as future home-owners and workers, could effect change by demanding responsibly sustainable homes and buildings. Then they were told how the work they were about to do would have a positive impact on the project. Still, broad participation in the project did not begin until the construction phase of the home, so most volunteers were not involved in the design of the home at all.

Ultimately, with each *Extreme Makeover* and Drury design-build project, participation was invited from the entire university. Inserting non-architecture students into the design dialogue quickly moved to the beginning of the process (Fig. 3.7).

Fig. 3.7 Eggstreme Chicken Coop, 2010. Photo by J. Hoffpauir

During the design charrette (a way of quickly generating a design solution) for the *Egg*streme Chicken Coop, non-architecture students were picking up markers, drawing on the board, and bringing critical-thinking skills from their various liberal arts disciplines to the conversation. Their contributions were varied in approach because of the diversity of their majors. Problem-solving skills also varied greatly, as did opinions on creating hierarchies of important project issues. This created lively dialogues between architecture and non-architecture students that challenged the architecture students in ways they had not been challenged before, but that they might often encounter with clients in their professional careers. This was the first project to reveal the many benefits of applying the whole-school approach and including liberal arts students from the beginning of the design process.

As the whole-school approach was developed, many unique actions contributed to its development. During the Joplin Volunteer Tribute mentioned above, colleagues collaborating on the project, Keith Hedges and Dr. Regina Waters, created what we called the *Drury SmartMob!: A Flash Mob with a Cause*. Social media was used to entice volunteers' participation in a short, high-impact task to help construct the tribute. As the SmartMob! workday grew near, hints via social media were sent out and eventually the location and service task were revealed. When the two busloads of SmartMob-ers arrived in Cunningham Park, they were 120-plus strong. Their task was to lay 12,000 square feet of sod to create a green carpet for the new tribute, which they completed in less than 45 minutes. The group was so energized and enthusiastic about helping that they continued laying sod, restoring 80 percent of the grass in the six-acre park before heading home (Fig. 3.8).

The first instance of incorporating liberal arts students in the early phases of a large-scale, long-duration project design was the Butterfly Garden and Overlook in Cunningham Park. Funded by the TKF Foundation, in partnership with Cornell University, the USDA Forest Service, Joplin Parks and Recreation, and Forest ReLeaf of Missouri, this project was a healing garden for those affected by the tornado, as it allows them to sit within nature while they grieve or reflect.

In this project, collaborations with a music-therapy professor, Dr. Natalie Wlodarczyk, greatly influenced the concept of the design and further revealed that transdisciplinary collaborations could enrich the experience and outcomes. During the ten-day blitz-building of the student-designed elements of the garden, music-therapy students hosted a "rejuvenation station," to

Fig. 3.8 Drury SmartMob! volunteers at Cunningham Park, 2011. Photo by Mark Miller

provide live music that the volunteers requested, to keep up the spirits and energy of the core team of students and volunteers.

The most substantial trial of the whole-school approach to date was our participation in the US Department of Energy's Solar Decathlon, leading to the creation of our competition home, called ShelteR^3. In fall 2013 Drury University and Crowder College, a two-year community college in Neosho, Missouri, partnered in applying to compete in the DOE's 2015 Solar Decathlon. In this competition, 20 collegiate teams were chosen as finalists and spent almost two years designing and building energy efficient houses powered by the sun. In the final competition, the teams and their houses were judged in ten contests to determine an overall winner. The winning team should produce a house that meets the following criteria:

- is affordable, attractive, and easy to live in;
- maintains comfortable and healthy indoor environmental conditions;
- supplies energy for cooking, cleaning, entertainment, and commuting;
- provides adequate hot water; and
- produces as much or more energy than it consumes.[5]

(**For photos, see the** Solar Decathlon 2015 website at http://www. solardecathlon.gov/2015/photos-gallery-crowder-drury.html)

The Solar Decathlon is predominantly an engineering-school competition, but the Crowder-Drury team believed Drury's liberal arts, whole-school approach to design-build could successfully compete against the traditional engineering-based teams.

Through personal experiences and participation in the Volunteer Tribute, and Butterfly Garden and Overlook projects, students and professors had witnessed the devastating damage in Joplin and heard the tragic, as well as inspirational, stories of survivors and heroes. These experiences fostered an overwhelming desire to assist in mitigating the devastation of similar disasters. When discussing the Crowder-Drury team's potential design concept for the Solar Decathlon, it was quickly agreed that the team would use the competition as an opportunity to attempt to create a home that would be tornado resistant. Adding this additional (though not required) layer of complexity to the already-difficult requirements of the competition was naïve, yet motivating and inspiring to the team.

The Crowder-Drury Solar Decathlon team believed that much of the structural devastation and loss of life in Joplin, as well as in many other tornado-hit cities, could be avoided if we designed buildings to resist the high winds and impact of flying debris from such storms. Working out the design details of a solar-powered, tornado-resistant home was a rigorous academic and real-world challenge for the students, but the team felt compelled to take on the challenge.

Additional conceptual inspiration came from a logistical challenge all competitors had to face. Entrants had to build the structure at the home university, ship it to Irvine, California, and reassemble it in time for October 8, 2015, the start of the competition. The process then had to be reversed when the competition ended.

Working out this logistical challenge and coupling it with our goal of disaster resistance led students to discover two additional potential uses for the competition house: a disaster-response command center and disaster-relief housing.[6]

ShelteR³: Respond, Recover, Resist became the concept and name of our competition home. (More details can be found on the team's website: http://shelter.drury.edu/)[7] (Fig. 3.9)

Fig. 3.9 ShelteR³
Conceptual Diagram,
2013. Credit: Marshall
Arne, Associate Professor,
Drury University; Jonas
Gassmann, Architecture
Team Leader

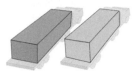

RESPOND
Truck-in both
side units

RECOVER
Assemble Units
•Disaster Response
Command Center
•Relief Housing

RESIST
Expand Units
•Post Disaster Housing

Respond, Recover, Resist Concept

Disaster Response
Two prefabricated modules (a living/sleeping area and kitchen/bath) are
whisked via flatbed truck into a community that has been devastated by a
natural disaster. The units are removed from the truck using a Binkley
system and then joined to form a disaster-response command center or
emergency-relief housing. Roof-mounted flat solar panels generate elec-
tricity and heat. The home or command center is self-sufficient and able to

function before power and water are restored. Innovative, impact-resistant cladding and structural details protect the structure from future storms and lend a sense of safety and security.

Disaster Recovery

Eventually the community begins to rebuild from disaster and residential housing takes priority over disaster response. The structure is easily adapted to fit those evolving needs. A foundation is laid and the two modules are separated by 20 feet. The resulting space is covered with window walls on both ends to create a gracious living area between the bedroom and kitchen and bath. Additional solar arrays are added on the roof for increased energy production. The innovative, high-impact resistant cladding covers the exterior of both modules to continue to protect occupants from future storms. A second layer of transparent, impact-resistant folding doors can be easily closed minutes before a storm, effectively sheltering the central living space from flying debris. Cabinetry, customized to the owners' needs, helps separate living areas from the bedrooms. An exterior storage shed is added and helps define an outdoor deck.

Disaster Resistance

The house need not be limited to post-disaster scenarios. In disaster-prone zones, the house offers a smart way to prepare for the possibility of high winds and can be prefabricated or built on-site. Innovative technologies can be adapted to new construction design or retro-fitted in existing homes.[8]

From the initial conceptual development of ShelteR³ through the entire two-year competition, students and professors from across the campus participated. Nine professors from seven disciplines mentored more than 100 Drury students from 22 different majors on this project (Fig. 3.10).

TACKLING THE CHALLENGE OF THE COMPETITION

With an emphasis on how well houses perform in energy consumption and how livable they are, student decathletes compete in ten contests during the Solar Decathlon. Each contest is worth a maximum of 100 points, for a competition total of 1000 points.[9]

The decathlon, with its ten contests and many sub-categories of contests, became the perfect vehicle for further exploring the whole-school

Fig. 3.10 ShelteR^3, Ariel view. Photo by Evan Melgren, public relations/communications team leader, Solar Decathlon

design-build methodology. Our faculty team looked at the ten contests from a liberal arts perspective and encouraged students to participate in or lead any contest team regardless of their majors. While the decathlon, in general, is about designing, building, and operating a solar-powered house, the members of our diverse liberal arts team could quickly see a role for themselves in the ten contests. The contests focused on architecture, market appeal, engineering, communications, affordability, comfort zone, appliances, home life, commuting, and energy balance.

ORGANIZATION

In our team, responsibility for the contests was divided between the two schools; however, any student from either school could co-lead and/or be a member of any team. Administrative and management tasks were divided between the institutions. Student leadership roles and a hierarchy of roles were created. Students applied for leadership positions and were selected based on an application and references. Teams were created that aligned with the organization of the competition, and faculty mentors were established and assigned to teams. Committees within the contest teams were formed to manage each category of the contest. A fundraising committee was formed. Student participants chose to work on contest teams based on their personal interests and enthusiasm for the particular contest.

Emphasis was placed on maximizing the number of leadership opportunities, and the organizational structure promoted diversity in the teams. The mixing of problem-solving approaches within the teams improved students' learning outcomes and exposed students to methods outside of their comfort zones. For example, in the communications team, students in a professional program of the school of business were exposed to the creative problem-solving tactics of the arts students as they worked together on competition deliverables. In turn, the arts students learned from the analytical process of the business school students.

In addition to team roles and leadership positions, all the students participating were encouraged to participate in all aspects of the project, including the conceptual development. This promoted two important outcomes: a feeling of ownership in the project for the non-architecture students and a rigorous, lively dialogue about design for everyone involved.

During the development of the design, it was observed that a nursing student was challenging architecture students on the livability of the home and the potential work flow if the home were being used during a disaster response. Designers should, of course, think about and address these issues but are rarely challenged in this way by peers outside of their discipline while they are in school.

As noted earlier, the future architect must have the ability to communicate well and understand how different groups occupy and use a building. While we argue that all architecture students at Drury are receiving a liberal arts education, working with students from 22 distinctive majors on the Solar Decathlon project created a unique transdisciplinary, engaged-learning experience that should deepen architecture students' preparation for the profession.

The liberal arts and business students gained some professional skills needed for successful employment in their fields. John Munschauer states in *Jobs for English Majors and Other Smart People:* "There are just two types of jobs: 'professional work' that requires special training in law school, medical school, architecture school, and so forth, and 'trait-oriented work,' for which employers seek workers with traits such as communications skills, imagination, reasoning ability, and sound judgment."[10]

Participation in a whole-school design-build project is an engaged-learning experience that *trains* the future professional and develops the *traits* employers are seeking. Cross-pollination of training-oriented thinkers and trait-oriented thinkers challenges both groups to think critically and solve problems in ways they are not normally challenged to do in their respective disciplines, thereby blurring the line between training and trait development for both groups.

Every decision we made called on the liberal arts in some way during the competition. For example, during the competition in Irvine, time was set aside for the public to tour the Solar Village and the competition houses. Each team conducted tours of their home and educated visitors about the technical aspects of the home. Scripts, tour routes, brochures, signage, and guide stations were created by a collaboration of architecture and communications students; all team members practiced until each one became an expert on every aspect of the home. In our case, the tour included special features of our home: disaster resilience, the three R's of ShelteR^3, and highlights of our liberal arts applications in the competition. Notable aspects of this last feature included the student/professor art exhibit curated by an arts-administration major, and the custom furniture and dishes designed by an alumnus and a professor.

Many rewarding stories of students' personal and professional growth developed as a result of participating in the whole-school projects. For example, a communications student asked if the professor thought ShelteR^3 was in the style of the Beaux Arts. When asked how he was familiar with the Beaux Arts, he said that the Solar Decathlon project and "hanging out with the architecture students" had caused him to develop an interest in architecture so he checked out books on architecture to educate himself about style and typologies. He also said that knowing more about architecture would help him develop a strategy for the communications contest for the competition. Later, during the last summer before the competition, when all of the architecture students were off on their required internships, this student taught himself an architectural 3-D modeling software so that he could create a model of the house to use in the required competition video (http://shelter.drury.edu/). The student's motivation to engage in learning beyond the requirements of his courses and the application of critical thinking that this student was displaying was exactly the outcome we hope for in all liberal arts students and very much the outcome we strive for in a whole-school engaged-learning experience.

Additional examples of participants' growth include accounting students who learned fundraising skills; a graphic-design student who learned to write weekly blogs; architecture students who learned cost-estimating; many students in different majors developing leadership and public-speaking skills; a business-administration student who learned grant writing; physics students who learned solar design; an architecture student and a physics student who developed leadership and management skills; and a student who "hated the outdoors" but changed her mind when she spent the summer learning to weld while building the house. And naturally, they all learned about sustainability, architecture, and disaster resilience.

From the nursing student who challenged the architecture students about design, to an economics major who delivered a TED-style talk at the competition's opening ceremonies, to the architecture student who says she will never again be afraid of speaking to a crowd, students surpassed their own expectations, became leaders, and learned from one another.

In developing every mandated deliverable of the contest we approached the design of the home and the competition from our liberal arts perspective. Our team constantly looked for and created opportunities for students to showcase what liberal arts diversity could bring to a very technical competition. The resulting home was rich in concept, challenged the students, and showcased the best in liberal arts education through multiple layers of interventions. ShelteR^3 delivered the message that we can design for resilience using the strength of a liberal arts education.

The competition was long and fierce; the field of university teams was impressive and strong. After the dust settled on the two-year endeavor, our Crowder-Drury, ShelteR^3 team took 8th place in the field of 20 competitors. Being the smallest college/university with the smallest budget by more than one and a half million dollars to our next closest competitor (others had multiple millions more in their budgets) we feel we gave our competitors a run for their money, literally.

Mid-way though the competition we were ranked as high as 4th place but we made a few rookie mistakes toward the end, including running out of water in our storage tanks taking us completely out of the last hot water creation contest and stopping a washer in the spin cycle of the laundry contest to save energy just to run the dryer longer. But the one mistake our team made that the faculty will never forget and most likely cherish forever is when the student decathletes forgot to plug in the electric car for the commuting contest on the last night because they were more focused on creating a surprise "thank you" party for the faculty on the beach. The

Fig. 3.11   ShelteR³, Impact resistant doors created by Kawneer. Photo by Evan Melgren

image of the students gathered together, standing on picnic tables with big smiles and signed posters thanking us for creating the experience for them will forever be burned into our memories and our hearts (Fig. 3.11).

SUCCESSES AND DIFFICULTIES OF THE WHOLE-SCHOOL APPROACH

Difficulties

Design-build projects, with or without a whole-school approach, require deep passion and dedication from the faculty who lead them. Time commitments from participating faculty are well beyond that of a typical faculty workload. Faculty are not compensated for the additional workload.

Faculty must mentor students throughout the project in ways that go well beyond a normal classroom experience. Administrative infrastructure and support are needed for the faculty and students to successfully execute these endeavors.

Releases from normal teaching loads are mandatory to provide faculty members with the added time commitment of a design-build project. However, the extraordinary time commitment and lack of compensation can be draining for faculty over the long term. Communication across the team is critical for long-term engagement of students and a successful final product.

Successes

Working with transdisciplinary teams has steadily increased the rigor of the work and improved the design outcomes. Everyone can have input and impact on design, which creates a sense of ownership in the project for each student.

Typically, due to the academic demands of the program, students in architecture do not meet as many students in other majors as most college students do over the course of their education. However, in the whole-school project we see new friendships formed and long-term professional connections begin to develop for students in all majors. Non-architecture majors become comfortable and socialize in the building housing the school of architecture.

Intimate work sessions with staff, faculty, and large numbers of local volunteers helped students understand that we are designing and building for others rather than ourselves, created a heightened sense of community, and reinforced giving in a selfless way.

The unique experience of a whole-school design-build project on their resumes sets students apart from others with the same degree and makes the students more competitive as they enter the job market. The leadership skills developed by students willing to take on those roles further set them apart from their peers.

A wide variety of opportunities may develop for students as a direct result of participation and leadership in the projects, including internships, fellowships, employment, and, in one case, the chance to conduct a presentation at a Congressional briefing in Washington, D.C. Opportunities for faculty include student help with their scholarship, some of which embraced behavioral research combined with design research.

Aligning design-build projects with institutional values opened doors within the university and fostered support from upper administration, which is key to successful projects at the scale of the case studies. Some prospective students chose Drury University in order to have a whole-school design-build experience.[11]

CONCLUSION

Whole-school design-build at Drury University has created tributes, healing gardens, bunks for kids with special needs, a structure with LEED platinum status, chicken coops, and a disaster-resilient home, among many other projects. The community groups served will benefit for years to come and, hopefully, the students will carry the experiences, special moments, lessons learned, and friendships with them for a lifetime (Fig. 3.12).

Project Collaborations

C-Street Farmers Market: Traci Sooter, Q. Scott Ragan, Myra Miller, 2005 third year architecture students, Shane Aaron, Liz Aiello, Lindsay Barcomb, Lalima Chemjong, Stacy Hancock, Elizabeth Hilgedick, Jason Hudspeth, Chandra McAllister, Luke Pullman, Daniel Richards, Chad Thompson, Tim Uelk; 2005 Advertising and Public Relations course

Fig. 3.12 Crowder-Drury team at Solar Decathlon Competition, 2013. Photo by Evan Melgren

students; Special Thanks: to Tom Bonebrake, Michael Buono, Mary Collette, James Mann, Tim Nelson.

Extreme Makeover: Home Edition, "Camp Barnabus," Purdy, MO: Traci Sooter, Stanley Rone; Architecture Design-Build students: Adam Kreher, Alexander Antonuk, Chad Thompson, Chandra McAllister, Daniel Richards, Dennie Sanders, Elizabeth Hilgedick, Fred Decker, Jamie Craighead, Jason Hudspeth, Lalima Chemjong, Lance Windsor, Lindsay Barcomb, Luke Pulliam, Ryan Stewart, Shane Aaron, Stacy Hancock, Tracy Steinhauser; Special Thanks to: Michael Buono, Cindy Howell, Laura Martin, Jenifer Martin, Diana McGinnis, Dana Sooter, Robyn Sooter, Sharon Sooter, Shelia Martin, Angie Woodcock, Linda, and Danny Woodcock

Extreme Makeover: Home Edition, "Collins Family," Murfreesboro, AR, 4-H Barn: Traci Sooter, Q. Scott Ragan, Dr. Valerie Eastman, Chris Smith, Donna Smith, Angie Woodcock; Drury University students, faculty, and staff: Amy Ehlers, Andrew Mattson, Bethany Kehlenbrink, Carly Rickerson, Chad Walker, Chris J. Smith, Deann Place, Donna Smith, Donovan Ross, Emily Taylor, Jeffrey Terranova, Juan Chavez, Lannette Guerra, Leah Landers, Mary Tickner, Michael Brown, Nikolas Chkautovich, Paul Davis, Rachel Shanks, Bo Roberts.

LEED Platinum Habitat for Humanity Home: Traci Sooter, 2007 Third year design studio students; 2008 Drury Design-Build students: Christopher Blackard, Anna Boehm, Juan Chavez, Nikolas Chkautovich, Cody Craddock, Amy Ehlers, Andy Mattson, DeAnn Place, Heather Ray, Bo Roberts, Adam Schmitz, Rachel Shanks, Jeff Terranova; The "Dream Team": Kevin Baird, Laura Bergman, Craig Culbertson, Christine Friederich, Lindsay Greer, Tyler Hellweg, Anna Kangas, Bethany Kehlenbrink, Audrey Mc Namera, Bryon Oster, Geoff Vaughn; Dr. Valerie Eastman, Dr. Wendy Anderson, Pastor Roger Ray, Q. Scott Ragan, Thomas Storlozzi, "B," Drury fall 2007 freshman class, 100+ Drury faculty, staff, and student volunteers; Special Thanks to Todd Parnell, McGinnis Wood Products

Extreme Makeover: Home Edition, "Hampton Family," Fair Grove, MO, Eggstreme Chicken Coop: Traci Sooter, Stanley Rone, Bethany Kehlenbrink; Drury University students, faculty, staff, alumni, and friends: Alexander Reyland, Andy Mattson, Ann L. Saunders, Audrey McNamera, Beth Nichols, Beverly Walker, Bill Scorse, Bryon Oster, Christopher Coonce, Conrad Remington, Darrin Teaford, David Beach, Derek Shultz, Donald Weber, Drew Reap, Eric Biffle, Happy Brazeal, Ivy Hurst, Jacob

Cordonnier, Jared Hoffpauir, Jatanna Gatewood, Jeff Hoener, Jessica Eli, Jessica Reed, Joel Thomas, Joseph Algiere, Kelly Marten, Kevin Baird, Kirsten King, Kuleya Bruce, Linda Brown, Lynne Reed, Mark Miller, Mary McFarland; Matt Trtan, Mike Hampton, Nelson Nichols, Pete Radecki, R Haraldson, Rebekah Wissmann, Dr. Regina Waters, Robert Deal, Robyn Sooter, Ryan Podolsky, Saori Nakayama, Sara Hornor, Susan Church, Tiffany Fahrig, Tony Decamp, Tywanna Walker. Special Thanks to: Michael Buono, Charles Taylor

Extreme Makeover: Home Edition, "7 Houses in 7 Days" The Volunteer Tribute, Joplin, MO: Traci Sooter, Nancy Chikaraishi, Rufus Louderback, Keith Hedges, Dr. Regina Waters, Courtney Swan, Drury SmartMob!; 2011 third year architecture class: Alexander Price, Andrew Allmon, Ashley Clayton, Brenda Varela, Brennan Scott, Christopher Grosser, Christopher Kemp-Baird, Cody Hearne, Elyse Coulter, Emily Biagioni-Paulette, Emily McVey, Erin Sikorski, Halie McCarter, Ismail Diken, Jacquelyn Paulsmeyer, Jake Roberts, Jonathan Hays, Justin Robben, Kevin Rogan, Kirsten Whitehead, Kyle Presnell, Laura Harmon, Mathew Stockstill, Natalie Endejan, Nicholas Fish, Paden Chambers, Ryan Kimmel, Samuel McBride, Sean Arkin, Victor Schmick, William Miller, William Toedtmann, Young-Soo Yang, Zachary Davisson, Zolfar Hassib, 200+ Drury community volunteers; Special Thanks to: Todd and Betty Parnell, Michael Buono, Chris Cotten, Angie Woodcock, Linda and Danny Woodcock

Butterfly Garden and Overlook: Funded by TKF Foundation, Walmart Foundation; Drury University: Traci Sooter, Nancy Chikaraishi, Keith Hedges, Dr. Natalie Wlodarczyk, Dr. Jennifer Silva Brown, Dr. Peter Meidlinger, Jayon You, Sam McBride, Jon Hays, Ryan Osborne; Joplin Parks and Recreation: Chris Cotten, Steve Curry, Jeremy Glenn, Joplin Parks and Recreation crew; Cormell University: Keith Tidball; USDA Forest Service: Erika Svendsen, Lindsay Campbell, Nancy Falxa-Sonti; Forest ReLeaf of Missouri; Donna Coble; Great River Associates: Jerany Jackson, Ryan Evits; Drury Design-Build students: Eric Foster, Olivia Freese, Stacie Good, Michael Ligibel, Grace Lounsbury, Madison Miles, Kanna Matsuo, Jacob Nentrup, Olivia Snell, Lauren Southard, Josh Storey, Brian Vanne, Trevor Wellman, Brandon White; Special Thanks to the Joplin Community, Chris Cotten, Todd and Betty Parnell and the Butterflies

Crowder-Drury Solar Decathlon competition house, ShelteR³: Respond, Recover, Resist: Drury University: Traci Sooter, Nancy Chikaraishi,

Marshall Arne, Keith Hedges, Kelley Still Nichols, Dr. Regina Waters, Dr. Steve Mullins, Dr. Peter Meidlinger, Dr. Rick Maxson; Dr. Saundra Weddle, Nelson Nichols, Ryan Osborne, David Cogorno, Rebecca Miller, Brian Shipman, Dr. Jonathan Groves; Andrea Battaglia, Debbie Huff, Mike Brothers; Consultants: Art Boyt, Q. Scott Ragan; Drury Student Leaders: Alaa AlRadwan, Mat Stockstill, Jonas Gassmann, Evan Melgren, Corey Marquardt, Swapnaneel Nath, Emma Reynolds, Vikas Jagwani, Alex Viehman, Cody Stepp, Brian Vanne, Lukas Kriem; Michaela Cantrell, Ahmed Altheiban, Avery Smith, Tina Haberberger, Chase Snider, Greg Snapp, Travis Bond, Ray Horner, Ashley Hesterberg, Wing Lam, Elisha Segrist, Sarah Watts, Kiah McCarley, Pema Wangzome, Joe Vander Pluym, Camille Hoang-Van, Evan Johnson; Drury Team Members: Kevin Abernathy, Bader Al- Shawaf, Yasmeen AlTamimi, Nick Alexander, Abdullah AlSahafi, Nick Ammann, Jessie Barton, Sara Beck, Alexandria Brewer, Rebekah Burleigh, Darwin Campbell, Christopher Cassity, Tamara Cartwright, Daniela Carvajal, Brittany Carver, Jessica Caudill, Jin Chang, Kyle Clingan, Mitch Daniel, Kevin Daroga, Jantzen Davis, Cameron Derossett, Irene Detrinidad, Ghada Elhaffar, Wayne Elliott, Eric Foster, Olivia Freese, Chesney Fries, Ivan Garnica, Brett Green, Megan Goosey, Julia Hartman, Michael Hightower, Camille Hoang-Van, Luke Huff, Tiara Hughes, Quoc Huynh, Trey Johnson, Addison Jones, Beatriz Juan, Phil Kean, Hwani Lee, Michael Ligibel, Albert Lloyd, Patrick Lopez, Grace Lounsbury, Thomas Louzader, Danny Loza, Michael Loza, Jamie Lu, Jordi Ma Lu, Zoe Mack, Kevin Madera, Madison Miles, Sam McBride, JR McClelland, Miranda Middleton, Stephanie Monroe, Ricardo Moreno, Andrew Newman, Kayla Nichols,Rafaela Noboa, Gbeminiyi Olugbenle, Jacky Paulsmeyer, Andres Pena, Melyssa Prenger, Alex Price, Ennis Randle, Scott Robinson, Brandon Roellig, Ryan Ruzycki, Shahad Sadeq, Bryce Schmidt, Tasha Symonds, Nicole Shaul, Lauren Shelton, Kyrie Simmons, Kevin Still, Lauren Southard, Xiadi Sun, Caleb Swadley, Shauntae Taylor, Rubi Trinh, Leo Vandeuren, Kim Velten, Alex Walker, Helin Wang, Tyler Weber, Abigail Weller, Samantha Williams, Micha Willis, Jeremy Womack, Tony Yue, Junye Zhou, Victoria Ziegler; Crowder College: Terry Clarkson, Kevin Newby, Russ Hopper, Jarren Welch, Matt Keeton, Mathew Lawson, Brandon Forkner, Janie Redding, Brock Cullen, Nicholas Jarosz, Daniel Mahoney, James Cantrell, Gage Harmon, Ashley Douthett, Contractors: Brandon Butcher, Steve Grauerholz; Gale Perry, Heriberto Sote; Special Thanks to: Carol Gaskill, Katherine Beseau, A.T. Kilani, Suzanne Ferguson, Robert Weddle

Special Thanks to: Nancy Chikaraishi. Professor of Architecture, for taking the leap of faith and collaborating since 2011; Keith Hedges, Associate Professor of Architecture, for being the positive, calm collaborator in a storm, and Drury University for supporting this innovative work.

Notes

1. U.S. Department of Commerce, National Oceanic and Atmospheric Administration, National Weather Service, Central Region Headquarters Kansas City, MO, June 2011. *NWS Central Region Service Assessment: Joplin, Missouri, Tornado—May 22, 2011*; http://www.nws.noaa.gov/om/assessments/pdfs/Joplin_tornado.pdf.
2. Mark Rohr, *Joplin: The Miracle of the Human Spirit*; (Tate Publishing, 2012).
3. Lynn Iliff Onstot, *Fact Sheet—City of Joplin—May 22, 2011 EF5 Tornado*. Public Information Office. July 1, 2013.
4. Traci Sooter, Nancy Chikaraishi, and Keith Hedges, (2014) *Whole School Design-Build in the Liberal Arts Tradition*, ACSA Fall Conference, Nova Scotia.
5. NREL, U.S. Department of Energy, *Solar Decathlon, 2013*, retrieved July 17, 2016, http://www.solardecathlon.gov/2015.
6. Sooter, Traci (2015) "It's All in the Details_ Two Missouri Schools Team up to Design Tornado Resistant Home," (2015). Accessed October 11, 2016, http://www.thenatureofcities.com/2015/07/19/its-all-in-the-details-two-missouri-schools-team-up-to-design-tornado-resistant-home/#respond.
7. "Crowder-Drury Solar Decathlon Team Conceptual Statement for ShelteR³" *Crowder-Drury Solar Decathlon Team, Drury University*, 2013, (U.S. Department of Energy 2015 Solar Decathlon).
8. Ibid. Crowder-Drury Solar Decathlon Team, Drury University 2013.
9. NREL, U. S. Department of Energy, *Solar Decathlon,* October 5, 2015, accessed October 11, 2016, http://www.solardecathlon.gov/.
10. John L Munschauer, *Jobs for English Majors & Other Smart People*. Third Ed. Peterson Nelnet Co., May 9, 1991 (first published May 1, 1981).
11. Ibid. Sooter, Traci, Chikaraishi, Nancy, Hedges, Keith (2014).

CHAPTER 4

Playing Chopin, Playing Barthes: Bringing Musical Practice to Reading

Steven Pane

To prepare a generation of "creators and empathizers, pattern recognizers, and meaning makers,"[1] students and their faculty need experience crossing disciplines—engaging ideas, problems, and questions not contained within a particular discourse. Yet interdisciplinarity is a messy thing. Unlike a multi-disciplinary approach,[2] interdisciplinarity is a practice; since there is no preexisting disciplinary language upon which to call, an interdisciplinary journey means creating a new discourse, such as borrowing a practice from one discipline and applying it to another. For example, what if we applied the process of studying music to studying an academic text? And what if in the telling of this interdisciplinary story, we stayed close to the nature of music itself—as a phenomenological art that unfolds in time. The result would be a language in which a musical word like "play" finds a place and function in the world of reading texts.

This is our interdisciplinary journey. Using a phenomenological approach, we'll follow an undergraduate pianist as she learns Frédéric Chopin's Ballade Op. 52, No. 4 in F Minor and transfers her musical approach to understand Roland Barthes's essay "The Death of the Author." Although a background in Barthes or music (even the ability to

S. Pane (✉)
University of Maine Farmington, Farmington, ME, USA

© The Author(s) 2018
N. H. Hensel (ed.), *Exploring, Experiencing, and Envisioning Integration in US Arts Education*, The Arts in Higher Education, https://doi.org/10.1007/978-3-319-71051-8_4

read the inline musical excerpts) is unnecessary, I strongly suggest listening multiple times to Chopin's Ballade No 4.[3] It is a terrific piece and adds an invaluable aural dimension to our project.

Let us now turn to our pianist.

A PHENOMENOLOGY OF PLAYING

Our student is a first-year undergraduate music major studying piano at a liberal arts college. The Chopin ballade she will practice shortly is fiercely difficult and is, at the moment, beyond her capabilities. Nonetheless, it will deepen her pianism more than works at her current level. In a few months she will perform the ballade, barely, but will give a strong performance when she returns to the piece three years later for her senior recital.

But we are getting ahead of ourselves. At the moment our pianist is in a small practice room seated in front of the piano; she plays the opening of the ballade up to where the music pauses on the fermata (Fig. 4.1-E).

She stops playing and reads something she wrote on the inside cover of the score,[4] a quote by Daniel Barenboim about how music emerges from and returns to silence: "[The musician] bring[s] it into the world. The sound does not exist in this world ... it is ephemeral."[5] This is her conceptual starting point for the opening of the ballade. The challenge is to get the quiet right-hand octaves (Fig. 4.1-A) to emerge from nowhere—as if the continuation of some music existing prior to the piece. *This will be very hard,* she thinks. *Louder openings are easier.*

Playing from the beginning again she becomes aware of the myriad of notes, articulations, and contrary dynamic markings. *Is all this noise any way to emerge from silence?* She reaches the fermata (Fig. 4.1-E), stops, and sees another contradiction: The music is searching, yet its repetitiveness (same melody fragment, same harmonies) keep it in neutral—*a momentum that moves nowhere.* The fermata pauses the momentum and waits. *Waits for what?*

She jumps to the middle and plays her favorite moment (Fig. 4.1-C), where the music opens up: The right hand makes a wide stretch and the left reaches down and plays the lowest note heard so far. *This feels good,* she thinks as her body sinks into the keys. *Perhaps I could set this moment up as a peak for the opening?* She starts from the beginning again and aims for this moment. On the way she realizes her unimportant, accompanimental 16th notes are drowning out the melody. She adjusts, on the fly, pulling back the volume, quieting the accompaniment but, unfortunately, the

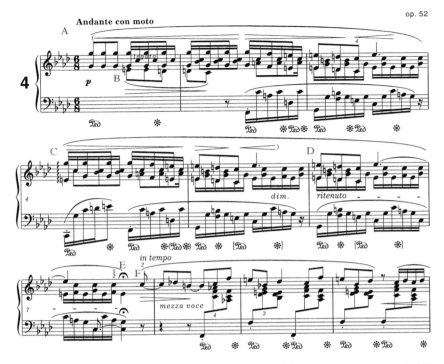

Fig. 4.1 Frédéric Chopin, Ballade No. 4 in F Minor, opening, mm. 1–10. Frédéric Chopin, "Ballade op. 52, no. 4 in F minor," in *Ballady op. 23, 38, 47, 52,* edited by Jan Ekier, and Pawel Kamin' ski (Kraków: Polskie Wydawnictwo Muzyczne, 2015) 48

melody as well. *Playing the accompaniment softer isn't enough. I have to shape[6] the melody so it emerges from the background.*

Because there is so much going on at once, she decides to concentrate on shaping one part; she plays just the melody:

This isn't a melody; it is a fragmented fragment: the fragment itself (Fig. 4.2-X), *part of the fragment,* (Fig. 4.2-Y), *then just the fragment's last four notes* (Fig. 4.2-Z). This is what pianist Alfred Brendel calls foreshortening,[7] when fragments are repeated in a series and the last one, or last few, are truncated. Musically, foreshortening can either intensify or pull back the momentum; here, it's winding things down. She decides to try the last fragment (Fig. 4.2-Z) as an echo of the preceeding one (Fig. 4.2-Y). She plays the melody alone again (Fig. 4.2-X), builds up to the high point (Fig. 4.2-Y), and concludes with an echo (Fig. 4.2-Z). *Nice.*

Fig. 4.2 Frédéric Chopin, Ballade No. 4 in F minor, opening with melody extracted, mm. 1–7

She returns to the beginning, this time playing all the notes, and suddenly notices the left-hand entrance is a secondary melody.[8] She starts again, gently brings out the left-hand entrance (Fig. 4.1-B), and continues through to her moment (Fig. 4.1-E), making a dramatic arc. *Cool.* When she reaches the foreshortened fragment (Fig. 4.1-D), she plays it like an echo and quietly eases into the fermata. *Okay, it sounds like something now.*

And it doesn't work. Rather than emerging from Barenboim's silence, the dramatic shape she's etched tramples on the music's ambiguity. *Too operatic.* She's frustrated but reminds herself that difficult music takes a ton of practice before it becomes hers, in her hands, in her body. The difficulty, however, is not simply dexterity, but teaching her body to integrate her thoughts, emotions, and technique to express a wide emotional spectrum in sound.

She continues to practice, yet things seem to get worse. She channels her teacher's voice: *Things have to fall apart in order to come together at a higher level.* Worried that it will sound terrible at her next lesson, she remembers that good teachers value an inchoate beginning as much as a final performance—each stage brings a different set of expectations and priorities. Still, she wonders whether she will ever play this piece well.

Looking at the clock, our pianist jumps up, grabs her stuff, and races out of the practice room. Running across campus she arrives just at the start of her first-year seminar. Today the class begins "The Death of the Author," an essay by Roland Barthes. It is early October and the class is told things will start to get tough, but with challenge comes reward. *Lovely,* our pianist thinks, still frustrated about the ballade.

A student is asked to read the first line:

In his story *Sarrasine,* Balzac, describing a castrato disguised as a woman, writes the following sentence[9]:

Our pianist tunes out the class. She lets her eyes scan the page and notices the punctuation demarcating phrases. She begins organizing the sentences as musical ideas. She stops for a moment—*too much Chopin*—but then resumes: (1) "In his story *Sarrasine,* Balzac," (2) "describing a castrato disguised as a woman," (3) "writes the following sentence."

There are three short melodic fragments, separated by commas, leading to a cadence on the colon—similar to Chopin's fermata (Fig. 4.1-E), except Chopin's fermata-stop is trying to think of where to go next. Here the colon commands us to stop and prepare for:

This was woman herself, with her sudden fears, her irrational whims, her instinctive worries, her impetuous boldness, her fussing, and her delicious sensibility.

With the entrance of another's voice comes a change in the sound. *Let's make the opening string instruments and "this was woman herself" a wind instrument—sounding at a distance, but still commenting on the present moment. Perhaps an English horn. It has an older sound, matching the shift to a more poetic prose.*

Her concentration is momentarily broken as she hears the class break out in pained expressions of shock—the instructor has just explained what a castrato is. She returns to her work.

Okay, after the colon, "her" is repeated six times, and that's not counting "herself." She organizes each "her" as the beginning of a melodic fragment: her sudden fears, her irrational whims, her instinctive worries. *Playing these fragments requires shaping each repetition as distinctive to avoid monotony—yet not so unique that we lose momentum toward the final repetition.* She starts looking at the progression of the words:

fears, whims, worries, boldness, fussings, and then ... surprise: delicious sensibility.

A joke—a buildup of expectation through foreshortening and then a deceptive cadence[10] on "delicious sensibility."[11] She quietly verbalizes the passage, building momentum as the list unfolds, then suddenly imagines herself playing "delicious sensibility" softly and with a wink. *Cool.*

Another student reads the next passage of Balzac. Our pianist tunes in to follow along.

> Who is speaking thus? Is it the hero of the story bent on remaining ignorant of the castrato hidden beneath the woman? Is it Balzac the individual, furnished by his personal experience with a philosophy of Woman? Is it Balzac the author professing "literary" ideas on femininity? Is it universal wisdom? Romantic psychology?

Our piano student counts. Six question marks. *Lots of expressive possibilities—wait, there were six "hers" in the previous quote. Barthes is balancing the flow of text. And like the "hers" quote, he uses foreshortening, except it ends differently. Rather than the playful deceptive cadence ("delicious sensibilities"), the momentum moves forward as the questions seem to gobble themselves up. It is also contradictory; despite the structural assertiveness of short rhetorical questions, we seem increasingly lost. Questions lead to more questions.*

She is momentarily distracted by a student who is unhappy Barthes writes this way: Can't Barthes just get to the point?

Refocusing, she reads ahead on her own:

> We shall never know, for the good reason that writing is the destruction of every voice, of every point of origin.

"We simply will never know" stops the momentum of the previous questions, but then we resume the push toward instability with a dissonant "destruction of every voice." She notices more foreshortening ("every point of origin"), though here it brings things to a stop. She quietly verbalizes the phrases with a breath-length silence after "origin."

She reads on.

> Writing is that neutral, composite, oblique space where our subject slips away, the negative where all identity is lost, starting with the very identity of the body writing.

This sentence is different from anything so far—no foreshortening. It is also the first sentence that could stand on its own. Yet in spite of the assertive structure the message delivered is ominous, we are losing identity.

She is again distracted, this time by the instructor's voice talking about the difference between "work" and "Text" in Barthes. The instructor reads something to the class:

the work can be held in the hand, the text is held in language, only exists in the movement of a discourse (or rather, it is Text for the very reason that it knows itself as text); the Text is not the decomposition of the work, it is the work that is the imaginary tail of the Text; or again, the Text is experienced only in an activity of production. It follows that the Text cannot stop (for example on a library shelf); its constitutive movement is that of cutting across (in particular, it can cut across the work, several works).[12]

The class is not appeased. More objections surface: Is it really pronounced "ball-sack"? Tuning out the class again, our pianist returns to the top of the text. *Castrato?* A surprising image to open with and is like many musical works that start by knocking us off our balance.

Damn. She's been called on. She has no idea what the question was. This instructor is nice, but young and sometimes stymied when students don't find the material interesting. She sympathizes. Most of her friends aren't into classical music. You have to give it time, she would tell them. Let it become a part of you, then it gets better with time.

Rather than asking to repeat the question, she fesses up: "Sorry, I've been pretending these sentences are musical phrases—shaping them how I'd play notes on the piano." The class is amused but intrigued. Sensing this, the instructor asks her to explain.

Our pianist walks the class through her process with a few students jumping in and offering their own sentence phrasings. Still fixated on the castrato, several offer ways to play the opening: "Cas-trAAA-to!" The instructor laughs, though nervously. "You guys are stealing the energy in the room." Then he adds, half seriously, "I hope we aren't trading academic rigor for silliness." The instructor thinks about how some of his colleagues slam this generation of students for a lack of seriousness in their reading and writing. *But Barthes would love this playing of his prose.*

Dividing the students into small groups, the instructor asks them to play the text as our pianist had done. "Use your body, read it aloud to each other, perform it—make it part of you, make it your own," he says. There is a great deal of energy in various parts of the room, and this carries over after they return to share their "playings." Amid the fun and wayward phrasings of various sentences, the instructor notices the students seem motivated to keep trying until they find a convincing rendering.[13]

Class ends. Students leave. The instructor returns to his office and pulls Barthes's *Image, Music, Text* off the shelf. He turns to a passage in "From Work to Text": *"Playing" must be understood here in all its polysemy: the text itself plays ... and the reader plays twice over, playing the Text as one plays a game, looking for a practice which re-produces it, but, in order that that practice not be reduced to a possessive, inner mimesis (the Text is precisely that which resists such a reduction), also playing the Text in the musical sense of the term.*[14]

The instructor reflects on how this was the messiest of the classes so far. Rather than the planned walk through the text, the class wrested control, barreling through their misreadings, yet using the mistakes to reflect on what might work better. It was a good class. They took risks. That's where learning begins, for students and instructors.

THE MOTILITY OF THE BODY AND THE PLEASURE OF THE TEXT

In the opening quote of the chapter, Barthes writes about a *muscular* playing where the body, rather than transmitting, *controls* and *inscribes* the music. For example, our pianist's muscular practice embodied everything from an unconscious stroke of the key to her most complex cognitive thought. In playing, the mind/body dualism collapses amid a synesthesia of senses, as hearing, seeing, touching meld to advance the project at hand. Merleau-Ponty calls this the motility of the body, something violinist and philosopher Elizabeth Behnke describes in "At the Service of the Sonata: Music Lessons with Merleau-Ponty":

> we find that with Merleau-Ponty and other phenomenological writers, "the body" need not be taken as an "object" manipulated by an ego or "subject" somewhere "inside" it. It is an immediate living presence, "mine" not because I reflect on it from a unique point of view, but because I hold sway through it; "consciousness is in the first place not a matter of 'I think that' but of 'I can.'" My body is not fundamentally a thing that I cause to move, but an original motility, radiating a field and domain of powers and possibilities, through which I am engaged in the world.[15]

Since motility collapses mind and body, approaching music from Cartesian "pure thought" is to operate at a deficiency. Music is conceived from and created by the body's motility, the point from which it engages the world.

In poetry, like music, we speak of body, yet not so much in academic reading since we usually guide students to read contemplatively—carefully, silently, pencil in hand. Certainly essential and beloved, silent reading is invaluable, but need it be the only way into a text? For students grappling with a tough read, playing the text, shaping the sentences as our pianist did, creates a physical engagement transforming the academic reading experience into something deeper than the data-mining method encouraged by textbooks. For students, the text itself—its syntax, form, grammar—becomes its own bodily motility brought to life through the intent of play. This may raise the dilemma that occurred to the instructor: What about the shapings of text that go against the grain of the how the text is usually understood? *CastrAAAto*. Does the teacher offer praise for mere creative expression or does accuracy count, and are corrections worth interrupting the students' self-driven process?

The answer is neither. The dilemma need not exist. The practice of musical phrasing is not just trying stuff out, but trying stuff out as part of a larger intent. Near the end of her practice session, our pianist develops a phrasing she ultimately rejects for being "too operatic"[16]; it provided a shape, *felt good even*, but did not match her conception of an opening emerging from silence. This will be one among legions of phrasings she will try out and reject. And a good teacher will encourage her to accept these legions as the very material constructing her path toward a performance-ready version.[17]

In the classroom, before students play a text, they need to understand that it is not about right or wrong phrasings, but *having at it*—taking the needed risks to construct a path toward an embodied understanding. Like a toddler learning to walk, a musician struggling with a tough piece or an instructor trying a new approach to teaching, the resulting wobbliness, tortured phrasings, or awkward interactions are not misfires, but the stuff of learning itself. Like the piano teacher, the instructor works alongside students, helping them cultivate their own questions as they work toward a convincing reading. This is rigorous work for both student and instructor as it eschews the comfortable teacher gives/student receives model for an improvisation of dialogue. *Okay, do you wish to make the case that the CastrAAAto is the dramatic centerpiece of the Barthes essay? If so, how would the rest of the text need to play? If not, then why does Barthes lead off with a castrato?*[18]

Let's turn to student writing. Playing, as we are using the term here, cuts across the composer/performer and reader/writer roles, helping students see their own reading and writing as inextricably linked. Grammar, rather than a set of laws, becomes an expressive tool for shaping the textual body; the inchoate first draft is just as valued as the final version, and

Barthes, no longer the indecipherable "genius," becomes the students' ally—one who can help them become better writers. At the next class, the instructor might strengthen the reading-writing integration by adopting the centuries-old practice of musical embodiment: copying and recontextualizing the work of another. Students can experiment with co-opting Barthes's syntactical structures to express their own ideas in writing: from practicing foreshortening to borrowing the structures he uses to sustain long sentences in the expression of complex ideas. With writing, this aspect of playing pushes the Chopin Ballade and "The Death of the Author" toward "open works" that the pianist and reader are invited to remix. As Barthes writes, "to compose, at least by propensity, is *to give to do,* not to give to hear but to give to write."[19]

In *The Philosopher's Touch: Sartre, Nietzsche, and Barthes at the Piano,* Francois Noudelmann gives us an image of Barthes's own classroom:

> Barthes loved wavering; he loved the suspension of power and its territorial drive. It was the same with his status as a professor: He dreaded magisterial discourse. During his seminars, attended by an ever more numerous public, his voice would tighten with mistrust; he did not want to give a doctoral ring or kick to it. Barthes confessed that he hoped instead to create an atmosphere of hashish-smoking: 'Everything is there, but floating.' Speech frees itself from meaning and from the law. Accompanying curls of smoke and melopoeias, speech becomes more like music: Sprechgesang[20] and cannabis. Barthes dreamed of himself as Pierrot Lunaire (Moonstruck Pierrot), who could escape what Sartre had already called the spirit of seriousness.[21]

Playing—in all its polysemy—is playful. And it is in the creative space of play that musicians are particularly receptive to experiencing the *pleasure* of the music. This is not something they receive, but create in their own rendering of the piece. In spite of her frustrations with the ballade, our pianist has moments of joy at the keyboard, moments when she emotionally connects, embodying the sentiment of a particular passage—*I love this here*. Barthes seeks the same in reading—"the pleasure of the text is that moment when my body pursues its own ideas." A musical approach applied to academic reading puts students at the center of an interdisciplinary practice, and by embodying and shaping the text themselves, they can become Barthes's pleasure-seeking readers. A welcome change from the associated drudgery of assigned readings, this can be liberating for a student, a kind of birth—the birth of a playful reader.

NOTES

1. Daniel H Pink, *A Whole New Mind: Moving from the Information Age to the Conceptual Age* (New York: Riverhead Books, 2006), 1.
2. Multi-disciplinary inquiry views a subject from two or more different disciplinary perspectives.
3. Multiple recordings of the Chopin Ballade are available on various streaming services. Given the focus on the physical experience in this chapter, viewing a video performance is recommended (e.g., You Tube, Vimeo).
4. The score is the sheet music.
5. Daniel Barenboim, "The Phenomenon of Sound." Daniel Barenboim, 2004, accessed June 17, 2016, http://danielbarenboim.com/the-phenomenon-of-sound.
6. The musical terms "shaping" and "phrasing" are used interchangeably, referring to how a musician uses momentum, volume, and other expressive tools to turn a group of individual notes into a sonic idea.
7. Alfred Brendel, "The Process of Foreshortening in Music," in *Alfred Brendel on Music: Collected Essays* (Chicago: Cappella Books, 2001) 58.
8. A secondary melody, like a descant, interacts with the main melody.
9. Roland Barthes, "The Death of the Author," in *Image, Music, Text*, trans. by Stephen Heath, (New York: Hill and Wang, 1977) 142. Is our pianist shaping the sentences of Roland Barthes or Stephen Heath? Clearly it is both, and given the focus on the prose, Heath's voice plays an important role.
10. A "cadence" is a pause in the momentum of music. There are different types of cadences depending on what is happening musically, much like punctuation marks: a colon pauses differently than a semicolon and a sentence period pauses differently than one concluding a paragraph.
11. A "deceptive cadence" occurs when the music prepares the listener for one kind of chord, but then delivers a different, unexpected one.
12. Roland Barthes, "From Work to Text," in *Image, Music, Text*, trans. by Stephen Heath, (New York: Hill and Wang, 1977) 157.
13. It is not necessarily the students with a musical background who have an affinity for phrasing sentences.
14. Barthes, "The Death of the Author," 162–163.
15. Elizabeth A Behnke, "At the Service of the Sonata: Music Lessons with Merleau-Ponty," in *Merleau-Ponty: Critical Essays,* ed. Henry Pietersma (University Press of America, 1989) 24. Behnke quotes from Maurice Merleau-Ponty, *Phenomenology of Perception,* trans. by Colin Smith (London: Rutledge & Kegan Paul, 1962), 137.
16. An operatic reading would involve larger gestures of sound at the expense of the intimate character the pianist wishes to achieve.

17. Since a performance or recording can never achieve a definitive ideal, a pianist's process of shaping and reshaping never ceases.

18. Although dealing primarily with writing, David Bartholomae's idea of risk applies to reading as well as music. He compares two college-placement essays: the first is grammatically sound and the second is riddled with errors. Yet, Bartholomae argues that the *second* essayist is stronger because, unlike the first, the writer takes the risk of engaging more complex ideas in a less familiar discourse. The first writer, in contrast, will need to be pried loose from safe, but constrained prose in favor of writing a "muddier and more confusing prose" in order to reach college level of writing. David Bartholomae, "Inventing the University" *Journal of Basic Writing* Vol. 5, No. 1 (1968): 20.

19. Roland Barthes, "Musica Practica," in *Image, Music, Text,* trans. by Stephen Heath (New York: Hill and Wang, 1977), 153. Barthes further writes about the loss of "muscular playing" as part of a wider cultural move away from the body. In "Musica Practica" Barthes provides a history of this change as the amateur pianists at the parlor piano gradually gives way to the long-playing record. "Musical activity is no longer manual, muscular, kneadingly physical, but merely liquid, effusive, 'lubrificating,' to take up a word from Balzac."

20. "Sprechgesang" or "Sprechstimme" asks the singer to approximate the pitches indicated in the score. The result is a voice which plays in the space between singing and speaking. In Arnold Schoenberg's *Pierrot Lunaire* (1912) the entire soprano part is written in *Sprechstimme*.

21. François Noudelmann. *The Philosopher's Touch: Sartre, Nietzsche, and Barthes at the Piano,* trans. by Brian J. Reilly (New York: Columbia University Press, 2012), 99.

CHAPTER 5

On and Off Screen: The Cinema and Media Studies Minor at Valparaiso University

Timothy J. Tomasik

At the risk of invoking a well-worn trope in contemporary examinations of higher education, I begin by stating the obvious: we now live and teach in the age of the Internet. In spite of our best efforts to deny this reality, or to forestall an irreversible embrace of it, we have to face facts. Most members of the professoriate were born and educated in an era before the Internet existed or was widely available. The vast majority of our students were born in an era in which access to the World Wide Web is a given. For these students, printed books are no longer considered the primary carriers of knowledge, civilization, and culture. The visual cues of words on a page are gradually being superseded by moving images on a screen that are enhanced through dynamic colors, formats, and sounds. Hyperlinks can virtually transport an individual from a YouTube video of a French protest, to a hyper-realistic multi-user game with players in Russia, and then to a Google Earth photo of a neighborhood street in Beijing—all in the space of mere seconds. To paraphrase Joe Young and Sam Lewis by way of Bob Marley, how do we keep our students down on the farm after they have seen Paris?

The advent of the Internet is of course not the first time our epistemology has been challenged by the invention of a new medium of communication.

T. J. Tomasik (✉)
Valparaiso University, Valparaiso, IN, USA

© The Author(s) 2018
N. H. Hensel (ed.), *Exploring, Experiencing, and Envisioning Integration in US Arts Education*, The Arts in Higher Education, https://doi.org/10.1007/978-3-319-71051-8_5

65

Near the end of the Middle Ages, a period in which knowledge was transmitted primarily via manuscripts, the invention of movable type and printed books transformed the way knowledge was organized and disseminated. The rapid reproduction of essentially identical texts cast the nets of collective wisdom much wider and in so doing created more distance between the reader and the author or source of authority. An ever-growing book market encouraged wider readership while limiting the hold over knowledge by an elite minority. Moreover, the material conditions of the book itself created new ways of reading. Rather than being limited to a linear reading from beginning to end of an unrolled scroll, readers of printed books could skip from section to section and even make use of new tools such as page numbers, indexes, and tables of contents in order to find specific information without having to read the entire text. From this perspective, hyperlinks on the web are simply distant cousins of index entries. Both help readers navigate the vast array of knowledge available and avoid information overload.

Given the inherently visual nature of our interface with the Internet, it is no coincidence that the field of visual studies has achieved a new prominence within the humanities. Since visual media are not confined to only one or two disciplines, they represent an area of great potential for interdisciplinary debate and collaboration. Like the printed book in relation to manuscripts, new visual media come loaded with technological advances, but even within such transformation, it is clear that older media are still very much a part of the new. Kindles and iPads promise storage of and rapid access to thousands of books within a small electronic device, but the designers were careful to retain the page turning features of actual printed books. Likewise, the Internet offers algorithmically rendered images of distant worlds, but the interface still takes place with a spectator gazing at a rectangular screen. Books and film, though "outdated" by the contemporary standards of our students, still inform the rapidly growing new media. As Lev Manovich puts it in *The Language of New Media*, "A hundred years after cinema's birth, cinematic ways of seeing the world, of structuring time, of narrating a story, of linking one experience to the next, have become the basic means by which computer users access and interact with all cultural data."[1] If we want to reach our students across the epistemological and technological divide between computers and books, one way is through the mediating functions and theories of cinema.

It should come as no surprise that we are already using cinematic functions and film in this way. Many humanities courses use films for a number of purposes: as a supplemental text, an illustrative example, or a springboard for discussion. As suspicious as we may be of the links between cinema and popular culture, we cannot deny in our pedagogies the attraction this medium holds for the vast majority of our students. It is true that we are, by and large, adept at modeling how to be effective readers of books and other texts. Are we as adept at teaching students how to be critical spectators? Can we harness students' attraction to film art to make our students into more critical spectators and thus by extension more critical thinkers? In short, to what extent can cinema studies contribute to an integration of the arts with disciplines more firmly rooted in professional practices?

To answer such questions, this chapter will examine the curricular design of the interdisciplinary minor in cinema and media studies (CMS) at Valparaiso University. Given the widespread and varied use of film on campus, it was clear from the beginning that this minor would be an interdisciplinary program. The minor focuses on a complicated art form that mixes a variety of media, both images and sound. Cinema studies in general also reflect trends in web-based interfaces that increasingly rely on video instead of text. In practice, the CMS minor channels the traditional critical modes of the liberal arts while engaging topical questions about the modern world and encouraging experiential learning through practical application. This combination of critical thinking, complex questions, and practical experience lies at the heart of the CMS minor, attributes clearly reflected in contemporary debates on higher education.

Indeed, it is its link to experiential and interdisciplinary learning that positions the CMS minor at Valparaiso firmly within contemporary pedagogical trends. The Lumina Foundation's Degree Qualifications Profile (DQP), for instance, focuses on the powerful drivers of "broad and integrative knowledge," which assume students receive instruction in a variety of different fields. Examining the boundaries between different fields pushes learners to ask new and more powerful questions. The DQP then takes the resulting knowledge a step further by championing "applied and collaborative learning" that creates a space for "practical skills crucial to the application of expertise." Critics may be quick to decry what on the surface could be read as a call for vocational skills over the traditional pillars of the liberal arts. However, the DQP is positing the importance of "addressing unscripted problems in scholarly inquiry, at work and in other settings outside the classroom."[2] Applying practical skills in this way may lead to what the Association of American Colleges and Universities describes in its "LEAP Challenge" as a "signature work."[3] Students integrate their knowledge from a variety of fields by completing a major or capstone project allied with their interests and passions.

In many ways, the field of film and cinema studies offers great potential as a testing ground for some of the pedagogical hypotheses and aspirations evoked above. Inherently interdisciplinary, film studies from its beginnings eschewed many of the academic constraints maintained in traditional disciplinary departments. Early attempts at studying film in academic settings tended to privilege the aesthetic qualities of film, analyzing them much like literary works. Since many early films were in fact adaptations of literary works, such work often found a welcome home in English and foreign language departments. As film studies began to coalesce into a more readily identified and independent field, the emphasis on aesthetic qualities began to shift. Thomas Leitch argues that at its inception as a recognized field, film studies "had staked its insurgent disciplinary claims by rejecting the aesthetic appreciation of literature and developing a competing methodology of cultural critique rooted in the revolutionary intellectual ferment in France during the 1960s and 1970s."[4] As such, within its own relatively short history, film studies has shifted from aesthetic analysis to cultural critique, thereby opening it up to larger and more complex social questions.

In order to situate Valparaiso's CMS minor within this larger continuum of film studies, we begin by examining how film programs at other institutions stake their disciplinary claims. Focusing this examination on the institutions that belong to the consortium of New American Colleges and Universities (NAC&U)[5] of which Valparaiso University is a member, will allow us to draw on a representative sample of institutions that are comparable in size and institutional mission. Of the 24 member institutions, fewer than half have any sort of film or cinema program.[6] The majority of those programs are housed within a particular department, typically Communication or English. Four of these programs, a mix of both minors and majors, do not require any specific production-type courses.[7] Only seven programs require coursework in video or film production, but six of those seven programs are majors rather than minors.[8]

The motion pictures major offered at Belmont University "covers writing, editing, producing, directing movies & actors, location sound recording, cinematography, post production and distribution."[9] In addition to a large number of courses that focus on filmmaking techniques, students must take at least two courses on the history of film.[10] The emphasis in this program is thus on preparing students to become professional filmmakers. Likewise, the BA in multimedia studies at California Lutheran University includes a track in "high definition digital cinema," but most of its requirements involve production-oriented coursework.[11] At this same institution, the Department of Communication offers a "film and television production" track, which encourages students to take some non-production courses such as an elective, Politics in Film, and a required course, Film Theory.[12] In the Department of Communication and Theatre Arts at John Carroll University, students can integrate a "visual media" track into a communication studies major. In addition to core courses in communications, students take a minimum of 15 credits either with a video concentration, which highlights television, radio, and journalism, or a film concentration, which emphasizes film and television history along with screenwriting. Both concentrations require a further nine elective credits in film or video directing.[13] Like John Carroll, Widener University offers a major in communication studies in which students must complete a 12-credit concentration. In the film studies concentration, "Students learn cinematography, storytelling, and editing and create pieces using industry-standard equipment. Students find their storytelling voices in screenwriting and directing classes. They have opportunities to take their filmmaking skills to a higher level through an editing class and learn sound and color correction and more in classes like Visual Effects for Film and Television."[14] The University of New Haven's BS in communication offers a similar mix of coursework in its "film production" concentration. In addition to a variety of production courses at all levels, students must take at least one course on the history of film.[15] In all five of these major programs, students are encouraged to explore both the critical and production side of film studies.

At Wagner College, students in the Department of Art, Art History and Film can obtain a major in film and media studies. This major can be further focused by adding a concentration in film making/digital arts, which focuses on the production side of film, or a concentration in film studies and media criticism, which "is humanities-based, and focuses on the theory and criticism of film." Wagner also offers a minor in film and media studies, which melds elements from both majors:

> The interdisciplinary minor in film and media studies will encourage students to become media literate and will foster creative engagement with the world. It will accomplish this goal by advancing awareness of media's effect on perceptions of critical social issues and by fostering both creative and practical skills of production and management. Courses in the minor address: film form and aesthetics; the history and politics of cinema, television, radio, and the internet; the business of film and media; multimedia production; and graphic computer arts.[16]

Roger Williams University offers a minor in film studies that is similar in scope to Wagner's. After two core courses, one an introduction to film studies and the other called Curation and Festival Production, students choose four electives from two categories: production-oriented courses and film studies courses in the humanities and social sciences. The description of this minor highlights not only the interplay between the critical and production sides of the field, but it also foregrounds its importance outside of the professional realm:

> Using an interdisciplinary framework, students within the minor have the opportunity to investigate both the professional aspects of cinematic studies—its evolution and the techniques of the filmmaking process—as well as critical approaches to the field, such as the relationship between cinema and other cultural productions, the international dimensions of the medium, and the power of visual culture in contemporary life. Therefore, the minor introduces students to the major issues in cinema—history, aesthetics, theory, and production—as grounded in the larger cultural and international factors that inform film, other modes of communication, and indeed our everyday lives. The goal is to have students become informed viewers of visual culture, equipped with critical skills that will be useful, not only in media careers, but in other aspects of life as well.[17]

Besides Valparaiso University's CMS minor, the minors at Wagner and Roger Williams are the only film studies minors among NAC&U institutions to include both the critical and production sides of this field. While Valparaiso's program did not consciously model its own curriculum after these programs, the parallels among them will highlight the importance of integrating the arts within the evolving contours of a twenty-first century liberal arts education.

Valparaiso University instituted its interdisciplinary CMS minor in fall 2013. It was designed in part to revitalize an aging minor in film studies that at the time had not been completed by any student in quite a few years. This minor had been created and maintained by a group of faculty from the English Department at Valparaiso University. The objectives for this minor were described as follows:

> The Film Studies Minor offers an opportunity to discover the place and significance of an important twentieth century art which has also been a social force. Film can be studied for its artistry, its historical development, its influence on human perceptions of the world and its relation to such subjects as national cultures, technology, politics, mass media, theater and religion. The minor in Film Studies allows the small scale but concentrated study of one important art, and through it, modern times.[18]

After completing an initial core course, Film Aesthetics, offered by the English Department, students were asked to take at least three additional courses, one each from three separate categories: film and literature, film and society, history of film. Many of the courses from the first and third categories came from the Department of English or the Department of Foreign Languages and Literatures. Courses from the second category came from other departments such as history and political science. In 2012, when conversations about revisions to this minor began, the film aesthetics course had not been offered for several years due to staffing issues in the English department, and enthusiasm for other courses in the minor had waned, resulting in a mostly defunct program.

In the fall of 2012, three faculty members met to envision a new film studies minor at Valparaiso. Coming from a background in French litera-ture, I was at that time embarking on a four-year professorship aimed at exploring and encouraging interdisciplinary collaboration at my institu-tion.[19] My initial foray into this professorship focused on film studies. With that emphasis in mind, I contacted colleagues in the Departments of Art and of Communication whom I thought might be interested in revising the film studies minor. Liz Wuerffel from Art brought to the table her experi-ence with video art, exemplified by "The Welcome Project," an initiative she began in collaboration with a colleague in the Department of English, Allison Schuette.[20] Peter Lutze, then a recent arrival at Valparaiso recruited to chair the Department of Communication, brought his own expertise in both filmmaking and film studies. The four of us were able to draw up the main parameters for a revised minor in films studies and then enlist the col-laboration of colleagues in departments across the university.

Unlike the majority of cinema studies programs at NAC&U institu-tions, the CMS program at Valparaiso does not have a departmental home. As an interdisciplinary minor, it is organized through an administrative committee of faculty from the Departments of Communication, Art, Foreign Languages, Sociology, and History. Though the programs at other NAC&U institutions do occasionally require coursework from a number of different disciplines, the Valpo CMS minor has made such interdisciplinary coursework a defining feature of the program.

One of the primary objectives of this minor is "to study the role of films and other digital media as artistic expressions and cultural forces."[21] Early on, in discussions about the nature of the minor, it was decided that the integrated study of both product and production was to be another defining feature of the minor. That is, we wanted students to study cinema critically, as an art form, but we also wanted students to experience the practical production side of making films and videos. Thus, within the

curriculum of the minor, students are required to take a general introduction to cinema course and at least one "production" course, either an
introduction to video production or a course on digital video art. The
introduction to cinema course, Communication 270, provides experience with basic concepts in film analysis. In this course, students "will
employ these concepts in analyzing and describing the varied styles, functions and social contexts of classical Hollywood, documentary, avant
garde, and world art cinema."[22] Though this course is not a prerequisite
for other courses in the minor, advisors tend to steer students to this
course first. However, students often do come to the minor from the
production side of the equation.

Students can fulfill the production requirement of the CMS minor
through one of two courses. One is Communication 271, Cinema
Production. This course is described as, "A practical, hands-on overview
of single camera field production techniques, including pre-production,
camera operation and aesthetics, lighting, sound recording, and non-
linear editing." Here the primary focus is on the technique and technology associated with film production. Along the way, the course "emphasizes
the language of audio-visual storytelling through a series of individual
projects."[23] These projects allow students to put theory into practice. The
production requirement can also be met with Art 324, Digital Video Art.
The focus in this course is the creation of video art, "with an emphasis on
developing experimental techniques and understanding the function of
time in this medium." Students work on their projects both independently
and collaboratively and throughout the course "observe a portion of the
history and aesthetics of film, video, and audio art."[24] Through these two
core courses, students engage from the start with the dynamics of production and criticism.

Beyond the core introduction to cinema and the production course,
students are also required to take two courses in the category of "history/
culture." These courses often include a geographical focus (World Cinema
Studies, French Film Studies, German Film Studies, and North American
Indian on Film) or a historical emphasis (History through Film). Such
courses are offered by the Departments of Communication, Foreign
Languages and Literatures, Geography, and History. The remaining credits required for the minor can be taken from any of three main categories
or from among a wide variety of electives offered by other departments,
notably among them the Department of Theater (Writing for Stage and
Screen) and Department of Sociology (Hollywood Goes to High School
and Mass Media and Society). Though all students are required to achieve

a minimum curricular expertise in the production and critical sides of the minor, they can complete it with coursework that engages their particular interest in the field. As our course catalog reads, the CMS minor "allows the small-scale but concentrated study of one important art form, and through it, our contemporary world."[25] For us, the study of cinema and digital media focuses on a complicated art form that mixes a variety of media. This art form is a particularly compelling one for the current generation of students whose lives are constantly inundated with video inputs from a variety of sources. By examining critically and practically the visual reality around them, students can pose fundamental questions about the world they inhabit. The CMS minor thus channels the traditional critical modes of the liberal arts while engaging with topical questions about the modern world. Since we also require direct experience with video and film production, insights and influences from the larger tradition of cinema can be applied to real-world projects that provide experience that can be of use in a future profession.

To provide a concrete example of how the CMS minor navigates the boundaries of criticism and production, I offer a description of one of my own courses, French Film Studies, with a particular focus on the final project in the course. At its most basic level, this course "examines film as an artistic medium in the context of French cinema from its origins to the present."[26] We typically begin with the earliest films in French such as the short vignettes of the Lumière brothers alongside George Méliès's classic 1902 *Voyage dans la lune* (*A Trip to the Moon*). After sampling a variety of films from the main historical currents of French cinema (silent era, surrealism, poetic realism, new wave, etc.), we view a more contemporary French film, the title of which changes from year to year. According to the course description, we focus on "cultural and historical context, cinematic technique, and instruction in the practice of writing critical analyses of film." Since my own training comes from literature and cultural studies, I am much better at presenting the course as an introduction to classic French cinema, but I endeavor to inject a minimum of technical acumen regarding cinematic technique. In terms of writing, I ask students to write a formal sequence analysis or close reading of a scene from one of our films. This exercise encourages them to view the films not just from a historical perspective, but from a technical, formal viewpoint that emphasizes cinematic practice and technique.

For the final project in the course, students have an option to do one of two presentations. For those students more attracted to the critical side of the CMS minor, I allow them to choose a film by one of the directors that we studied, but a film that was not shown in class. Students prepare a visual presentation on this film, putting it in historical context and opening a dialogue with what we learned about that filmmaker or others throughout the course. As part of this visual presentation, they are also required to provide a brief sequence analysis of a scene in the film. For those students drawn to the production side of the minor, I offer the option to create and screen (with director's commentary) an original short film. Though the topic of the short film is entirely of their choosing, I ask them to shoot the film in the style of one of the filmmakers studied in the class. After the screening, the student directors discuss why they chose a particular filmmaker's style and how they incorporated that style into their own productions. The last time I taught this course, one student produced a comic film set on Valparaiso's campus, inspired by Godard's *Au bout de souffle* (*Breathless*), relying heavily on his particular style of using jump cuts. In her presentation, she pointed out how the shooting of the film was not difficult, but that the editing necessary to achieve Godard's jump-cut pace took enormous effort. Another student created a much more introspective and symbolic piece in homage to Luis Buñuel's and Salvador Dalì's, *Un chien andalou* (*An Andalusian Dog*). While the student's film was not quite as visually shocking as the infamous 1929 surrealist film, the dramatic screening did spark an animated discussion in class. This particular presentation pushed the boundaries of the assignment along with the tolerance of the student spectators.

One characteristic of this assignment is that it privileges neither the production nor critical side of the minor. Both groups of students present at the same time and feedback is offered from them for both types of projects. In the final days of the course, these students encounter the technical complexity of how to produce, shoot, and edit a film, while applying their critical acumen to films not yet encountered in the course. Application, in both cases, is key. This "signature work," in the parlance of AAC&U's LEAP Challenge, provides students with an occasion to apply what they have learned to a new context. In presenting the results of their work to other students, they also benefit from feedback as well as the knowledge that their own initiative has helped enlarge the knowledge base and technical expertise of their peers.

CMS students at Valparaiso can take their limited experience in the minor and apply the skills learned in the professional realm, either through continuing in a film studies school or in the context of video production in a variety of work places. At the same time, these students have learned to put their knowledge of film into a historical and cultural context, letting them hone their critical thinking skills within the arena of one particular kind of artistic production. The production side of the minor encourages creativity and demonstrates how integrating a curriculum in the arts can provide a basis for essential life skills that can be pursued and exploited in the workplace. The critical side of the minor demonstrates the fundamental methodologies of the liberal arts, illustrating how art informs culture and history and vice versa. The interdisciplinary nature of this minor challenges students to question the boundaries of knowledge even as they affirm the rich possibilities afforded by the intersections of different disciplines. Through the integration of the arts into what might be considered a technical and professional minor, CMS students at Valpo are able to develop at least two different worldviews simultaneously. Empowered by their own creativity and critical acumen, they transcend the boundaries between producer and consumer. In the end, this education is one that they will have acquired from experiences on both sides of the camera, both on and off screen, as spectators, critics, and creators.

NOTES

1. Lev Manovich, *The Language of New Media* (Cambridge, MA: MIT Press, 2001), xv.
2. The Lumina Foundation, "The Degree Qualifications Profile," accessed November 15, 2016, https://www.luminafoundation.org/resources/dqp, 5.
3. Association of American Colleges and Universities, "The LEAP Challenge: Education for a World of Unscripted Problems," accessed November 15, 2016, https://www.aacu.org/sites/default/files/files/LEAP/LEAPChallenge Brochure.pdf, 2.
4. Thomas Leitch, *Film Adaptation and Its Discontents*, (Baltimore: Johns Hopkins University Press, 2007), 5.
5. The 24 member institutions of the NAC&U are Arcadia University, Belmont University, California Lutheran University, Drury University, Hamline University, Hampton University, John Carroll University, Manhattan College, Nazareth College, North Central College, Ohio Northern University, Pacific Lutheran University, Roger Williams University, St. Edward's University, Samford University, The Sage Colleges, University of Evansville, University of La Verne, University of New Haven, University of Scranton, Valparaiso University, Wagner College, Westminster College, Widener University.

6. The following details are gleaned from the websites of the relevant institutions. In total there are 11 programs with a film orientation. Arcadia University has a cinema studies minor offered within the Department of Communication. Belmont University offers a major in motion pictures. The Communication Department at California Lutheran University has a concentration in film and television production; this same institution also offers a BA in multimedia, which includes a track for high definition digital cinema. Hampton University offers an interdisciplinary program in cinema studies. John Carroll University offers a film track as part of its visual media major in communication. At Roger Williams University, there is a film studies minor offered within the Department of Communication & Media Studies. The English Department at Samford University offers a film studies concentration as part of that major. The University of New Haven offers a BS in communication, which offers a film production concentration. Wagner College offers a major in film and media studies, while Westminster College provides a film studies minor. At Widener University, the major in communication studies includes a film studies track.

7. These four institutions are Arcadia University, Hampton University, Samford University, and Westminster College.

8. These seven institutions are Belmont University, California Lutheran University, John Carroll University, Roger Williams University, University of New Haven, Wagner College, and Widener University. Only Roger Williams and Wagner offer film minors that include a production component.

9. Belmont University, "About the Motion Pictures Program," accessed November 15, 2016, http://www.belmont.edu/motionpictures/about/index.html.

10. Belmont University, "Motion Picture Degree Requirements," accessed November 15, 2016, http://www.belmont.edu/motion-pictures/courses/requirements.html.

11. California Lutheran University, "Multimedia," accessed November 15, 2016, http://catalog.callutheran.edu/undergraduate/coursesofinstruction/multimedia/.

12. California Lutheran University, "Communication," accessed November 15, 2016, http://catalog.callutheran.edu/undergraduate/coursesofinstruction/communication/.

13. John Carroll University, "Visual Media Track," accessed November 15, 2016, http://sites.jcu.edu/russert/pages/programs-of-study/undergraduate-programs/major/visual-media-track/.

14. Widener University, "Concentrations, Communication Studies," accessed November 15, 2016, http://www.widener.edu/academics/schools/arts_sciences/undergraduate/social_sciences/coms/concentrati ons.aspx.

15. University of New Haven, "Communication," accessed November 15, 2016, http://catalog.newhaven.edu/preview_program.php?catoid=9&poid=1629&returnto=806.
16. Wagner College, "Film and Media Studies," accessed November 15, 2016, http://wagner.edu/art/academic-programs/film-and-media-studies/.
17. Roger Williams University, "Film Studies," accessed November 15, 2016, http://rwu.edu/academics/schools-colleges/fcas/degree-offerings/film-studies.
18. Valparaiso University, "Film Studies Minor," accessed November 15, 2016, http://www.valpo.edu/registrar/assets/pdfs/ucat12s2.pdf, *General Catalog 2011–2012*, 234.
19. Valparaiso University, "Baepler Professorship Offers Opportunities for Interdisciplinary Growth," accessed November 15, 2016, http://www.valpo.edu/news/2012/01/25/baepler-professorship-offers- opportunities-for-interdisciplinary-growth/.
20. Valparaiso University, "The Welcome Project," accessed November 15, 2016, http://welcomeproject.valpo.edu/.
21. Valparaiso University, "Cinema and Media Studies," accessed November 15, 2016, *General Catalog 2016–2017* http://www.valpo.edu/registrar/assets/pdfs/ucat16v2.pdf, 363.
22. Ibid., 97.
23. Ibid., 97.
24. Ibid., 77.
25. Ibid., 363.
26. Ibid., 148.

CHAPTER 6

A Lasallian Commitment to the Arts and Liberal Arts

Heidi Laudien

Established in 1853 *by the Institute of the Brothers of the Christian* Schools, Manhattan College draws its inspiration from the heritage of John Baptist de La Salle, the innovator of modern pedagogy and patron saint of teachers. Among the hallmarks of this Lasallian heritage are excellence in teaching, respect for human dignity, reflection on faith and its relation to reason, emphasis on ethical conduct, and commitment to social justice. As such, the college's mission is to provide a contemporary, person-centered educational experience that prepares graduates for lives of personal development, professional success, civic engagement, and service to their fellow human beings.

Manhattan College believes that the performing, literary, and visual arts are a core component of that educational experience and, therefore, seeks to weave these courses into the broad liberal arts foundation its students receive. For example, in January 2016, students and faculty traveled to Italy to participate in the 500th Anniversary of the Jewish Ghetto in Venice. The 20 participating students had taken either the religious studies course that addressed the religious, social justice, ethical, and historical issues related to the ghetto, or the art history course studying visual depictions of those issues. While it would be impossible to fully describe the

H. Laudien (✉)
Manhattan College, Riverdale, NY, USA

© The Author(s) 2018
N. H. Hensel (ed.), *Exploring, Experiencing, and Envisioning Integration in US Arts Education,* The Arts in Higher Education,
https://doi.org/10.1007/978-3-319-71051-8_6

many ways in which our students are exposed to the arts, in this chapter I will detail six specific courses and programs of study that illustrate the commitment of the college to providing arts opportunities for the students.

CHILDREN'S LITERATURE

"Lions and tigers and bears! Oh my!"[1] Children's literature today is as varied as the lives and lifestyles of our twenty-first century children, and unlike other genres, is defined by its audience. In English 365, a required course for all Secondary Education majors in the School of Education at Manhattan College, students explore a range of children's literature from pre-school picture books through young adult texts dealing with contemporary issues. Taught by Dr. Heidi Laudien in the Department of English, this course is interdisciplinary, calling upon the disciplines of religion, philosophy, and the fine arts, specifically illustration. The course places an emphasis on genre studies and theories of narration with a particular sensitivity toward cultural consciousness and diversity. Students also spend a substantial amount of time considering issues of how the audience shapes the reading/learning experience. In addition to reading the primary texts, students engage in a substantial amount of secondary reading that explores contemporary controversies in children's literature ranging from learning differences to ideas about diversity.

As a required component of the course, students visit a publishing house in New York City and have the opportunity to meet with children's book authors throughout the semester, which gives students a unique opportunity to gain an inside glimpse into the entire process of authoring, editing, illustrating, and publishing children's books. Of the several authors Laudien has brought to campus, John Hulme, co-author of *The Seems: The Glitch in Sleep*, was particularly well received by the students. *The Seems: The Glitch in Sleep*, the first novel of *The Seems* children's series released in 2007 by Bloomsbury Publishing, tells the story of 12-year-old Becker Drane who works as the Fixer for the Seems—a secret organization that makes sure the world keeps running according to the "Plan." The text tackles themes relevant to the lives of all students such as suffering and its place in the world. The text also raises important ethical questions and the idea of social justice, making it an ideal interdisciplinary text between the fields of literature, philosophy, science, and religion. In order to prepare for the author visit, Laudien required the students to read the text and develop a series of questions to ask the author during a question and answer session, which followed the author presentation. From Hulme's talk, the students learned about the writing process, the impetus behind the text, stories about publishing, and the demands on the writer. They also learned specifics about the process of co-authoring a text and making writerly compromises. The question and answer session became a thought-provoking conversation about Hulme's personal interests, his ideas for the series, his writing process, and several lively personal anecdotes. Bringing in the author of the children's text enriched the reading experience and allowed the students to see the actual person behind the text. Such question and answer sessions are particularly engaging because the students are allowed to voice their (often) candid responses to the text directly to its author.

Following the author visit, students were required to write a personal response and to answer a course evaluation. Repeatedly students mentioned this experience as the "highlight" of the course, noting, "I've never met a children's author before," and "I can't believe how down-to-earth Mr. Hulme was and how willing he was to share his story with us." Another student remarked, "This author talk convinced me that I want to go into children's publishing some day." Students felt both an ownership and a mastery of the material, especially when their questions were met with thoughtful responses by the author. Hulme commented that he was impressed by the level of investment in the text on the part of the students, and he noted that he had not previously considered many of the questions posed by the students with respect to the text's form and content. Meeting the author behind the art proved to be mutually rewarding.

In the spring of 2017, Laudien will bring in Dr. Christine Seifert, professor at Westminster College in Salt Lake City, Utah, and author of *Whoppers: History's Most Outrageous Lies and Liars* (YA nonfiction, 2015, Zest); *Virginity in Young Adult Literature After Twilight* (nonfiction/scholarship, 2015, Scarecrow); and *The Predicteds* (YA fiction, 2011 Sourcebooks Fire). The Manhattan College students enrolled in the course will be required to read *The Predicteds* and also prepare questions to ask the author. Seifert will also lead a workshop on authoring young adult texts during which the students will create outlines for young adult texts that they will later compose and revise throughout the semester. At the semester's close, Laudien will compile the student-authored texts and submit them for publication consideration. The premise for their stories can be grounded in their area of expertise. For example, a current math education student is working on a book for second graders on navigating math problems, and another student of education in kinesiology is writing about the topic of movement, the body, and the importance of living a healthy lifestyle. In this way, the students bring their own unique interdisciplinary perspectives and interests to the writing of their children's texts as they call upon learned material in their respective disciplines.

Venice, Italy: 500th Anniversary of the Jewish Ghetto 2016

In 2016, 20 students participated in a three-credit January intersession program cross-listed in Religious Studies and Performance Arts when Manhattan College's Holocaust, Genocide and Interfaith Education Center joined the Venice Center for International Jewish Studies for the commemoration of the 500th Anniversary of the Venetian Jewish Ghetto. Drs. Mehnaz Afridi, Shaul Bassi, Murray Baumgarten, and Kathleen Sunshine led the program, acting as organizers and liaisons to supervise and direct the service and logistical aspects of each day. Drs. Savoy and Francis presented the formal classes and were responsible for the fulfillment of all academic requirements for the full three-credit course. This collaboration offered Manhattan students an extraordinary opportunity to experience life in Venice and participate in the celebration of its history as a crossroad of international Jewish experience.

Two faculty members taught the historical and interreligious dimensions of the ghetto through an analysis of architectural and artistic expressions. "Venice and the Art of Three Religions" was a required class that used the Centro Veneziano di Studi Ebraici Internazionali as a base and the city of Venice as a classroom to explore the intersection of Judaism, Islam, and Christianity in the art and architecture of Venice. Another class on religious studies explored Venetian Jewish ethnographies and the dynamic ways in which Venetian Jews developed their various identities in Venice through interaction with Venetian culture. The class also looked at religious images and representations of Jews and Judaism in Venetian religious history. Additionally, students produced a mural and physical design of the old ghetto and presented it to the local community as a gift.

The two classes offered by Drs. Daniel Savoy and Philip Francis were part of the Religious Studies and Visual and Performing Arts core requirements. The classes, in cooperation with the Centers, culminated in an academic and service-learning component, a fundamental core of Manhattan College's Lasallian educational experience. Through the analysis of religious and artistic symbolism, the students explored the intersections of visual and intellectual representations of Venice, Italy. The Venice Center provided relevant speakers such as a Venice-based English professor who was an expert on the Jewish ghetto and others including Dr. Shaul Bassi, Ca'Foscari University in Venice, Professor of English and an expert on the Jewish ghetto, Venice; Dr. Michele Brignone, Oasis Center Muslim-Catholic Dialogue, Mestre, Venice; Mohamed Al Ahdab Director of Islamic Cultural Center, Morghera, Veneto; and Leonore Rosenberg, wife of Rabbi Bahbout Orthodox, Head of Jewish community, Venice, who spoke about relationships between the three religions. From these lectures the students learned about the importance of interreligious relations, religious tolerance, and the specific struggles of those who once lived in the Jewish ghetto. It was clear that these lectures served to broaden our students' perspectives by encouraging them to think beyond their own experiences and to consider what it would have been like to be forcibly segregated and surveilled because of religious difference.

These course offerings were transformative for the Manhattan College students. One of the most important lessons for the students was learning about the history of the oldest Jewish ghetto and then meeting the community and listening to their challenges even to this day in a Catholic environment. The students also had a chance to meet Muslims in the area and learn that they had become the new "other" of Venice. Working in another culture among different peoples and traditions strengthened their understanding of the differences and similarities in a multiplicity of religious groups. This person-centered experience allowed the students to engage with various cultures, perspectives, and traditions, hence furthering the development of the students as individuals and citizens of the world. Lasallian values teach us about the ethics of other faiths, their acceptance, and understanding the suffering of others. Our students learned how to become self-critical and more faithful to inclusivity. With its emphasis on respect for human dignity, reflection, and faith, this study abroad trip reinforces the values of a Lasallian education, one invested in the education of the complete student who is committed to respect and reverence of others.

THEATRE IN THE CITY

"Theatre in the City," taught by English and Drama scholar Dr. Deirdre O'Leary, is an upper level course designed to introduce up to 15 Manhattan College students to the unrivaled theatrical offerings of New York City. Students view current listings at the start of the semester and decide which shows they would like to see. Over the course of the semester, students see approximately twelve shows, highlighting the variety that New York theater offers, from off-off Broadway avant-garde productions to star-studded Broadway revivals of the theater classics, like last season's production of "Waiting for Godot" with Sirs Patrick Stewart and Ian McKellan.

Since Manhattan College offers a class on the "History of the American Musical," O'Leary limits the musicals to one per semester—one that is either historically significant or canonical, or one that broadens the form. Students also attend after-show conversations and interviews with cast and crew, and to date they have met with actors Jonathan Groff and Bill Crudup. Because the students study the plays before and after seeing the performances, they report that this course opens their eyes to theater as a multidimensional and collaborative art form and not just a pleasant evening out.

Viewing live performances of plays is beneficial to the students' comprehension of the plot, theme, and vocabulary, which are significantly altered after viewing the performance. Theater performances are also a critical way to teach students about history and theater history, whether they are seeing *Henry V* or *All My Sons*. Seeing a play about a specific period of world history has undeniable pedagogical importance, but also seeing a play like *Tis 'Pity She's a Whore*, staged faithfully in the style of English Jacobean performance, has much to teach the students about seventeenth century staging and acting styles in addition to the insights they can gain from a Jacobean audience's expectations of gender, violence, and sex, for example. These plays are not produced in vacuums. As O'Leary states, "they grow up in the soil of a specific society, and seeing a play like *Lysistrata* tells us much about the culture of the playgoers as much as the skills of the playmakers."[2]

O'Leary's selection of the plays for the semester is based on several criteria. She includes four or five plays from the Western canon which have included Arthur Miller's *A View from the Bridge*, Tennessee Williams' *The Glass Menagerie*, Thornton Wilder's *Our Town*, and Samuel Beckett's *Waiting for Godot*. Students often have some familiarity with these plays, either from high school or from other classes or just general knowledge that they exist. Prior to seeing a performance, they are required to read the play and turn in a short writing assignment, such as a thematic analysis or information on the original production. Every production analysis that the students do is guided by three questions: What is the production trying to do? Is it a fond, faithful restaging of an American classic, and if so, why? And what is the reasoning behind such a choice? O'Leary seeks out productions that reveal a new interpretation of a canonical work. For example, Ivo van Hove's 2016 Tony Award winning revival of *A View From the Bridge* did just that. Arthur Miller's 1956 classic was stripped of every culturally specific prop and set decoration and the actors were placed in a bare, stark metal ring onstage. With the audience on three sides, the playing space more easily referenced Greek theater of the fifth century than the Brooklyn docks where the play is actually set. The students were encouraged to question how the design choice reveals new truths about the play. Specifically, she asked the students to consider how the production team radically remade this American period play into a stunningly contemporary, vital commentary on one man's (Eddie Carbone, played by Mark Strong) existential battle with fate. From there, she asked the students to consider how the production team (director, designer, playwright, actors) tried to accomplish this goal. Finally, in an effort to lead students away from simply stating their like or dislike of the production, she asked them to consider if the production successfully met the goals of the first two questions. By posing such questions, O'Leary encouraged critical thinking and analysis.

Understanding the critical interpretive lens a director, designer, or actor uses in bringing a canonical work to the stage becomes an essential goal of the student's learning. The course aims to engage students in larger questions such as: What happens to these plays when directors, designers, and actors collaborate to reveal seemingly new messages in old(er) texts? Is a new interpretation in some ways a disservice to the wishes and artistic vision of the author? How do we consider the role of the author in the age of director? Students grapple with these larger questions in longer, end-of-semester papers where they incorporate performance theory and reception theory.

In addition to one musical and one Shakespearean production, O'Leary always tries to include a few new works that are not yet published and/or reviewed. This is a challenging exercise because it is difficult for the students to observe, take notes, digest, and critically analyze something they are only seeing for approximately two hours. This requires students to be active listeners and observers, something we are always trying to instill in our other classes at Manhattan College. They must "read" the design and performances as a text alongside their understanding of the plot. O'Leary states, "Over the last few years, I've come to really value these productions because the students cannot find reviews and analyses on the Internet. They must figure it out for themselves and stand by their interpretations."[3]

Sometimes the students will see something that is quite baffling. The 2016 production of *Fondly, Collette Richland* by famed experimental theater company Elevator Repair Service was no exception. Students exited the theater alternately laughing and complaining about being bewildered as to what it all meant. They quickly realized that there were almost no reviews to help them interpret the play and they would have to sit and think about what they had just seen. They had to draft their own critical responses without the crutch of someone else's interpretation telling them whether it was good or not. It is this type of exercise that encourages the students to see things from multiple perspectives and carry over their critical and analytical thinking skills to other courses and aspects of their lives.

O'Leary also has introduced a semester-long scavenger hunt/trivia quiz. Questions refer to persons and places of interest in the neighborhood where the students see a show. The questions/tasks are designed to help the students explore other parts of New York City and gain a first-hand view of New York's unique theater history. The students must familiarize themselves with the questions prior to going to the theater and allow themselves enough time to take photos (if required). For example, when visiting the Union Square Theatre (located inside NY's former Tammany Hall) to see a production of "The 39 Steps," students were asked to determine the significance of Tammany Hall and to figure out which politician is most famously associated with it. They were asked, "What is the most unloved piece of public art in New York City?" and "Whose residence now houses the most respected member's only theater club in NYC?" Questions such as these encourage the students to engage not only with the play under discussion but also with the cultural and historical place in which it is being performed. When seeing the play *Fondly, Collette Richland*, the students were asked to find the theater that is largely credited with being the first and most significant American experimental theater. O'Leary told them that "everyone who is, was, or ever dared to someday be innovative has performed in, directed, designed, or wrote a show that was produced here"[4] and asked "Who is the woman who is referenced in the title of the theatre?" Another question in this assignment included, "What theatre was home to the bloodiest theatre riots in America? What was the death toll? What is playing there now?" Questions such as these encourage the students to engage with theater culture and history and were viewed by the students as an innovative way to learn course material. Manhattan College student Sera Pisani (class of 2016) wrote of the course the following:

Taking "Theatre in the City" was my first introduction to the rich culture of performance and drama in NYC. Not only was I able to learn about a concentrated genre of literature, but I was also given the opportunity to see it come alive through extremely specific components of design, style, and interpretation. Perhaps the most fascinating aspect of the course was experiencing each text in vastly different settings. While most people are never exposed to off Broadway theaters, we had the opportunity to experience and compare off-off Broadway, and Broadway itself, even watching some experimental theater. As the course progressed, my rhetoric and understanding grew regarding the industry, and by the end of the course I was familiar with terminology, historical context, and important figures in the current theater scene today. Literature itself is inherently performative, so combining it with an education of theatrical adaptation was exhilarating and inspiring. Drama is meant to be seen, not read, so creating an educational space where the texts could be experienced the way the playwright intended was truly incredible.[5]

As the semester progressed, students answered longer response questions such as the following: Write about the experience of traveling to different theaters in New York. How familiar were you with the different Manhattan neighborhoods before this class? Did you see any parts of New York City that you hadn't seen before? What was your favorite neighborhood, and why?

By the semester's close, the students are challenged to respond to reflection questions such as, "What do you think are the qualities of good theatre criticism?" and "What is the most challenging aspect of watching theatre?" Research suggests that "culturally enriching field trips have significant educational benefits for students whether they are to see an art museum or live theatre."[6] Undoubtedly, "Theatre in the City" is a course that fosters knowledge, cultural consumption, historical inquiry and critical thinking skills. It further provides a unique opportunity for Manhattan College students to make connections between the world of theater and their own worlds.

MUSIC AND ROMANTICISM

"Music and Romanticism" taught by Professor and Founder of the Visual & Performing Arts Department, Dr. Mark Pottinger, explores how music in the nineteenth century reflects the culture's dominant concerns (e.g., Romanticism, Naturalism, Realism, Historicism, and Nationalism) and how this powerful force contained the seeds of the very uncertainty and socio-political anxiety that characterizes our understanding of the modern era. According to Pottinger, "in the nineteenth century, composers explored music's potential to express deeper and more powerful emotions, than any other time in Western history, including those of unconscious dream states. The old 'Classical' musical structures such as the music of Haydn and Mozart began to crumble under the weight of this emphasis on feeling."[7] Understanding how this came about is one of the main objectives of this course. Although the primary focus of this course is music, a reading knowledge of music is not necessary for success. The students in this course devote a significant amount of time to learning how to listen actively and intelligently to Western music from the United States and Europe. The approach is interdisciplinary and incorporates visual arts, history, philosophy, and literature in order to perceive the major intellectual and political cross-currents of the era. The aim of the course is for students to reflect upon the watershed moment when reason (empirical truth) gives way to imagination (platonic idealism). As Pottinger suggests, "the students learn to see that their observations of everyday phenomena such as politics, economics, technology and ethics are highly defined by a constant reverberation observation of the thing in isolation and that which can only be inferred through an awareness of a larger perspective of the interconnectedness and development of all life—a microscopic vs. a telescopic view."[8]

Manhattan College offers minors in Art History, Digital Media Arts, and Theater, and a major in Art History that began in 2010 and currently has 17 majors. Many changes have occurred over the past several years in the department, due in large part to the pivot toward New York City as a central focus for the college-wide curriculum. The College supports the understanding that the study of music, art, or theater is like any other object-focused study in the humanities, where one is able to examine the human project in all its fullness. Such a move by the College thus replaces the long-held idea that the study of the arts simply makes one a well-rounded person. Courses such as "Music and Romanticism" are a testament to the College's commitment to support the integration of the liberal arts and fine arts.

Akin to reader-response theories, Pottinger suggests that "the student must be seen as an active agent who imparts 'real existence' to the music and completes its meaning through interpretation through her own eyes." He goes on to suggest that "as we look forward to teaching future students the rudiments of music history—the classroom and its select set of resources must be expanded to embrace the multiplicity that a living history brings: an interconnection between the world of ideas and the world of experience."[9] Thus one of the exciting features of this course is a scavenger hunt at the Metropolitan Museum of Art in New York City and a four to five page photo essay response afterwards. In the essay, the students must provide six images with an explanation that attempts to define aspects of the images. For example, they might tackle subjects, genres, narratives, authorial intent, emotionality, or the size of the artifact and how such images define romanticism. In the Musical Instrument Museum section the students are required to take a picture of a characteristic nineteenth-century instrument. They are then asked, "What in the appearance of the instrument as well as its perceived sound captures the nineteenth century desire for a 'romantic' sound? In other words, what is a 'romantic' view of sound and how does this instrument represent that vision?" They are next asked to locate the American Wing, the parlor/salon rooms and take a picture of a characteristic nineteenth-century salon. They are asked several questions about this space including, "What are the objects in the room and what is their arrangement and historic style (e.g., Gothic revival, Renaissance revival, Greek revival)? Based on this answer and the image, they consider how then is bourgeois 'taste' defined in the nineteenth century?" From there, the students make their way to the Panorama room of the American Wing and consider how the room and the panorama indicate bourgeois desires for travel and luxury and how the room indicates the nineteenth century fascination with optics and science. Manhattan College student Mitchell Shaw (class of 2015) responded in this way:

> The panorama room displays the bourgeois desire for travel and luxury by making it possible for them to feel like they are part of the image on the wall for a period of time. The walls are painted in order to portray the palace and garden of Versailles. For a small fee people were able to come and feel as if they were actually at this place. This room also indicates the 19th century's fascination with optics and science because it had to be painted and displayed in such a way that caused the viewer to feel as if he was in the image. This was due to the angle of the walls, the way that it was painted, and the lighting around the image.[10]

For the remaining questions the students are asked to take a picture of a nationalistic or heightened nature scene and consider what makes the image a part of the Romantic Age and to take a picture of both a nineteenth-century portrait and an eighteenth-century portrait to notice the differences in the portraiture of individuals between the 1800s and 1700s and reflect on why such differences might exist.

In addition to the scavenger hunt assignment, students of "Music and Romanticism" are required to attend a live music event. In the fall of 2015, students attended a performance of Beethoven's 3rd Symphony at Carnegie Hall in New York City. Following the concert the students were asked to write a reaction paper to the event and to make specific connections between the course material and the music. As Pottinger purports, "as instructors we have come to learn that students desire an immediate application to their learning—one that is easily utilized 'on the ground' as it were, toward goals that exist outside the studied material."[11] A course such as "Music and Romanticism" does just that—the students project abstract and philosophical ideas onto real material that they must find in pre-selected galleries, and in this way, they become aware of the "reality" of nineteenth-century thinking in everyday objects. In short, the scavenger hunt teaches the student critical thinking to look beyond the object to understand latent ideas that are not defined by the surface alone. Music helps to "ring" this true by the fact that it exists on a time line, whereby new ideas are prepared by the present, creating expectations for the future.

Pottinger suggests, "Listening to music with this critical perspective on the articulation of ideas (the rhetoric of form and timbre) then forces one to want to understand all that comes to define the sounds that we hear, including technology, economics, history, philosophy, science, gender and racial studies."[12] The study of music via found objects in museums and the like is the study of life and all of its complexities, making the student a sympathetic learner of the world. In the end, the scavenger hunt and the accompanying assignments of this course demonstrate a synthesis of the studied material with the student's own lived experience.

MODERN DANCE: THOUGHT AND MOTION

"Modern Dance: Thought and Motion" is a cross-listed course in Theatre and Kinesiology that introduces the art of modern dance and topics that shape current thinking about the purpose and value of dance in Western society. Currently taught by Lisa Johnson, BFA, M.Ed., the course focuses on the birth of modern dance at the turn of the century until the 1960s. Students read and watch videos on prominent choreographers of the time who created dance works in response to their respective contemporary cultural moments and their places within it. The students create a warm-up and modern technique routine based on some of the dance artist's work they study. This calls upon the unique sensibilities of the students and requires them to work together through a creative process. By incorporating learned techniques from the dances they have studied and meshing them with their own creative impulses, they learn how to put theory into practice.

They later co-create a dance piece, choreographed in part by the instructor. The students are given guided instruction, yet for the most part they are in control of the piece. The idea of constructing original movement can be daunting for some students at first, but it proves to be a satisfying component of the course because the students are actively creating, problem-solving, and making decisions together to determine the final outcome. Over the course of the semester the students develop more self-confidence from the focus on mental and physical presence and ultimately overcome their fears of physical movement in front of their peers. The course covers a broad range of topics that examine modern dance through the lens of autonomy and body-mind centering to include the following:

- The Feldenkrais method, the onset of a new dance
- Isadora Duncan Technique, community and agency
- Arts and society development, American ideals
- Pioneers Martha Graham and Dorish Humphrey, verbal communication
- Art criticism/Edmund Burke Feldman, non-verbal communication
- Jose Limon/narrative assessment, contemporary performance field study
- Immersion observation, the power of spirituality
- Alvin Ailey/allegorical assessment, the post-modern crusade
- Merce Cunningham/Judson Dance Theatre and Lincoln Archival Library Field Study
- Baryshnikov and modernism.

Sharon Oliensis, professional dancer and guild certified Feldenkrais Practitioner, instructs a Feldenkrais session (a body/mind method) and Lori Belilove, artistic director of the Isadora Duncan Dance Company and Foundation, does a class highlighting the history and dance technique of her work. The course fulfills three credits in both Theatre and Kinesiology. The students develop their critical thinking skills through discussions and collaborative work. They attend a dance performance and listen to two guest specialists who conduct master classes.

Students engage in critical analysis of weekly readings and/or showings of video. Through the application of dance, movement experiments and discussion, the students develop an awareness of body articulation. The course further seeks to foster creativity, self-identification, independent thinking, and the ability to develop world views. Although no dance experience is necessary, students are expected to actively participate in the creation of dance throughout the course. The class content and physical practice is designed to acclimate dancers and non-dancers alike.

The course requires that students learn to become active participants. Participation applies to discussions, video critiques, physical application, field studies, response papers, and the student's overall conduct in class. It also includes a written critical exam on a dance piece viewed in class. This course is a collaborative effort—the student's mental and physical presence is required and reliant upon other classmates. One of the major assessments for the course is a midterm paper. Each student writes a historical assessment on a modern choreographer while highlighting a societal, philosophical, or other critical aspect of work that may seem relevant. The students are encouraged to include personal reactions to their findings and give a brief presentation on the selected artist in class. Additionally, a final paper is required in which students present an argument or formulate a philosophy related to a chosen topic in dance or movement.

The culminating exercise in the class is a final movement exam. This is a three-part physical exam based on two exercise sequences and the execution of class choreography, which is developed during the term. The student's progress throughout the semester is a significant component. For example, how the student applies herself to physical work and refines movement phrases reflects her overall class progression. At the semester's close, an informal showing is conducted and the student is evaluated on her ability to demonstrate memory/knowledge of dance material and performance skills.

The learning outcomes for the course are quite specific. The purpose of this class is to gain knowledge of contemporary dance and develop a well-rounded understanding of self and the surrounding world. Students hone skills through critical thinking, oral and written communication, creativity, and physical practice that explore space, rhythm, dynamics, coordination, and movement techniques that support a fluid functioning body.

CONTEMPORARY DANCE COMPOSITION

"Contemporary Dance Composition" is another offering that is cross-listed in Kinesiology and Theatre. This course looks more closely at dance developments of the 1960s to the present. This is a choreography-based course, somewhat like music composition, where the students experiment with craft, improvisation, and innovation. The students examine post-modern dance choreographers and use their "toolbox" of highly original strategies as a springboard to create their own dances. This course has a lab/process focus where students create their own solo studies and then transform its motif/movement vocabulary into a piece of group choreography typically in trios, quartets, and so on depending on the size of the class. The students learn about current dance artists and are introduced to the principles in modern dance and practical methods that explore the craft of choreography. The class includes warm-up and movement exercises that investigate improvisational skills, self-expressive content, principles of design, and developmental techniques intended to foster the creative process. Assessment of readings/video based on post-modern choreographers and dance composition methods are implemented to provide historical reference in relation to constructional devices used in the artistic process. The students learn to cultivate reasoning, creativity, body articulation, communication, and expressive attributes in the individual as well as to develop an understanding of others and the art form itself. The students play with choreographic structures and exchange between dances to really submerge into the creative process. Students examine several topics of study to include the following:

- Improvisation: The Body as an Instrument, Developing a Motif
- Meaning and Movement, Chance and the Element of Randomness
- Merce Cunningham, Music and Dance
- A Creative Approach, Evaluation of Experimental Concepts
- The Judson Dance Theatre, Choreography and Performance Skills, Methods of Construction
- Lar Lubovitch/Movement Orchestration and Contemporary Dance Field Study
- Cultural Analysis

Readings and video selections emphasize post-modern dance developments and related aspects in dance composition. Students are expected to read course materials and come to class prepared to share their ideas and impressions about it. Students are also responsible for movement assignments, which progress from solo studies to group work. Throughout the term, students learn to exercise their abilities as viewers and contribute to the development of one another's dances. This is implemented in the form of discussion labs, critical observations, record keeping, and experiments conducted in a supportive and constructive manner.

The student's progress in the course is evaluated along a broad spectrum of criteria to include the following:

- problem-solving aspects that identify different movement and phrase material strategies, manipulation of counts, and patterns of development and design;
- developing a descriptive common vocabulary through the creative process, discussions, and assessments on both historical study and choreographic feedback;
- kinesthetic intelligence based on the ability to control one's bodily motions, develop a sense of energetic direction, understanding of weight distribution, fine and gross motor implementation of physical gestures, and movement in time and space;
- transferring one's own movement into alternative idea/s and the ability to teach peers dance material (i.e., learning the difference between imitation and interpretation);
- visual/spatial awareness that involves the capacity to arrange shapes and patterns in space, recognize its strengths and weaknesses, and bring forth images that enhances a piece of choreography and interpretation of it;
- musical/rhythmic quality; understanding of tempo, phrasing, syncopation, and tone;
- interpersonal engagement and persistence of self-identification, movement tendencies, concentration, concept development, memory, and reflection; and
- intrapersonal ability to notice and make distinctions among other individuals by observing characteristics, interacting with environment, experimenting, explaining, and developing a sense of understanding larger than one's own.

Through movement studies, students learn how to utilize self-actualization, motivational factors, distillation of ideas, process-oriented skills, developmental tools, constructive methods, communication of meaning, and refinement of the final outcome. After viewing a live contemporary dance performance, the final class paper consists of a cultural analysis of it. Students ultimately learn that everything a culture uses and produces reveals something about that culture to the living entity and observer. Students learn how to describe movement, analyze its compositional attributes, and contemplate its relationships and meanings when assessing a piece of art. Students are encouraged to think about what they see and what they feel as revealed in the choreography and consider how it relates to their society and contemporary culture.

These courses are just a sampling of the many ways in which Manhattan College is committed to the integration of the liberal arts and fine arts. It is clear that courses that integrate the fine arts will have a lasting impact on students, regardless of their careers. A study of the fine arts is integral to the Manhattan College experience and we believe it deserves institutional investment. The role of the arts fosters creativity as one of the core values of education and therefore it should play a central role in the curriculum of any twenty-first-century student. As Martha Nussbaum suggests when describing the role of the arts in challenging ideology, "artists always ask the imagination to move beyond its usual confines, to see the world in new ways."[13] Manhattan College recognizes that the arts serve to enrich the lives of our students and to strengthen personal growth, professional success, civic engagement, and service to their fellow human beings. Thus Manhattan College encourages students, regardless of major, to engage with and challenge ideology through artistic endeavors and to encourage students to develop an understanding of artistic expression.

NOTES

1. Frank L. Baum, *The Wizard of Oz.* Directed by Victor Fleming. (1939; Los Angeles: MGM Studios), film.
2. O'Leary, Deirdre. Interview by Heidi Laudien. Personal Interview. New York, June 15, 2016.
3. Ibid.
4. Ibid.
5. Pisani, Sera. Interview by Heidi Laudien. Personal Interview. New York, July 5, 2016.
6. Greene, J., Hitt, C., Kraybill, A., Bogulski, C. (2015) Learning from Live Theatre. *Education Next*, 15, no.1 (accessed July 12, 2016, EducationNext.org).

7. Pottinger, Mark. Interview with Heidi Laudien. Personal Interview. New York, July 1, 2016.
8. Ibid.
9. Ibid.
10. Shaw, Mitchell. Interview by Heidi Laudien. Personal Interview. New York, July 12, 2016.
11. Pottinger, Mark. Interview by Heidi Laudien. Personal Interview. New York, July 16, 2016.
12. Ibid.
13. Martha C. Nussbaum, *Not for Profit: Why Democracy Needs the Humanities.* (Princeton NJ: Princeton University Press, 2010), 23–24.

CHAPTER 7

Mindset: Entrepreneurship and the Arts

Jennifer Blackmer

The University Title Generator is a nifty website that offers hours of fun, along with a not-so-subtle critique of the concept of "academic bloat."[1] It's a handy, clickable tool that helps enterprising would-be administrators create their next academic position, and even suggests possible salaries:

- Lead Vice Liaison to Facilities Partnerships to the Subcommittee for Neighborhood Compliance ($88,000)
- Lead Assistant Chancellor of the Committee on Academic Services ($209,000)
- Vice President of Academic Compliance of the Subcommittee on Strategic Employee Planning ($350,000)

I wasted about 20 minutes laughing at these ridiculous concoctions until I came to the disheartening realization that my own title, associate provost for entrepreneurial learning, could have been generated by this satirical exercise. Indeed, I spent 18 months after I was promoted to this "buzzwordy" rank on a whirlwind tour of my campus (8 colleges, 1200 faculty, and 46 departments), explaining why and how a playwright and screenwriter could find herself in the

J. Blackmer (✉)
Ball State University, Muncie, IN, USA

© The Author(s) 2018
N. H. Hensel (ed.), *Exploring, Experiencing, and Envisioning Integration in US Arts Education*, The Arts in Higher Education,
https://doi.org/10.1007/978-3-319-71051-8_7

position of promoting entrepreneurship. If I had a dollar for every time a colleague asked me what starting a business has to do with learning art, history, science and philosophy, I could—well, I could start a business.

The word "entrepreneur," in all of its forms, is certainly loaded. Apart from being a current academic trend, entrepreneurship connotes hot tech start-ups and multi-million-dollar public offerings. The irony, of course, is that the most celebrated entrepreneurs, including Bill Gates, Steve Jobs, and Mark Zuckerberg, never graduated from college—and yet we study what they did, appropriate their processes, and are now charged with making those activities the core of the collegiate learning experience. At the end of the day, this forces us to ask some tough questions: Do universities have a right to co-opt the entrepreneurial experience? Are we simply using a new word to explain the same old routine of going to classes, listening to lectures, taking multiple-choice tests? Does one even need to go to college to make something new?

The key difference at my institution, in my view, is the incorporation of the word "learning" into my job description. Entrepreneurial learning is not about the teaching of entrepreneurship; it's about cultivating entrepreneurial thinking in both teachers and students, encouraging them to embrace the tools of the entrepreneur as a way to build successful careers and lives. One can effectively do this regardless of the area of expertise. Indeed, while the most familiar modes of entrepreneurship involve business start-ups, it has become clear to me over the course of a 20-plus year career as an artist and writer that I have truly been my own entrepreneur. To co-opt the expression of my friend and colleague, novelist Cathy Day, I have been "CEO, COO and CFO of the small business called Jennifer Blackmer, writer." Real examples of entrepreneurial behavior are found all over the humanities and the arts, particularly in the creative person's ability to embrace risk, think critically, be both flexible and reflective in her processes, and ultimately build a career. Accordingly, students who choose to study and practice the arts find themselves thoroughly prepared for a number of possible careers, whether directly in the arts, in related fields, or in areas entirely different from what they may have imagined when they first set foot on campus. In the words of Carol Geary Schneider, past president of the Association of American Colleges and Universities, "Entrepreneurship is simply a shorthand title for learning how to apply knowledge, skills and judgment under conditions of uncertainty."[2] And, as time, tech, and higher education march on, uncertainty seems to be the new norm.

Risk-Taking: Something from Nothing

May, 1993. The previous year I'd graduated college with a bachelor of science in theater, summa cum laude. I'd just completed an internship in stage management at the Indiana Repertory Theatre. I'd had a great year and learned more than I ever thought possible, but it was over. Done. Kaput. I was officially unemployed. To commemorate this transition, I went to lunch with a graduate student I'd become friends with during countless hours in the rehearsal room. He was also unemployed but was very much looking forward to returning to LA. I, however, wasn't in a particularly celebratory mood:

ANDREW: You're grumpy today.
ME: I'm not grumpy. I'm scared. I have no idea what I'm going to do next. (Thoughtful pause.)
ANDREW: What you do next is direct *Julius Caesar* on the steps of the war memorial in downtown Indianapolis.
ME: Huh?
ANDREW: You heard me. Direct *Julius Caesar* on the steps of the war memorial. (I stare at him.)
ME: I can't do that!
ANDREW: Why not?

I opened my mouth to reply before I realized I didn't exactly have an answer to his question. Why couldn't I do that? *Why couldn't I?* So I picked up the phone, made a few nervous calls, assembled a spirited group of actors and a musician and put on a show. (It wasn't *Julius Caesar*, and it wasn't at the war memorial, but that doesn't matter.) We needed money, so we raised money; we needed postcards, so we made postcards; we needed a press release so we wrote one of those, too. It was scary and exhilarating, and the show was a hit. Empowered, I moved to Chicago, got a "day" job, and did it again. And again, and again, and again, and again, and before I knew it, I'd built a theater company. Together we learned how to write articles of incorporation and apply for tax-exempt status. We created an operating budget and cut deals on space rentals. If I didn't know how to do something, I asked an expert, or I looked it up (my "day" job, at a bookstore, came in handy in more ways than one.) For six years, my colleagues and I made theater, and people came to see it. There is nothing quite so gratifying as putting something (in this case, art) into the world where it didn't exist before. If someone had told me then that

I was an entrepreneur, I would have laughed in her face. But that's exactly what I was, and I did it because there wasn't much else I could do. The tidy myth of "go-to-college-graduate-get-a-job-work-forty-years-at-the-same-company," ubiquitous when I was an undergrad, never applied to the arts. A student chose to study theater, art, English, or music at her own risk, with eyes wide open and no guarantee of employment. As young theater majors, we were told on our first day of college that if we could do anything else with our lives and be happy, then we should go do that. A life in the arts is difficult, harder than anything we've ever done, we were told, and we should be prepared for late nights, poverty, and sacrifice. Models for success were few and far between; "famous" actors were less than 1 percent of the total number of performers out there, and we'd be doing well enough just to eke out a living.

Those of us who remained after this pep talk were reminded of the inevitability of failure over and over again. Failure became a constant companion, not a bad one, necessarily, but definitely something to learn from and overcome the next time. By the time we graduated, we were prepared for the worst. What I found in the real world, however, was anything but the worst—I found a sphere full of opportunity, and I also found that I had learned the skills to identify and take advantage of it. And while I spent time in the sandbox of the real world, making something new, I cavorted with failure, embraced it, ran away from it, and had the time of my life.

Critical Thinking: Everyone's an Entrepreneur

Scott Carlson's article for *The Chronicle of Higher Education*, "How to Assess the Real Payoff of a College Degree," opens with the story of Dimitrius Graham, a music major at Morgan State University.[3] When asked why he went to college, Mr. Graham replied: "I can't not go to college ... there are so many things I could do because I have networked so much. College is full of opportunities."[4] His explanation is not unusual; for as long as there have been applied-arts majors, students have been asked to explain their choice of them. Lately, however, this same scrutiny is being applied to all majors, as well as to the act of going to college itself. In 2011, The Pew Research Center conducted a survey of 2142 Americans ages 18 and older; a majority of them (57 percent) stated that the higher education system in the United States fails to provide good value for the money invested in college degrees.[5] Only 22 percent of those surveyed feel that they can adequately pay for college, and "by a small but statistically significant margin, the public says that the main purpose of a college education should be to teach work-related skills and knowledge (47 percent) rather than to help an individual grow personally and intellectually (39 percent)."[6]

Into this volatile stew drops the skepticism of politicians who promise to hold accountable those responsible for the massive amounts of student-loan debt, and this discussion has coalesced around the concept of ROI—return on investment. "Looking at college explicitly in terms of its return on investment, measured in starting salaries and potential earnings, is something new—a confluence of anxieties about the rising cost of college, mounting debt among students, a flaccid economy, and the ubiquitous vocabulary of the market," says Carlson.[7] He notes that the ROI perspective is everywhere now: in the US Department of Education's College Scorecard; the college "ROI Rankings" from PayScale, a salary-ranking company; and in recent best-selling books assessing the value of college.[8] Even *The Chronicle of Higher Education*, which routinely features op-eds critiquing the concept of ROI, created a tool, College Reality Check, which compares an institution's "net price" with expected time-to-graduation and potential earnings in the workforce.[9]

Those of us in the arts and humanities have decried this perspective, saying that ROI is merely one measure of a student's success after college. ROI presupposes a time-limit, suggesting that starting at a specific salary immediately following graduation is the only way to reap the investment in college and mitigate the damage of debt. "There is at least some evidence that fields with high starting salaries are fields where you plateau early," says Dennis P. Jones, president of the National Center for Higher Education Management Systems.[10] He suggests that "it's the students in the broader-based arts-and-sciences fields that end up in the CEO positions, but it takes a long time to get there."[11] There is much debate about how to quantify what counts for success in a particular field of study. Is there room, for example, for the former actor who builds a successful career as a project manager in an ad agency? How about a stage manager who takes a position managing cases for the FBI?

And then there's the largest question of all: What, exactly, defines success?

Perhaps entrepreneurship can provide a middle-ground in which these extremes may be met and explored. Reframing the ROI debate through the lens of entrepreneurial learning allows us to imagine a world in which the arts and humanities can hold as much sway as the fields with more direct links to the office or the boardroom. In order to do this, however, "entrepreneurial" must become more than a buzzword; its meaning must be unpacked, and the competencies of the entrepreneurial mindset uncovered and explored.

Research supports the notion that college students, now more than ever, respond to high-impact practices that encourage collaboration and "tinkering." The growing body of work on the effectiveness of project-based learning, community-engaged scholarship, and undergraduate research, conducted by organizations such as the Association of American Colleges and Universities, the New American Colleges and Universities, and the Council on Undergraduate Research (to name just a few), suggests that twenty-first century college students expect to "co-create" their own educational experiences, in much the way they create videos online and communicate with the world immediately, whenever and wherever they wish. Entrepreneurial learners learn by doing.

Theorist John Seely Brown notes that "there are several pedagogies that exist today that we as educators are not yet taking advantage of to best prepare students for the 21st century workscape."[12] These pedagogies, he suggests, are designed to teach learners to become resilient in the face of rapid change, and they center on the concept of "pulling" knowledge from sources (such as the Internet) rather than having knowledge "pushed" into them (from experts in, say, a lecture class).[13] This type of learning can only exist in the age of the Internet, where a new "pro-am" (professional-amateur) system of scalable mentorship is emerging. As an example, Seely Brown cites the cooperation between professional astronomers who "created a network of stargazers triangulating observations with telescopes as capable as the professional grade 200-inch Hale telescope at Palomar Observatory. ... Professionals realized that if they collaborated with amateurs they could solve many astronomical mysteries in a mutually beneficial way."[14] He goes on to propose that, within this uniquely collaborative combination of knowing, making, and playing, the entrepreneurial mindset is born.

So what is the entrepreneurial mindset? A 2014 compendium created by the UK-based National Centre for Entrepreneurship in Education (NCEE) offers several examples of entrepreneurial-based pedagogies applicable to fields across disciplines, from performing arts, to science, technology and the humanities.[15] "The entrepreneurial mind is seen as being central to wider employability, in general, as well as a wide range of personal and organizational contexts. This demands that the concept, while still incorporating the establishment of new ventures in business, also embraces opportunity-seeking ... in any context along with capacity to design and grow organizations of all kinds."[16] Activities suggested by Gibb and Price have specific learning goals that coalesce into a list of desirable proficiencies for entrepreneurs—the mindset. The mindset is not a fixed trait, but a series of transferrable skills and behaviors that can be taught, cultivated, and practiced, including:

- opportunity recognition
- flexibility and adaptability
- creativity and innovation
- initiative and self-direction
- communication and collaboration
- networking capacity
- critical thinking and problem solving
- negotiation capacity
- persuasive capacity
- risk-taking
- capacity for reflection and analysis[17]

The compendium goes on to list forty-four different activities that can foster these potential outcomes, including debate, speed-networking, role play, shadowing, critical incidents, selling exercises, case studies, and others. What connects these tools is the student-centered nature of every activity; in each example, students make choices and engage in questions that compel them to "pull" necessary information from all sources in order to complete the assignment or project. Through these activities, learning goals are met—students initiate action, collaborate, communicate, network, negotiate, solve problems, persuade, take risks, and reflect on their successes and failures.

Assessment can take the form of rubrics evaluating outcomes of individual projects, surveys, and peer-reviews, pre- and post-course exams, and reflective writing activities. Programmatic assessment (an area that we are just beginning to explore at my institution) examines these measurable outcomes over several disciplines and a longer period of time, and will provide some much-needed support for our efforts. In the meantime, unofficial anecdotal evidence suggests that students experience greater transformations through these activities than they would through traditional lecture-based learning.

REFLECTIVE FLEXIBILITY: A LIFE IN THE ARTS

Much has surprised me in my short time as an academic administrator. Perhaps most surprising, as I've digested the latest "cutting-edge" research on high-impact student-driven learning and the entrepreneurial mindset, is how familiar it all seems. Sure, I was an entrepreneur as a 20-something theater-maker in Chicago; that's an easy connection to make—yes, I did, in effect, start a business. What's more fascinating to me, however, is how the list of attributes desired by entrepreneurs also describes the necessary attributes of the artist. In other words, the actual process of making art can also foster the entrepreneurial mindset:

- Opportunity recognition: The artist must understand the context in which the art she creates will be received. Is there an opportunity here for my voice to be heard? How and why?
- Flexibility and adaptability: Every piece of art undergoes a process of creation, and every single one of those processes repeatedly hits snags and obstacles. Indeed, if the artist doesn't hit a major obstacle, then he's doing something incorrectly. Artists must adapt to the changing circumstances of their creation, and do so purposefully.
- Creativity and innovation: While this may seem like a given, artists learn through practice that creativity is never a magic "bolt of inspiration." It is, rather, a muscle that must be exercised. The artist must be open to innovation to allow the muscle to grow and be healthy.
- Initiative and self-direction: Art is never made without somebody making it. These artists must be self-directed to get themselves into the studio or lab and make new things. If they don't do it, someone else will.
- Communication and collaboration: Art is never created in a vacuum. While some artists are soloists, the project is never finished until an audience has the chance to weigh in. Some forms, like theater and film, are inherently collaborative, and the whole is always worth more than the sum of its parts.
- Networking capacity: Beyond the fairly obvious fact that most artists build careers through personal networks, there is also the notion that art is about the Human condition: Humans are explored only when we know them, so networks provide not only opportunity, but also inspiration.

- Critical thinking and problem solving: The artist is always of two minds—the creative mind and the critical mind; one cannot exist without the other. The creator gives herself over to what she is making, but the critic evaluates worth as a measure of the truth that the artist sets out to explore. Every artistic process is a series of problems to be solved.
- Negotiation capacity: Every piece of art is a negotiation between the artist and its inspiration, with the audience as the intended recipient. In many art forms, such as the theater, negotiation is the principal behavior through which choices are made.
- Persuasive capacity: Every piece of art is an argument with a point of view. The artist must master the art of persuasion in order to encourage his audience to consider the ideas behind his work.
- Risk-taking: It has often been said that there is no great art without great risk. While risk to life and limb may not always be a part of the process, there is always the risk that the audience will misunderstand intentions or, worse, not care. Saying anything as definitively as the artist must say it is a risky activity.
- Capacity for reflection and analysis: Artists must always reflect on the successes and failures of the work that they put out into the world. Only through repeated reflection will an artist understand her voice—and once she does understand it, it will undoubtedly change. Artists must continuously ask questions of the world around them, to inspire their voices and challenge their developing perceptions.

So not only does building a career in the arts require entrepreneurial attributes such as flexibility and opportunity recognition, but the *actual creation of art, any type of art,* also requires them. It is here, within the act of cultivating this artistic/entrepreneurial mindset, that we offer young artists stellar opportunities to be successful in the world of work, sometimes even more successful than their peers who studied more "appropriate" fields such as business or technology. The applied practices of making art cross those boundaries, in knowing, making, and playing, is what John Seely Brown advocates in educating all students for the twenty-first century workplace. Artists, therefore, seem to be natural entrepreneurs.

In the same way, participation in the arts can provide practical models for all students hoping to develop the mindset of the entrepreneur. This is certainly not a new idea; the vast majority of general education and core curricula across higher education offer courses that provide at least some exposure to the fine arts. These encounters, however, are typically in the form of introduction or survey courses such as music appreciation or art history. What would happen if, instead of sitting in a music appreciation lecture, a biology student was offered a blank piece of staff paper and encouraged to compose a song? What would happen if an anthropology major was given a play to read, and then told to write one herself and read it out loud among a group of peers? What would happen if an accounting major was given a paintbrush and a canvas and a problem to solve? Perhaps entrepreneurship and entrepreneurial thinking, long seen as only the domain of business, is best taught as an art, preparing students with an artistic toolbox, encouraging them to dance with failure like an artist does, open and willingly, with eyes clearly focused on the horizon.

On the first day of every semester, I share with my playwriting students that the worst piece of advice I ever received was to "write what I know." Sadly, this unfortunate directive is ubiquitous, almost cliché. Young writers, especially college students, hear it time and again. They take it to mean that, in order to write with an authentic and truthful voice, they are only "allowed" to relate what they've experienced in life thus far which, for a traditional undergraduate, is practically nothing. I see students across our campus embodying this bad advice in other aspects of their lives as well; they silo themselves into smaller and smaller possibilities until the only options they can see for themselves, and for their futures, are dismally few and prescriptive—"My major is X, so I'm only qualified to do X." How many people have stopped themselves from pursuing something because they felt they were unqualified? In my case, that means I never would have started my theater company, never would have written my first play, and never would have taken the steps into the unknown that effectively launched my entire career.

Instead of directing my students to "write what they know," I tell them that in my class they're going to "write what they WANT TO know." The act of writing is not only one of reflection, but one of creation, where writers imagine possibilities and do the hard work required to make them so. It is my hope that the future of higher education finds the silos between all disciplines—art, science, business, technology, and the humanities—breaking down entirely, so that we may all be who we WANT TO be, learning from each other and inspiring each other along the way.

Notes

1. University Title Generator, www.universitytitlegenerator.com.
2. Beth Mcmurtrie, "Now Everyone's an Entrepreneur," *The Chronicle of Higher Education,* April 24, 2015, accessed April 26, 2015, http://www.chronicle.com/article/now-everyones-an/229447.
3. Scott Carlson, "How to Assess the Real Payoff of a College Degree." *The Chronicle of Higher Education,* April 22, 2013, accessed October 5, 2016, http://www.chronicle.com/article/Is-ROI-the-Right-Way-to-Judge/138665/.
4. Ibid.
5. Pew Research Center. "Is College Worth It?"| Pew Research Center—Pew Social Trends, accessed February 16, 2017, www.pewsocialtrends.org/2011/05/15/is-college-worth-it/.
6. Ibid.
7. Scott Carlson, "How to Assess the Real Payoff of a College Degree," *The Chronicle of Higher Education,* April 22, 2013, accessed October 5, 2016, http://www.chronicle.com/article/Is-ROI-the-Right-Way-to-Judge/138665/.
8. Ibid.
9. Ibid.
10. Ibid.
11. Ibid.
12. Brown, John Seely. "Cultivating the Entrepreneurial Learner in the 21st Century," March 22, 2015, accessed September 20, 2016, www.johnseelybrown.com.
13. Ibid.
14. Ibid.
15. Entrepreneurial Mindset Index, Network For Teaching Entrepreneurship accessed September 25, 2015, retrieved 29 October 29, 2015, from http://www.nfte.com/entrepreneurial-mindset-index.
16. Ibid.
17. Ibid.

CHAPTER 8

The Business in Music at Belmont University

Don Cusic and Beverly Schneller

If you go to the Ryman Auditorium in Nashville, Tennessee, you will see on display an aging playbill showing that in the cast of *Hamlet*, Ophelia was played by one Sarah Colley. And who was she? None other than Sarah Ophelia Colley Cannon. Her stage name was Minnie Pearl; her trademark straw hat with the price tag hanging on it graced any number of early television shows and stages in the twentieth century. Mrs. Cannon was a graduate of the Ward-Belmont School for Women, the precursor of Belmont College, which would become Belmont University in 1991. Her marriage, if you will, of Shakespearean theater (albeit a college performance) with a vaudeville-style comedy act involving repartee, singing, dancing, and written comedic material persists to this day at Belmont University through the curricular and applied-learning opportunities associated with the College of Visual and Performing Arts and the Mike Curb College of Entertainment and Music Business (Curb College). Outside of these colleges, students also experience the arts through the Artist's Studio track in the Honors Program, and in the university's general education program, called the BELL Core. (The acronym stands for The Belmont Experience: Learning for Life.)

D. Cusic (✉) • B. Schneller
Belmont University, Nashville, TN, USA

© The Author(s) 2018
N. H. Hensel (ed.), *Exploring, Experiencing, and Envisioning Integration in US Arts Education*, The Arts in Higher Education, https://doi.org/10.1007/978-3-319-71051-8_8

Consistent with the mission statement, Belmont strives to gradu ate students who will "engage and transform the world with disciplined intelligence, compassion, courage and faith." In this chapter, we will look closely at how the Music Business program in the Mike Curb College of Entertainment and Music Business was founded and structured to serve as a liberal studies-based professional degree program that draws on multiple resources across campus for its curriculum.

Internships and corporate partnerships give students "real life" and on the-job training in the entertainment industry. As one of nine colleges and the largest undergraduate college, the Curb College is constantly evolving while remaining true to the fundamentals of a humanities-based college education for its nearly 3000 students. The programs offered in Curb College—songwriting, film, music business, entertainment industry stud ies, and audio engineering technology—attract the majority of students enrolling at Belmont. When their enrollment is combined with roughly 1000 students in the College of Visual and Performing Arts, these two colleges account for more than 50 percent of the undergraduate popula tion of the university.

Belmont University is unique academically in that it is the only univer sity in the United States to offer the Music Business degree as a Bachelor in Business Administration.[1] While it attracts many would be artists and some with established entertainment credentials, Belmont also enrolls stu dents who want to learn the business of entertainment. It is typical to find musicians practicing in the gazebos on the quad; many civic-engagement projects are focused on students and creativity. The university has had students write songs with veterans, write and record songs with victims of domestic violence, and in 2015, the music-therapy program began a youth choir for children on the autism spectrum.

Such was the vision of Belmont President Herbert Gabhart who, with the help of music-industry executives in Nashville, started designing the Music Business program in the late 1960s. Gabhart's vision has been sus tained and expanded under the current leadership of President Robert "Bob" Fisher. There are two "histories" of how the Music Business pro gram came to be. The first is that a group of executives in the music indus try approached Gabhart and told him a college program was needed to educate future executives in the music business, offering their help and support for such a program. There was an announcement sometime around 1968 that music executives were working on this.

The other, more colorful, story is that Belmont, as a small Baptist College in desperate need of financial help, benefited from a bit of gossip. President Gabhart heard that Roy Acuff, a noted country singer at the Grand Ole Opry, had pinned a large sum of cash behind a curtain in a hotel where he was performing and had forgotten it when he left. (It was typical that Acuff hid his money like this when he was on the road and performers were paid in cash.) When President Gabhart heard this story, he thought there might be money to be found in the music business, so he sought out industry executives to help initiate a Music Business program for Belmont University.

There's a bit of truth in each of those stories. Music executives in Nashville did indeed encourage Belmont to start a program for future executives in the industry. And Belmont was, indeed, having financial difficulties and was desperate to find a way to attract more students. At the time, a big problem in the music industry was that there were lots of performers, but few business leaders whose training combined strength in accounting, law, project management, and ethics with the technical skills needed to make records and sign artists. By 1973, President Gabhart launched the program, moving it from the music department to the business college. With just three full-time faculty, the program offered courses in entrepreneurship, recording technology (with its own studio and record label), and related business curricula. Thus, from the outset, the Belmont Music Business program was rooted in applied, integrated, and practical learning.

The Bachelor of Business Administration in Music Business is a business administration-based degree program in which students concentrate their studies in a traditional AACSB accredited business curriculum with major field study in the Music Industry or Music Production. Because the program is equivalent to a "double major" in Business Administration and Music Business, students are not required to complete a minor area of study. Content areas for the Music Business degree at Belmont are divided among general education (BELL Core credits), credit hours in Music Business, and credit hours in Business courses, as shown in the following:

Business Courses 39 *credit hours*

Economics
Accounting
Entrepreneurship
Business Law I

Management Information Systems
International Business
Business Finance Principles of Marketing
Principles of Management
Business Ethics
Strategic Management

Major Area, Music Business *13 credit hours*

Survey of Music Business
Survey of Recording Technology
Music Publishing
Copyright Law
Senior Capstone (1 credit course)

Emphasis Area: *15–16 credit hours*

(Choose from Music Production or Music Business or Legal Studies)

Emphasis Area Electives:	12 credit hours for Music Business or Audio Engineering Technology; 6 credit hours for Legal Studies
Free Electives:	7–10 credit hours

Now over 40 years old, the Music Business program is a bellwether for a number of issues related to the future of arts education and balancing a traditional liberal arts curriculum with the professional education students need for success in the industry. Belmont has never been and has never wanted to take a conservatory approach to arts education. In recent years, the university has added undergraduate degrees in publishing and music therapy and a graduate degree in audio engineering technology.

Clearly, music business is not a traditional area within business education. It is a multidisciplinary and interdisciplinary area of study that relies heavily on courses outside the major, mainly in the BELL Core, to acquaint students with ethics, sociology, communication skills, and quantitative literacies. Since the Music Business program is a form of business within traditional business education, it is unique as a discipline. Across the country, when the study of entertainment, recording technologies, or music is included in a college curriculum, it is most commonly housed in music departments and in business schools.

Belmont's program flourishes in its own undergraduate college with a $10 million endowment from Mike Curb, owner of Curb Records, who not only supports Belmont's program but also has funded Entertainment and Music Business, as well as recording programs, at Arizona State University, Bethune-Cookman University, California State University-Channel Islands, California State University-Northridge, Daytona State College, Fisk University, Honolulu College, Rhodes College, UCLA, Vanderbilt University, and an endowed professorship at Claremont-McKenna University in business and law. In addition, Curb has been central in leading efforts to save the historic music studios on Nashville's Music Row. Through his Curb Foundation, he has endowed charitable programs at hospitals and in communities across the United States.[2]

Trying to fit the business of the arts into a liberal arts framework is an opportunity to think differently, as Mike Curb has done, about what an artist might need to know to be successful in the entertainment industry. In the words of co-author Don Cusic, "If classical music folks are elitist and business departments are 'practical,' the liberal arts folks are dreamers. They may be teachers but they're also artists and writers and dreamers. They read novels that don't have facts, paint pictures that don't look just like a person, sit around and think about things that involve more imagination than practical ways to make money." Thus, in the music industry, entrepreneurs and creative individuals, as part of the business world, are forced to measure success in personal and corporate profits, investments in entertainment ventures, and in the work of developing artists. Within the music industry, money is a by-product of a passion. It is almost antithetical to many humanists to consider that all creative products need to be monetized if they are ever to reach the public; and, to grasp that the public— the audiences who go to operas, plays, and rock concerts—are all consumers of products.

Music Business majors at Belmont are taught that the business is what enhances the creativity and the promise of some success. To achieve success, the students need to know how to communicate an idea, how to speak clearly and reasonably about the idea, and how to develop long-term plans for bringing the product to fruition. Why then is there an apparent disconnect between arts education and professional education?

First, for some in the academy, there's the issue of "utility versus utopia." A professional program involves education and training for a profession— at Belmont University that means the Music Business and Music Business-related fields. Among these are songwriting, audio engineering, and film.

The "utopia" is what a traditional liberal arts curriculum provides, which, to boil it down to an over-used cliché, is that it teaches students "to learn how to think."

There are conflicts. Many students just want to be employed in the music industry, or, at least, to have an opportunity to be successful in the music industry. Some want to be performers, some want to be musicians, some want to work for established record labels, publishing companies, booking agencies, PR firms, management companies, or in other jobs connected to the music industry.

Many liberal arts majors enter college with an eye on graduate school; they're already anticipating gaining a master's degree—and possibly a doctorate—along the way. The Music Business students, for the most part, have little immediate interest or desire for advanced degrees (except possibly law school). They plan to be part of the music industry, where academic credentials are, honestly, not always a gateway to success.

Pre-med, pre-law, pre-pharmacy, and nursing are all professional fields. Students must complete their course of study (and, often, pass a professional licensing examination) before they can enter that field. The entertainment industry isn't like that. While most major corporations demand a bachelor's degree as a gatekeeper, the entertainment industry is filled with entrepreneurs who had an idea and chased it. The proof is in the results; if someone can be effective in the entertainment industry—promoting an artist, promoting a song, booking an artist—nobody cares whether they have a degree or not.

Some in the academy believe that a Music Business program is more a "trade school" than a legitimate academic field. We certainly have courses with practical application (training vs. education and more practical "how to" courses than courses heavily doused with theory), but the liberal arts courses also are integral and tend to mollify those criticisms.[3]

There has been a drive at colleges and universities to foster a "creative campus" that will encourage students be grounded in the arts as a way to express their creativity. At Belmont, the Music Business program has achieved similar goals in several ways. First, there are regularly scheduled "showcases" during the academic year. We currently have showcases for "urban/pop," "country," "Christian," and "rock" music. Students hold auditions, select the acts that they will perform, and run the events, which are judged by a jury of peers. The showcases are scheduled during the academic year, generally two in the fall semester and two in the spring semester, usually aligned to "Preview Day," when prospective students and their parents are visiting campus. The showcases start at 7 p.m. and conclude by 9 p.m., demonstrating to parents and students what awaits them. These are full-blown concerts with each of the four acts performing three songs. They are held in the Curb Event Center, which holds about 8000, with top-of-the-line sound and lighting systems.

Another outlet is the Curb Café, an on-campus café with food, nonalcoholic beverages, and a stage. Students select the talent from applications and handle bookings for the café. This creates an opportunity for students to perform for the campus and the community. The intimate setting, with seating for about 45, provides a cabaret-like experience with a small stage and usually space for three to five performers.

There generally are two ways in the United States to go from being a "nobody" to a "somebody"—through sports and entertainment. We see this happen regularly. When someone moves into the category of a "somebody," he or she is seen constantly in the media and typically enters a social world with other celebrities and even world leaders. It is not unusual for a top entertainer or a top athlete to have dinner at the White House. Young people see this and aspire to this. Yet, if they want to reach that level, they need to know about a wide variety of issues. This is, essentially, a selling point for the liberal arts.

Curb College's faculty members stress that they are not in the entertainment business, which means the faculty can't let the rules of the entertainment industry overrule those of the educational enterprise; the two worlds must work in tandem. The Curb College faculty is drawn from a wide range of backgrounds and experiences. Some are touring artists, some are specialists in marketing and in consumer research, others are entrepreneurs, and still others are lawyers or former industry executives. What they all have in common is commitment to teaching the music business from a liberal studies standpoint, and so some also have taught a freshman seminar, the junior cornerstone coursework, and the capstone seminar. In the last three years, two faculty members in music business taught in the Honors Program. One taught an elective on the history of jazz and the African-American experience, and another faculty member joined an Honors faculty member to teach the first course in the Artist's Studio track on theories of creativity.

Beyond Belmont classrooms, students in music business and other programs offered in Curb College complete multiple internships in the music industry. In the Pipeline program, held in the summer, a selected group of students work as teams with faculty and corporate supervision to solve a specific entertainment or music industry business' problem. Students present their recommendations both orally and in the form of a recommendation report. About five years ago, the initial work of a Belmont Pipeline team had a direct impact on changes to the still-changing US Copyright Law. In the summer of 2015, Belmont was chosen as a site for the regional hearings on copyright reform sponsored by the US House of Representatives.

Students and faculty in the applied programs face a challenge in recognizing the intersections among the majors. Students come to college focused on accelerating through college to earn a degree and begin their careers. As such faculty members help them make the connections among the theoretical aspects of the liberal arts curriculum and find ways to adapt that knowledge so that they can pivot creatively, intellectually, and ethically as they engage in careers in the entertainment industry.

Classrooms can offer environments for students to explore and experience creativity. However, students have to be willing and able to envision how their learning will resonate with their professional interests, intentions, and goals. Since students enrolled in the arts programs may also be in the Honors program, this creates an additional opportunity to create their own learning plan, culminating with a thesis on a topic in the music or entertainment industry.

Establishing Value in Arts Educations

Though Belmont documents do not highlight the importance of creativity as a skill, it is implied and understood that students are expected to think critically and creatively.[4] Learning Goal 3 of The BELL Core states broadly and generically:

> *3. General Education seeks to help students develop an understanding and enriched appreciation of the arts, humanities, religion, social sciences, and natural sciences, including:*
>
> – *The conceptual frameworks of the arts, humanities, religion, social sciences, and natural sciences*
> – *The achievements in the arts, humanities, religion, social sciences, and natural sciences*

College specific learning goals in Music Business courses emphasize the primary professional knowledge needed to be successful in the field and within business settings. For example, all students majoring in Music Business take the Survey of Music Business course. As a multisection course, all the classes adhere to these learning outcomes:

During this course, the student will:

 - *Demonstrate an understanding of music-generated revenue*
 - *Identify the basic concepts of intellectual property ownership*
 - *Investigate the function of record labels and the types of recording deals*
 - *Research the role of management, touring, promotion, and publicity in artist development*
 - *Examine career opportunities within the music industry*
 - *Outline the financial aspects of the music production, recording, and distribution process*
 - *Discuss the impact of technology on business models*

Exploring the learning associated with these outcomes teaches the students how to move from being a creative person—an artist only—and challenges them to understand and apply the business principles needed to sustain their careers and those of others. In this way, they participate in a broader and deeper conversation about values—how to value themselves as creative, and how to value their creative products and those of others. As Oshin Vartanian and colleagues state in their book, *Neuroscience of Creativity*, in order for artists to be understood through their creative products, they have to be able to communicate "immediately. In other words, those novel combinations that we *value* (in poetic language, for instance) and thus regard as 'creative,' invariably involve relevance—even if the relevance is not immediately apparent."[5] This is the challenge that arts educators face—how to make the content of the traditional liberal arts relevant and immediate to their students. Belmont's Curb College does this through applied projects and internships.

APPLIED PROJECTS AND INTERNSHIPS

The key to the entertainment and Music Business program is internships. Students work in offices of entertainment-related firms and experience first-hand what it is like to work in the music industry. No lecture from a teacher—no matter how good the teacher or how good the lecture—can open the eyes of a student to what day-to-day life is like in the music industry as well as an internship. Internships are, of course, also helpful to the entertainment firms because the businesses have the opportunity to "audition" a potential employee and, in the end, perhaps offer him or her a job.

Students regularly intern at a major record label, an independent record label, publishing company, artist-management company, entertainment-marketing company, recording studio, production company, booking agency, concert-promotion firm, publicity company, radio station, or a number of other entertainment businesses.

Belmont Entertainment and Music Business students are required to register for internship credit (1–6 cr. hours) after completing their sophomore year. They must pass a required internship seminar (that discusses on-the-job behavior as well as lessons about the interview process); and have completed the four core introductory courses in Curb College (Survey of the Music Industry, Survey of Recording Technology, Copyright Law, and Music Publishing).

Curb College has made specific efforts to facilitate internships by hiring two career coaches who work only with Curb students, two full-time professional advisors who augment the work of the faculty advisors, and an additional staff person who manages the operations of the internship program and works collaboratively with a faculty supervisor and the primary staff in Belmont's Office of Career and Professional Development.

In fall 2015, the internship assessment was restructured to ask students to complete reflective writing that responds to prompts measuring to what extent the students used the knowledge gained in their classes in the internship and to what degree they felt prepared for their internship. The faculty supervisor, Internship Co-coordinator, and the students' faculty advisors are then able to review the students' portfolios and work with them to advance individual career readiness. The impetus for the change to learning associated with the internships came from faculty desiring to learn more about the relevance of what they were teaching to students' career needs. The change also stemmed from an institutional assessment goal of measuring the extent to which students recognize their learning and apply it outside of directed activities and in applied settings. In the 2014–2015 cycle of the National Survey of Student Engagement (NSSE), as well as in responses to our internal spring survey on student engagement, students' responses concerning the value of their learning, particularly recognizing how to use the skills and knowledge acquired in the BELL Core, were uneven and low. Since the majority of students taking the surveys are in the arts programs, this was an indirect indication that we needed to make the linkages stronger between the arts and the liberal arts education so that students see a direct value in learning both curricular areas thoroughly.

THE PIPELINE PROJECT

The Pipeline Project is an effort to bring undergraduate students into contact with businesses that want to develop the students' talents in creative, industry-focused problem solving with relevant and real-life applicability. In March 2015, for example, a group of students worked with Sea Gayle Music on an analysis of the impact of copyright laws on independent music publishers. Belmont students targeted specific areas that relate to licensing of new music and copyrighted music for other uses, and built on work from a 2014 Pipeline project on the impacts of copyright law, especially the unanticipated consequences of copyright law's lack of enforcement in the music industry. Sea Gayle President Marc Driskill said in a local news story about the students' work, "This project engages the voice of the next generation. These are important voices and we saw that engaging them this way would be beneficial to us all."[6] To be successful in the Pipeline projects and in internships, Belmont students apply skills learned in business, music business, and in the liberal arts core with its emphases on writing, speaking, teamwork, and problem solving.

THE EXAMPLE OF THE HONOR'S PROGRAM ARTIST'S STUDIO

In 2013 faculty in the Honors Program expressed a desire to support students in Curb College and The College of Visual and Performing Arts who enrolled in the Honors Program and thus were eligible to take the alternative liberal arts core. As a result, the Artist's Studio track was added to the Honors Program. This alternative liberal arts core emphasizes masterworks of Western literature, comparative religions, and broadly constructed historical survey courses with titles such as The Age of Exploration. In the Artist's Studio track, students take courses on creativity, perceptions of beauty and truth, and related aesthetically infused philosophical studies. These students generally will produce novels, poetry chapbooks, and visual-arts projects for their senior theses. The track draws between one-third and one-half of its enrollments from Curb College or The College of Visual and Performing Arts. Two recent thesis projects produced by 2015 graduates were a study of the selection of marching band instruments as a socially engineered, gender-based experience for young adults, and the second was a recording project of new music. Both of the students now are employed, one at record label here in Nashville and another as a music teacher in a local school district. These students are typical high-achieving graduates who use their professional knowledge in finding a meaningful career.[7]

THE ARTS EDUCATION OF THE FUTURE

Since 2000, arts programs have been on state and federal chopping blocks. By 2008, only 20 percent of school districts had been spared the closure or reduction of language, art, and music programs. Arguments for the value of arts education in building students' memory and attention span and for improving their ability to focus, grasp patterns, and communicate with others are seemingly ineffective in convincing lawmakers to restore funding. This is the case even though arts educators routinely argue, for example, that "the arts are life changing," that "students flourish when creativity drives learning," and that the arts help teach students how to be successful in many areas, including teaching them "to be human beings who can enjoy the deeper forms of beauty."[8]

Further, when you read scholarly articles on higher education assessment, creativity is rarely mentioned as a learning goal outside of arts programs. You will see mentions of creative problem solving, but the emphasis is on the solution to a problem, and less on the creative modes of inquiry that demonstrate intellectual risk-taking, synthesis of disparities, and the role of experience in communicating resolutions for real or fictional problems. In "How Critical Thinking Sabotages Painting," a March 25, 2016, essay published in *The Chronicle of Higher Education,* artist–educator Laurie Fendrich of Hofstra University argues that the overlay of assessment language regarding promotion of critical thinking when applied to painting classes hinders a student painter's ability to pursue "the fruits of direct observation in favor of the dubious pleasures of verbal abstraction" about art.[9] In other words, the rubrics used for critical thinking as the measure of success have deadened the aesthetic sensibility of the aspiring artist. There is more to her argument than we can address here, but her point that art students would do better to "take time to notice [what] is stirring, beautiful, and exhilarating" is as indisputable as it is essential.

To some extent in contrast to Fendrich, in 2011, George Kuh and Steven Tepper stated that creativity had to be consistently and thoughtfully taught.[10] They identified seven properties that creativity in education should possess, and we used these as models for our co-curricular and curricular efforts. They said the core skills and abilities associated with creativity are demonstrated:

- In the use of figurative language
- In making "what if" propositions
- In making "keen observation," that is, having a critical eye

- In risk taking and showing initiative
- Taking and making use of feedback
- Finding people to implement novel ideas
- Communicating in innovative ways

Kuh and Tepper underscore the serious need for creative thinking tied to writing and communication skills to once again be taught in ways that promote creativity in high school and in college general education courses. The reduction of creative activities in the foundational years of brain development may be restricting this generation's ability to understand the creativity of self-expression. If current students can't think creatively and cannot express it in written prose or other forms of creative works, they may find it difficult to face challenges in the classroom and everyday life.[11]

Kuh and Tepper are correct that "creative careers demand people who are entrepreneurial, resourceful, enterprising, and savvy about markets and opportunities," which is why Belmont continues to emphasize the importance of business within the study of music business. This is an industry that is constantly changing. It will only be through a solid grounding in the liberal arts and in applied learning that the students who will be the future of the entertainment industry can hope to succeed and simultaneously help the industry survive. The kind of learning that happens daily in arts education should empower students to lead, to create nimble and flexible responses to technological and legal changes, and to demonstrate ethical responsibility in dealing with the diverse people who make their careers in the arts.

NOTES

1. There are roughly 175 degree granting programs in music business or related fields (excluding audio engineering and recording technology), commonly designated by such terms as music merchandise and marketing, performing arts management, and music and entertainment industry studies. The University of the Arts in Philadelphia has a program entitled Music Business, Entrepreneurship and Technology, and more recent entrants to the field at the graduate level are the music industry programs designed by Steven Tepper for Arizona State University's Herberger Institute for Design and the Arts, http://herbergerinstitute.asu.edu/degrees/.
2. Mike Curb, http://www.mikecurb.com/about/bio.cfm and for information on the Minnie Pearl exhibit at the Ryman Auditorium in Nashville, TN, http://ryman.com/news/ryman-adds-minnie-pearl-museum-display.

See also, *Living the Business* by Mike Curb with Don Cusic (Nashville: Brackish Publishing, 2017), Curb's autobiographical account of his career in the music business.

3. David Bruenger, " Complexity, Adaptive Expertise, and Conceptual Models in the Music Business Curriculum," *Journal of the Music & Entertainment Industry Educators Association (MEIEA),* Vol. 15, No. 1(2015): 99–119. He provides a communication theorist's look at the critical thinking and systems thinking demonstrated in the traditional Music Business curriculum and argues for greater emphasis on adaptive reasoning to promote the kind of intellectual agility needed for contemporary industry work. Relatedly, Bence Nanay in "An Experiential Account of Creativity" in Elliott S. Paul and Scott B. Kauffman's *The Philosophy of Creativity, New Essays* (New York: Oxford UP, 2014) grapples with whether or not the industrial invention of rubber vulcanization by Charles Goodyear was based more of his extension of prior knowledge with rubber as a manufacturing substance; creativity as defined as originality; or simply being " lucky" in that he " managed to find" a workable way to make something new based on his experience in the field (25).

4. The BELL Core, http://www.belmont.edu/bellcore/.

5. Oshin Vartanian, et al. *Neuroscience of Creativity,* (Cambridge: MIT Press, 2013): 10.

6. Jessica Nicholson, " Belmont University, Sea Gayle Music, AIMP Celebrate Pipeline Project 4.0 Success," *Music Row, March 3, 2015,* retrieved August 27, 2016, http://www.musicrow.com/2015/03/belmont-university-sea-gayle-music-aimp-celebrate-pipeline-project-4-0-success/.

7. The Honors Program at Belmont University, http://www.belmont.edu/honors/index.html.

8. Stacy Boyd, "Extracurriculars are Central to Learning," *U.S. News & World Report,* April 28, 2014 (https://www.usnews.com/opinion/articles/2014/04/28/music-art-and-language-programs-in-schools-have-long-lasting-benefits); Marianna Fang, "Public Schools Slash Arts Education and Turn to Private Funding," *ThinkP*rogress, August 5, 2013 (https://thinkprogress.org/public-schools-slash-arts-education-and-turn-to-private-funding-f16ff3b0bda5); Sharon Noguchi, "Cutting Art, Music, Foreign Language, from High School Graduation Requirements Will Have a Big Impact," *San Jose Mercury* October 31, 2011 (http://www.mercurynews.com/2011/10/13/cutting-art-music-foreign-language-from-high-school-graduation-requirements-will-have-big-impact); and Fran Smith, "Why Arts Education is Crucial, and Who's Doing it Best," *Edutopia,* January 28, 2009 (https://www.edutopia.org/arts-music-curriculum-child-development). For whether or not creativity can be taught, see Berys Gaut, "Educating for Creativity," in Elliott S. Paul

and Scott B. Kauffman's *The Philosophy of Creativity, New Essays* (New York: Oxford UP, 2014). Gaut argues it can be taught, using examples from composition tied to math and from critical reasoning in philosophy.

9. Laurie Fendrich, "How Critical Thinking Sabotages Painting," *The Chronicle of Higher Education* March 25, 2016, retrieved March 25, 2016, http://chronicle.com March 25, 2016.

10. George Kuh and Steven Tepper, "Let's Get Serious about Cultivating Creativity," *The Chronicle of Higher Education*, September 4, 2011, retrieved March 19, 2016.

11. Beverly Schneller and Larry Wacholtz, "Teaching Creativity through the Poetry of Dana Gioia's *Pity the Beautiful*," conference presentation on teaching the Artist's Studio core course, The Critical Eye, College English Association annual meeting, Denver, Colorado, March 31–April 2, 2016.

CHAPTER 9

The Value of the Arts Within a Liberal Arts Education: Skills for the Workplace and the World

Ilene Lieberman and Mara Parker

Much has been written about the benefits of learning to play an instrument, creating an image on canvas, or moving in coordinated gestures. Aside from the importance of the artistic endeavor itself, proponents point to the skills developed by students of the arts: self-discipline, persistence, risk-taking, collaboration, problem-solving, careful and attentive looking and listening, empathy, and the ability to see an issue from multiple perspectives.[1] Such abilities are needed not just by visual artists, musicians, or dancers; they are of immense benefit to any person engaged in education, professional work, or simply day-to-day existence.

With their foundation in history and theory, academic classes in the fine arts prove equally beneficial in the development of key proficiencies. Liberal arts students who take courses in art history or music history are given a valuable opportunity to learn not only content, but also to develop new ways of thinking, communicating, and evaluating. Classes in these areas broaden a student's understanding of human nature and, consequently, offer new ways to think about the unknown and the familiar, new concepts and old ideas, and one's own and diverse cultures. Such courses teach our

I. Lieberman (✉) • M. Parker
Widener University, Chester, PA, USA

© The Author(s) 2018
N. H. Hensel (ed.), *Exploring, Experiencing, and Envisioning Integration in US Arts Education*, The Arts in Higher Education,
https://doi.org/10.1007/978-3-319-71051-8_9

students that communication can be achieved not just with the written or spoken word, but also with sound, shape, and gesture. Historically based arts classes teach students to hear and to see, to be comfortable with ambiguity, to examine an issue from multiple perspectives, and to develop sound methodologies for working through confusing and sometimes controversial issues. Such skills are valued by any number of professions, both within the arts and without.

Arts Interventions: An Introduction

The scientific community is beginning to understand the importance of arts education for the skills their students derive, particularly critical thinking "outside the traditional, reductive science paradigm."[2] Learning to "look closely" or "listen closely" can help develop skills that enhance clinical and scientific work.[3] This recognition of the value of arts education has appeared primarily at the graduate level, especially in medicine.

Arts programs have become standard at many prominent medical schools in the United States, including those at Harvard, Yale, Stanford, and Cornell. Such arts "interventions" (guided examinations of art works) are valued because they improve students' observational and visual diagnostic skills, ability to empathize, and ability to deal with ambiguity and uncertainty. In a 2004 study that examined teaching and learning in medicine, Rodenhauer, Strickland, and Gambala found that more than half the schools responding to their survey used the arts in learning activities. Most included literature, visual arts, performing arts, and/or music, and reported improved clinical skills and an ability to empathize.[4] What is interesting is that students do not study visual art or music as it applies to medicine. Rather, the works of art studied serve as a means of developing critical thinking and abstract skills that are then transferred to any field[5] that values critical thinking, enhanced awareness, unbiased inspection, accurate reporting, and an ability to consider multiple perspectives. Such skills are needed in law enforcement,[6] reading, writing, and mathematics,[7] to name but a few areas.

The use of art, particularly visual art, to improve observational and interpretive skills in clinical practice has been investigated and documented in numerous studies focusing on medical education.[8] Proficiency in visual observation allows students to gather and assemble data in a coherent and logical way, and heightens awareness of "pattern recognition, which focuses [not only] on identifying the familiar but also ... the ability to identify the unfamiliar."[9] Braverman argues that this is not something that can be taught formally through lecture, but rather can only be achieved through *experiential* learning,[10] that is, immersion with the primary material.

Boudreau, Cassell, and Fuks maintain that one learns "deep seeing" best through aesthetics. Internalized images do not simply function as a memory aid but rather as an incubator and generator for new ideas and perceptions.[11] As Wellbery and McAteer note, "deep seeing" means that students learn to observe with an open mind.[12] Boisaubin and Winkler contend that the art of truly seeing can only be achieved with intellectual discipline and attention. "Presuppositions, stereotypes, and prejudice ... [must] be suspended ... before the honestly inquiring eye and a new reality, even truth, can be revealed."[13]

DEVELOPING OBSERVATION SKILLS: VISUAL STRATEGIES

One reason the study of the visual arts is so prized at the graduate level is that it teaches the learner critical thinking and reflection. Observation skills, "honed through experience with the arts ... [fosters] attention, self-awareness, and critique."[14] Close observation, which Wellbery and McAteer argue is a scientific habit, leads to subjective engagement, and allows one to understand and monitor one's personal values, frustrations, and inner resources.[15]

What effect does learning to see have on students' work in other areas? Pellico, Friedlaender, and Fennie note that students who participated in arts interventions wrote more about what they saw than those who did not. This directly resulted in more objective clinical findings when examining patients. Pellico and her co-researchers argue that the use of artwork encourages seeing, observing, identifying, discriminating, and clustering data.[16] Jasani and Saks contend that students who take part in art classes [interventions] successfully transfer their newly developed observational skills to "real world" settings (e.g., medical) and are able to arrive at a broader set of interpretations, are open to multiple perspectives, and recognize the impact of context on perception.[17] Such skills fit directly with the goals of clinical observation.[18]

Two different strategies have been used by researchers to investigate and document these heightened observational skills and increased ability to empathize. The most frequently used approach is Visual Thinking Strategies (VTS). The approach was initially created for use with younger students to "teach critical thinking, visual literacy and communication skills."[19] Students are trained to observe color, light, shadow, contour, form, texture, pattern, line, symmetry, and balance.[20] Its application has been expanded to many audiences including medical residents, and at the graduate level, the methodology embraces the same goals of critical thinking, communication skills, and visual literacy as set out for younger students. VTS focuses on three questions:

> What do you see?
> What makes you say that?
> What else do you see?

To answer these questions, students work, with guidance, through a four-step process:

1. Observation: identify visual findings and record observations without judgment.
2. Interpretation: draw conclusions about the work's meaning and generate multiple interpretations.
3. Reflection: evaluate conclusions and question validity; personal beliefs and biases are explored.
4. Communication: share ideas with other students.[21]

VTS teaches students to observe; with practice, they develop aesthetic skills, learn to give evidence for interpretations, and take part in respectful dialogue. Using the three basic questions of VTS, students are asked to (1) look carefully at works of art, (2) talk about what they observe, (3) back up their ideas with evidence, (4) listen to and consider the views of others, and (5) discuss many possible interpretations.[22] VTS promotes unbiased observation, greater organization of thought, and deeper-level reflection. The use of this strategy leads to decreased use of subjective terminology in favor of increased consideration of multiple interpretations.[23] One of the major benefits of VTS is that this mode of thinking and analysis can be transferred to other settings. It provides students with a safe experience in which they learn to navigate uncertainty and divergent thinking in ways that often produce valuable new ideas.[24]

Thus, examining works of art becomes a practical experience in which to try out new reasoning skills. It trains one to be flexible and concretely illustrates that there is no single approach to problem-solving.[25] It encourages students to move beyond their comfort zone while simultaneously improving their ability to empathize and develop their perspective-taking skills.[26]

A second art program designed to cultivate skills of observation is the Art of Analysis program, developed at Ohio State University College of Medicine, and frequently referred to by the acronym ODIP (observe, describe, interpret, and prove). The program was specifically created to "encourage critical thinking skills, engender empathy, create a foundation for cooperative achievement, increase students' tolerance for ambiguity, and build visual observation skills."[27] Like VTS, ODIP was first used with younger students. In its earliest form, ODIP was piloted over a two-year period with a group of fifth graders. Researchers successfully documented the students' increased critical-thinking skills and greater depth of observation. Examining works of art, students were asked to consider the following:

1. What do you see? Try to find a detail no one else will notice. (Observe)
2. Describe what you see. What colors are present? How would you describe these colors? (Describe)
3. What's going on in this work of art? Make an interpretation based upon what you see in this work. (Interpret)
4. Prove your interpretations using visual evidence. What do you see that supports your interpretation? (Prove)

At the graduate level, students participating in the program were asked to answer additional questions by identifying works of art in the museum where the program took place, and articulating why and how those images depicted a particular concept. The questions were:

1. What does compassion/empathy look like?
2. What does cruelty look like?
3. What does (the act of) being humane look like?
4. What does selfishness look like?
5. What does being a good teacher look like?
6. Find a work of art that does/does not immediately appeal to you. Document why this is so? Use ODIP to interpret the work.[28]
7. Choose any two works of art that you are surprised to see installed next to each other, and make an argument for why they are side by side.[29]

A key component of the Art of Analysis program is oral discussion. This format teaches students to support their ideas and theories, and form proofs. It challenges the participants' presuppositions and observations. Students learn that the sharing of ideas often expands and alters their own viewpoint. Ambiguity is no longer a source of discomfort but rather a means by which one learns to respect the opinions and skills of fellow students.[30]

INCREASING PERSPECTIVE: DEALING WITH AMBIGUITY AND UNCERTAINTY

One of the most important benefits of studying the arts is that such study demonstrates the positive aspects of ambiguity. It helps us understand the many layers of meaning embodied in seemingly abstract works and the sensitivity, engagement, imagination, and reflection required in its interpretation.[31] Boudreau, Cassell, and Fuks contend that the study of both representational and non-representational works stimulates recognition and cultivates empathy.[32] Such an argument is not isolated. Numerous investigations over the past 20 years[33] point out that the study of the visual arts improves one's ability to empathize. Pellico, Friedlaender, and Fennie argue that viewing works of art teaches the dangers of self-selecting observations. Students who participated in arts interventions found that they no longer ignored conflicting cues; furthermore, they recognized the influence of their own backgrounds and understood how this affected their analyses.[34] Perry, Maffulli, Wilson, and Morrissey suggest that the study of visual arts leads students to recognize and understand the more complex and subtle patterns relating to human experience and emotion. Students who participated in arts interventions demonstrated an increased awareness of multiple perspectives, an appreciation of subtle cues from body language, and a healthy skepticism about initial impressions.[35]

Learning to deal with uncertainty and ambiguity encourages students to take responsibility for their own learning.[36] While uncertainty may make one uncomfortable, it presents an opportunity for growth.[37] Uncertainty and ambiguity move "the perceiver beyond the obvious into a realm where values, meanings, and priorities are weighed."[38] As Wellbery notes, just as one works through a painting's ambiguity, exploring the various possibilities, in the medical world (and in life in general), we meet people and situations that demand we read facial expressions, decipher body language, hear vocal inflections, and so on. One must be able to make sense of both overt and covert messages.[39]

Grappling with uncertainty is an opportunity to clarify values. Studying art provides us with a framework from which we can resolve uncertainty: One identifies which information is lacking, one recognizes that interpretation is a process that occurs over time, and one understands the contributions of context.[40] While Jeffrey Campbell has addressed this when dealing specifically with uncertainty in medicine, his comments can be applied to all professions and day-to-day situations.[41] He argues that one's ability to be effective and empathetic can be cultivated by developing a tolerance and healthy respect for uncertainty. Because of the abstract nature of the arts, varied interpretations are possible. Such contradictions are particularly useful as a pedagogical tool for they force students to collect information in an objective manner. Thus, one learns to accept and consider alternate interpretations.[42]

Learning to Listen: Music Interventions

Music education offers another entrée into the world of critical thinking, empathy, communication, and problem-solving. In an abstract fashion, it explores such themes as compassion, human dignity, loss, and sadness. It teaches us to listen not only to someone's words, but to what is "behind the words" by noticing cadence, volume, inflection, tone, tension, and pacing.[43] If, as Newell and Hanes suggest, the basis for empathy is knowing how to listen, then learning how to listen to music is the ideal means to develop that skill.[44] Like VTS, listening to and discussing music encourages the respectful sharing and consideration of ideas. It opens the student to divergent interpretations and ultimately to an exploration of possibilities not previously considered. Not listening means we lose a sense of connection and empathy; we stop paying attention. We revert to practiced and memorized behaviors, many of which may be detrimental to the understanding of complex situations.[45] Music education helps students develop a variety of ways of perceiving and thinking,[46] and to cultivate problem-solving techniques, comparison, classification, reflective processes, and the appraisal of activities.[47] It encourages critical assessment of listening, performance, interpretation, and creation. It fosters this individually and as an assessment of others' ideas.[48]

The analysis of a composition means that the listener must fully engage and be involved in the act of listening. This active listening requires focus as well as the knowledge, emotions, memories, and expectations that one brings to the experience.[49] These same skills can be applied when dealing with humans in any situation. One learns to hear a depth of cues and complex elements; one develops the ability to listen to pitch, rhythm, declamation, voicing, repetition, color, articulation, and direction.[50] Studying music teaches us to hear the interplay of multiple parts just as when we truly listen to people, we hear multiple strands. Learning to listen "encourage[s] breadth and simultaneity of attention, understanding which voices are concordant and which voices conflict, color or alter the meaning of what may otherwise appear as a primary melody."[51] It means that we can assess problems, recognize alternate solutions, and the like.

Understanding a composition challenges our expectations, our values, and our pre-conceived ideas. It teaches the importance of recognizing deviations from expected patterns. Discussions about music and an engaged exploration of it help us to move past the surface sounds and explore the inner meaning. Music is an essential pedagogical tool because it "reflects the nature of art itself: an exploration into the human condition via the mutual dialogue" among listeners.[52] Such analysis and criticism help us to explore and deepen our understanding of music at various levels of interpretation, aesthetics, structure, style, expressivity, and ideology-culture.[53] Newell and Hanes note that listening skills and cultural awareness are defining outcomes for medical students and that music is an ideal way to train students in these skills.[54] But such skills are not restricted to medical people. Rather, listening and cultural awareness are necessary for nearly any profession or personal experience.

ARTS EDUCATION FOR THE UNDERGRADUATE STUDENT: A TEST CASE

While the benefit of the arts is widely accepted at the graduate level, much less attention has been paid to its importance at the undergraduate level. One can easily argue that if enhanced observational and listening skills are crucial for those engaged in demanding professions, such skills are no less important for those who will be entering the general workforce, be it after four years of undergraduate education or after additional schooling at the graduate level. Moreover, the skills learned through a study of the arts are not simply for the employed. Rather, such skills are needed by any person who hopes to be an engaged and responsible citizen. Thus, the arts must be considered a cornerstone of the undergraduate liberal arts education.

How does one integrate the arts into an undergraduate curriculum, especially for those students majoring in such seemingly unrelated fields as biology, engineering, nursing, hospitality, and business? The following case study and plans for future curricular development discuss the use of the arts as a means of successfully teaching students to listen, think critically, discuss, reflect, and accept ambiguity and multiple perspectives.

During the spring of 2015, we offered a class entitled "Music, War, and the Art of Persuasion" to a group of students who were part of Widener University's Honors Program in General Education. None of these students were music or fine arts majors. A limited number had some musical background—either as an instrumentalist or vocalist—but in general, the students were primarily science and engineering students with a limited number of other majors represented (psychology, business, and English). The class was conducted as a colloquium, meaning it was a discussion-based seminar, led as much by the students as by the instructor. The course, focusing on music written by composers specifically in reaction to World War II and the Vietnam War, was designed so that students would be able to develop their listening skills and their ability to articulate what they heard, to learn to be comfortable with ambiguity, and to put together their own composition that expressed their personal view of a given world conflict. In essence, this course achieved for our undergraduates what the graduate courses discussed above accomplished for their students.

Each week, students were asked, prior to meeting, to listen to a specific number of compositions and answer a set of pre-discussion prompts and questions:

1. Describe your immediate response to the music.
2. What associations did the music have for you?
3. What did you notice about the medium?
4. What did you notice about the way the piece was structured (the way it was laid out)?
5. What idea/emotion/attitude do you think the composer was trying to convey?
6. What sounds were particularly interesting to you? Why?
7. What sounds might you want to store in your toolbox? Where do they occur in the piece (in other words, how will you be able to find them again?)?

8. If the composition has a text:

    - What did you notice about the text?
    - Does the music support the text or does it work against it?
    - Is any of the text repeated? What effect does this have?

9. Sum up your total response to this music. On reflection, what do you think it means and what features of the music stand out?

Students were expected to listen to the compositions and complete the directed listening assignments prior to meeting as a group. The class discussions, led by the students, moved from personal reactions to the compositions to reflective remarks on the attitude of the composer toward the military conflict.

Students offered thoughtful comments and listened attentively to each other, often using a classmate's idea as a point of departure for some newly considered concept. All students left class with a different perspective on the composition and what it meant. To ascertain how much their views had changed, students were then asked to respond to a post-discussion set of prompts and questions:

1. Describe your response to the composition.
2. Now that you know more about the composition, what associations does the music have for you?
3. What effect does the piece's structure have on the way you view/consider the work?
4. What effect does the piece's harmony and texture have on the way you view/consider the work?
5. Now that you know what the composer was trying to convey, do you think he succeeded?
6. What is the most moving/successful part of the work? What is the least successful part of the work?
7. What sounds might be useful to you in your own composition? (What sounds might you want to place in your toolbox?)
8. Sum up your total response to this music.

Both the pre- and post-discussion observations included questions about a "toolbox." The students' final project was an original composition. The "toolbox" was a shorthand means of assisting them to develop a compendium of sounds that could be used to convey ideas, emotions, or concepts.

While students could, if they wished, compose an original composition, as one student opted to do, they were encouraged to use GarageBand or a similar computer program that allowed them to manipulate pre-existing sounds/recordings (their toolbox) and from there, to create their own work. The students were given the task of (1) developing an understanding of ISIS and the crisis (restricted at the time) in the Middle East through an extensive examination of reputable sources; (2) arriving at their own conclusion as to whether the United States should be involved; and (3) writing a composition that would reflect their position and attempt to persuade their listeners (their classmates) to agree with them. All of this needed to be articulated both in conference with the instructor and in written format, as a final composition, and orally to their classmates.

The presentations were thoughtful both on the part of the individual presenters and the listeners. The setting provided students with a safe space in which to take a stand about a political situation and to present their ideas, not using the traditional means of a paper, but rather, with a musical composition—to speak, as it were, abstractly. As none of the students were composers, this meant they were asked to function far outside their comfort zone; most did so with a fair amount of trepidation. The level of nervousness during the presentations was quite high, and most probably was directly related to a feeling of vulnerability. Taking a stand on a contentious issue, writing a composition, and playing it for one's peers was intensely nerve-wracking and placed students in an uncomfortable position. In essence, they were required to take a risk they would not have chosen. Nevertheless, they presented with poise, and discussions were respectful and polite. The student views were varied and the discussions that followed indicated the diversity of thought. When asked about their musical choices and decisions, presenters could answer with confidence and easily articulate their process.

Students were asked to reflect on the compositional process.

Were some parts easy? Why?
Were some parts difficult? Why?
What problems did you encounter?
Was it what you expected?
How do you view the final result?
What would you do differently the second time around?
What is your view of the compositional process?
Knowing what you now know, how do you approach the act of listening?

Their responses to this last question were particularly interesting, for they reveal a newly discovered and intentional approach to listening. Among the responses:

> After the course ... my act of listening has significantly changed. I have become much more attentive to musical details, am able to pick out musical sounds. ... Before, I would either like or dislike a piece without attempting to interpret the deeper meaning. ... Now I can carefully listen and note changes in music, ... understand the purpose of using consonance and dissonance, and try to feel the emotions and message conveyed in specific compositions. Listening to music is not just a way to pass time and relax, but a way to understand and experience a composer's view on specific events.

> I now listen more intently for slight variations in musical structure and difference. I now listen to the timbre, tempo, dynamics, and harmony more keenly ... to determine the message that the composer was trying to convey.

> I think this class and my experience in creating this composition has had a significant impact on the way in which I approach the act of listening. ... I don't think I had ever been in a group or setting where I so deeply and critically analyzed a piece of music.

The course, in its outcomes, embodies the benefits of a music class (as well as an arts class) within a liberal arts curriculum. It teaches the students to listen deeply, to search for meaning, to acknowledge personal bias, to be comfortable with uncertainty, and to appreciate multiple perspectives. In short, it affords undergraduates precisely the competencies they need to tackle potential challenges and succeed in a complex world.

FUTURE PLANS: DEVELOPING THE "TOOLBOX"

We will continue to use the arts as a foundation to improve student skills in two new courses to be offered in the next academic year. "Art in the Aftermath," taught as an Honors colloquium, with students coming from diverse majors (nursing, biology, engineering, psychology, and business), will investigate the resilience of humankind in combating trauma, tragedy, and loss, by looking at the transformational role art can play as an agent for change and renewal. Through exploration across disciplines, and using much the same methodology as "Music, War, and the Art of Persuasion," students will consider the means by which creativity provides a basis for transcendence. The second arts course, "Learning to Look, Learning to Listen," will be offered to first-year nursing and social work students, and will use the approaches outlined above to cultivate the myriad skills future practitioners will need in their toolbox to succeed: critical thinking, empathy, observational acuity, engaged listening, and sensitivity to diverse populations. The capacity—rather, *the necessity*—of such courses in cultivating the competencies required in contemporary society assures the arts' continuing relevance in the workplace and the world.

The evidence supporting the benefits of arts programs at the graduate level has long been recognized and has, in fact, led to a reshaping of curricula. What has, up to now, not been recognized is that there is an equal benefit in incorporating arts classes into the undergraduate professional education. Observational, listening, critical thinking, and empathy are critical skills for all students. Our own findings, based on our test case, suggest that arts courses provide a unique preparation for both those who pursue graduate study and those who choose to enter the workforce.

We acknowledge that not all will see this benefit as transparent, nor do we assume that undergraduates in professional majors will automatically appreciate, yet alone accept, the applicability of the arts in their curriculum. One might view this as discomfort with an approach that challenges their expectations. Visual and musical intelligence provide a critical foundation for learning and for dealing with this uneasiness. As the research and our experiences have proved, arts education forms an integral part of professional programs, interacting *directly* with students' chosen fields and equipping them with the tools needed to flourish. Such learning experiences increase our students' proficiencies and their chances for success, and should, therefore, find their way into all occupational training.

NOTES

1. For an extensive discussion of the benefits of arts education (including dance, drama, visual arts, and music), see Richard R. Deasy, ed., *Critical Links: Learning in the Arts and Student Achievement and Social Development* (Washington D.C.: Arts Education Partnership, 2002). This compendium of more than 60 studies and essays examines the benefits of arts education and the transference of skills from one area (arts) to learning and behavior in other academic and social contexts. See also Louis E. Catron, "What Theatre Majors Learn," accessed December 20, 2015, http://lecatr.people.wm.edu/majorslearn.html; May Kokkidou, "Critical Thinking and School Music Education: Literature Review, Research

Findings, and Perspectives," *Journal for Learning through the Arts* 9, no. 1 (2013), accessed January 4, 2016, https://escholarship.org/uc/item/4dt433j3; "Long Term Benefits of Music Study," accessed December 20, 2105, http://www.wheaton.edu/CSA/Lessons/Long-Term-Benefits-of-Music-Study; Lisa Trei, "Musical Training Helps Language Processing, Studies Show," *Stanford Report* (November 15, 2005), accessed December 20, 2015, http://news.stanford.edu/news/2005/november16/music-111605.html; "20 Important Benefits of Music in Our Schools," *National Association for Music Education*, last modified July 21, 2014, accessed December 20, 2015, http://www.nafme.org/20-important-benefits-of-music-in-our-schools.

2. Rimma Osipov, "Do Future Bench Researchers Need Humanities Courses?" *AMA Journal of Ethics* 16, no. 8 (Aug. 2014): 604–609, accessed January 4, 2016, http://journalofethics.ama-assn.org/2014/08/ecas3-1408.html.

3. Ibid.

4. See Paul Rodenhauser, Matthew A. Strickland, and Cecilia T. Gambala, "Arts-Related Activities Across U.S. Medical Schools: A Follow-Up Study," *Teaching and Learning in Medicine* 16/3 (2004): 233–239.

5. Irwin M. Braverman, "To See or Not to See: How Visual Training Can Improve Observational Skills," *Clinics in Dermatology* 29 (2011): 344.

6. J. Donald Boudreau, Eric J. Cassell, and Abraham Fuks, "Preparing Medical Students to Become Skilled at Clinical Observation," *Medical Teacher* 30, nos. 9–10 (2008): 859, accessed December 18, 2015, http://dx.doi.org/10/1080/01421590802331446. For a recent assessment of such use in law enforcement, see Sarah Lyall, "Off the Beat and Into a Museum: Art Helps Police Officers Learn to Look," *New York Times*, April 26, 2016, http://www.nytimes.com/2016/04/27/arts/design/art-helps-police-officers-learn-to-look.html?_r=0. Art historian Amy E. Herman , *Visual Intelligence: Sharpen Your Perception, Change Your Life* (New York: Eamon Dolan/Houghton Mifflin Harcourt, 2016), explains such work with the New York Police Department in venues such as the Metropolitan Museum of Art.

7. Sheila Naghshineh, Janet P. Hafler, Alexa R. Miller, Maria A. Blanco, Stuart R. Lipsitz, Rachel P. Dubroff, Shahram Khoshbin, and Joel T. Katz, "Formal Art Observation Training Improves Medical Students' Visual Diagnostic Skills," *Journal of General Internal Medicine* 23 (2008): 995.

8. See studies by Charles L. Bardes, Debra Gillers, and Amy E. Herman, "Learning to Look: Developing Clinical Observational Skills at an Art Museum," *Medical Education* 35 (2001): 1157–1161; Jacqueline C. Dolev, Linda Krohner Friedlaender, and Irwin M. Braverman, "Use of Fine Art to Enhance Visual Diagnostic Skills," *Journal of the American*

Medical Association 286 (2001): 1020–1021; Nancy C. Elder, Barbara Tobias, Amber Lucero-Criswell, and Linda Goldenhar, "The Art of Observation: Impact of a Family Medicine and Art Museum Partnership on Student Education," *Family Medicine* 38 (2006): 393–398; Johanna Shapiro and Lynn Hunt, "All the World's a Stage: The Use of Theatrical Performance in Medical Education," *Medical Education* 37 (2006): 922–927; Deborah Kirklin, Jane Duncan, Sandy McBride, Sam Hunt, and Mark Griffin, "A Cluster Design Controlled Trial of Arts-Based Observational Skills Training in Primary Care," *Medical Education* 41 (2007): 395–401; Naghshineh, Hafler, Miller, Blanco, Lipsitz, Dubroff, Khoshbin, and Katz, "Formal Art Observation Training"; Pamela B. Schaff, Suzanne Isken, and Robert M. Tager, "From Contemporary Art to Core Clinical Skills: Observation, Interpretation, and Meaning-Making in a Complex Environment," *Academic Medicine* 86 (2011): 1272–1276; Andrew Jacques, Rachel Trinkley, Linda Stone, Richard Tang, William A. Hudson, and Sorabh Khandelwal, "Art of Analysis: A Cooperative Program Between a Museum and Medicine," *Journal for Learning Through the Arts* 8/1 (2012): 1–10, accessed January 7, 2016, http://escholarship.org/uc/item/36n2t2w9; and Gary E. Friedlaender and Linda K. Friedlaender, "Art in Science: Enhancing Observational Skills," *Clinical Orthopaedics in Related Research* 47 (2013): 2065–2067.

9. Lawrence T. O. Bell and Darrell J. R. Evans, "Art, Anatomy and Medicine: Is There a Place for Art in Medical Education?" *Anatomical Sciences Education* 7 (2014): 371–372.

10. Braverman, "To See or Not to See," 345.

11. Boudreau, Cassell, and Fuks, "Preparing Medical Students," 858.

12. Wellbery and McAteer, "The Art of Observation," 1629.

13. Eugene V. Boisaubin and Mary G. Winkler, "See Patients and Life Contexts: The Visual Arts in Medical Education," *The American Journal of Medical Sciences* 319, no. 5 (May 2000): 292.

14. Wellbery and McAteer, "The Art of Observation," 1629.

15. Ibid., 1626.

16. Linda Honan Pellico, Linda Friedlaender, and Kristopher P. Fennie, "Looking is Not Seeing: Using Art to Improve Observational Skills," *Journal of Nursing Education* 48, no. 11 (Nov. 2009): 648–649.

17. Sona K. Jasani and Norma S. Saks, "Utilizing Visual Art to Enhance the Clinical Observation Skills of Medical Students," *Medical Teacher* 35, no. 7 (2013): e1329, accessed December 20, 2015, https://doi.org/10.3109/0142158X.2013.770131.

18. For a list and discussion of these goals, see Boudreau, Cassell, and Fuks, "Preparing Medical Students," 859–861. The authors focus, in particular, on the need to articulate what one sees, to be aware of cultural determinants, and the potential for bias.

19. Jacques, Trinkley, Stone, Tang, Hudson, and Khandelwal, "Art of Analysis."
20. Naghshineh, Hafler, Miller, Blanco, Lipsitz, Dubroff, Khoshbin, and Katz, "Formal Art Observation Training," 992.
21. Jasani and Saks, "Utilizing Visual Art to Enhance the Clinical Observation Skills," e1328. See also Alexa Miller, Michelle Grohe, Shahram Khoshbin, and Joel T. Katz, "From the Galleries to the Clinic: Applying Art Museum Lessons to Patient Care," *Journal of Medical Humanities* 34 (2013): 434.
22. Miller, Grohe, Khoshbin, and Katz, "From the Galleries to the Clinic," 434.
23. Jasani and Saks, "Utilizing Visual Art to Enhance the Clinical Observation Skills," e1330.
24. Miller, Grohe, Khoshbin, and Katz, "From the Galleries to the Clinic," 435.
25. Ibid.
26. Shapiro and Shallit, "A Night at the Museum," 599–603.
27. Jacques, Trinkley, Stone, Tang, Hudson, and Khandelwal, "Art of Analysis."
28. This question allows students to become aware of their own biases and to view the work from a different perspective.
29. Jacques, Trinkley, Stone, Tang, Hudson, and Khandelwal, "Art of Analysis."
30. Ibid. Herman, *Visual Intelligence*, 98, develops strategies for seeing based on the acronym COBRA (camouflaged, one, break, realign, ask).
31. Jan C. Frich and Per Fugelli, "Medicine and the Arts in the Undergraduate Medical Curriculum at the University of Oslo Faculty of Medicine, Oslo, Norway," *Academic Medicine* 78, no. 10 (October 2003): 1038.
32. Boudreau, Cassell, and Fuks, "Preparing Medical Students," 859.
33. Philip Darbyshire, "Understanding the Life of Illness: Learning Through the Art of Frida Kahlo," *Advances in Nursing Science* 17 (1996): 51–59; Deborah Kirklin, Richard Meakin, Surinder Singh, and Margaret Lloyd, "Living With and Dying From Cancer: A Humanities Special Study Module," *Medical Humanities* 26 (2000): 51–54; Paul Lazarus and Felicity M. Rosslyn, "The Arts in Medicine: Setting up and Evaluating a New Special Study Module at Leicester Warwick Medical School," *Medical Education* 37 (2003): 553–559; Lisbeth Blomqvist, Kaisu Pitkälä, and Pirkko Routasalo, "Images of Loneliness: Using Art as an Educational Method in Professional Training," *Journal of Continuing Education in Nursing* 38 (2007): 89–93; Fatemah Geranmayeh and Keyoumars Ashkan, "Mind on Canvas: Anatomy, Signs, and Neurosurgery in Art," *British Journal of Neurosurgery* 22 (2008): 563–574; and Arno K. Kumagi, "Perspective: Acts of Interpretation: A Philosophical Approach to Using Creative Arts in Medical Education," *Academic Medicine* 87 (2012): 1138–1144.

34. Pellico, Friedlaender, and Fennie, "Looking is Not Seeing," 650.
35. Mark Perry, Nicola Maffulli, Suzy Wilson, and Dylan Morrissey, "The Effectiveness of Arts-Based Interventions in Medical Education: A Literature Review," *Medical Education* 45 (2011): 146.
36. Renée C. Fox, "Training for Uncertainty," in *The Student-Physician: Introductory Studies in the Sociology of Medical Education*, ed. by Robert K. Merton, George G. Reader, and Patricia L. Kendall (Cambridge, MA: Harvard University Press, 1957; reprinted 1969), 210.
37. Caroline Wellbery, "The Art of Medicine: The Value of Medical Uncertainty?" *The Lancet* 375 (May 15, 2010): 1687.
38. Ibid., 1686.
39. Ibid., 1687.
40. Ibid.
41. Jeffrey I. Campbell, "Art and the Uncertainty of Medicine," *Journal of the American Medical Association* 312, no. 22 (Dec. 10, 2014): 2337.
42. Braverman, "To See or Not to See," 345–346.
43. Glenn C. Newell and Douglas J. Hanes, "Listening to Music: The Case for its Use in Teaching Medical Humanism," *Academic Medicine* 78, no. 7 (July 2003): 715.
44. Ibid.
45. Peter Van Roessel and Audrey Shafer, "Music, Medicine, and the Art of Listening," *Journal for Learning through the Arts* 2, no. 1 (2006), accessed January 4, 2016, http://escholarship.org/uc/item/501997g9.
46. Kokkidou, "Critical Thinking and School Music Education," 4.
47. Ibid., 5.
48. Ibid., 6.
49. Van Roessel and Shafer, "Music, Medicine, and the Art of Listening."
50. Ibid.
51. Ibid.
52. Ibid.
53. Kokkidou, "Critical Thinking and School Music Education," 6.
54. Newell and Hanes, "Listening to Music," 715.

CHAPTER 10

Creative Writing for Professional Writing Majors

Mary Rist and Sasha West

As the other chapters in this anthology point out and as the STEM-to-STEAM movement in K–12 education suggests, the capabilities and habits of mind learned in practicing the arts are essential to lifelong success in a professional world that values flexible skills in decision-making, problem-solving, and empathy. These skills and habits of mind are cultivated in the visual and performing arts, but creative writing workshops offer another, though perhaps less visible, venue for artistic development. Universities often offer creative writing courses as part of the traditional literature major; however, this arrangement can obscure the professional value of the skills taught in creative writing workshops (including storytelling, attention to detail, empathy, and concern for crafting sentences). Such skills may be particularly important for writers training for positions in business and non-profit organizations who will write for ever-changing platforms and tell their organizations' stories to an increasingly diverse but segmented audience.

These are the kinds of writers enrolled in the Writing and Rhetoric BA Program at St. Edward's University, a small liberal arts university in Austin, Texas. We have found that both students and employers value the experience gained in creative writing courses taken as part of the writing major.

M. Rist (✉) • S. West
St. Edward's University, Austin, TX, USA

© The Author(s) 2018
N. H. Hensel (ed.), *Exploring, Experiencing, and Envisioning Integration in US Arts Education*, The Arts in Higher Education, https://doi.org/10.1007/978-3-319-71051-8_10

Based on our experience redesigning an undergraduate writing major and utilizing research into the role of creativity in professional success, this chapter argues for the inclusion of creative writing courses in the professional writing curriculum and describes a program in which creative writers participate with aspiring journalists, editors, and marketing writers in an undergraduate writing and rhetoric major. Programs like these allow creative writing students to learn editing, digital media skills, and rhetorical history, while the professional writing and journalism students benefit from the collaboration and critique of a writing workshop. This program foregrounds the habits of mind listed as essential to success in academic and career writing by the Council of Writing Program Administrators, the National Council of Teachers of English, and the National Writing Project. By helping young writers develop not only their creativity but also their curiosity, openness, engagement, responsibility, flexibility, and metacognition,[1] the St. Edward's writing major produces students ready to engage with the challenges of the twenty-first-century world.

While the BA in English is well known, the BA in writing is a relatively new phenomenon. Once considered "instruction in the basics of educated discourse,"[2] writing at the turn of the twenty-first century has become a skill in demand by employers and a program that has saved many English departments. The early 2000s have been called, by Weisser and Grobman, the "decade of the writing major"[3] as so many programs were established between 2000 and 2010. Curricula in the new writing majors vary considerably, with many majors still linked to literature programs. A growing number of other programs, however, pair a professional focus with a theoretical background from the ancient liberal art of rhetoric.[4] Spigelman and Grobman argue that a rhetorically based program gives students the tools to "appreciate the social, cultural, and ethical obligations of their future roles as rhetors,"[5] while also teaching workplace writing skills, since rhetoric has a history as a practical art. Dominic Delli Carpini argues that "there are many reasons why offering profession-based outcomes, while still staking a claim to geographies within liberal education, is more than just a compromise position."[6] Rhetorical tools of critical thinking and analysis allow students to use the practical skills they acquire in thoughtful, effective ways.

These professionally focused majors have proven to be successful within the humanities. Enrollments have been strong; for example, Florida State University reported 700 students enrolled in its Editing, Writing, and Media Program in 2013.[7] A 2015 anthology profiling undergraduate writing majors showed the average enrollment at 18 institutions, many regional state or liberal arts institutions, to be 67 majors with 8.6 full-time faculty positions.[8] Here at St. Edward's University, writing and rhetoric is the second largest major in the School of Humanities, enrolling almost three times as many majors as our colleagues in the literature program in 2015–2016.

Despite historical ties to the liberal arts, over time, writing and rhetoric programs tend to become more professionally focused and less humanistic or rhetorical. The story of the Pennsylvania State—Berks/Lehigh Professional and Technical Writing Program, formed in 2000, is instructive. After several years of operation, program administrators gathered data from students and from an advisory board of local employers who asked for more focus on professional skills, and so the program was revamped to meet this need. The department had learned that "despite our belief that theory is requisite to practice, we came to see that our majors needed to know Quark and FrontPage at least as much as Foucault and Foss."[9]

These relatively new professional writing programs have produced writing graduates who then can find jobs in a variety of fields. Weisser and Grobman[10] surveyed graduates of the Penn State—Berks/Lehigh's writing program mentioned above and found that their alumni reported holding jobs much like those reported by the alumni from the St. Edward's writing and rhetoric program who post their job titles on LinkedIn. Graduates from both programs are working in publishing or marketing or they hold communication positions in government agencies or non-profits. However, despite sending students into professions such as advertising and marketing, which reward creative thinking and writing, few of the BA or BS programs in professional writing offer much in the way of creative writing coursework.

Recently, Douglas Hesse, past president of the National Council of Teachers of English, among others, has argued that writing programs should embrace creative writing because creative and professional writing can complement each other effectively.[11] Creative writing workshops help to teach the habits of mind we want students to develop as undergraduates. In crafting new pieces, students practice the kind of innovation, imagination, and creativity that both employers and world leaders cite as necessary to the coming age.[12] Workshops themselves give students a practicum or lab experience in peer review, teaching them to give and receive criticism well, and to revise work in response to audience needs.

Thus, our core curriculum combines what professional writing classes can do well—teaching rhetorical awareness of audience and situation, use of form, translation of content—with what creative writing does well—examining the unknown, inventing new forms and structures, creating audiences as well as writing for them. This yields versatile, responsive, innovative writers who are better prepared to respond well to both the known tasks they will face in the working world and the new written forms technology will create in the future that we cannot possibly anticipate.

Courses in creative writing and professional writing have existed side-by-side in the Department of Writing and Rhetoric at St. Edward's since the department was formed in 1987. Beginning in 2002, the writing program offered separate concentrations for professional and creative writing. As part of our 2015 curricular review, however, we decided to require all students to take both kinds of coursework. We hoped to emphasize the value of both kinds of writing and their ability to cross-pollinate. There is a larger pedagogical precedent for this. In surveying the use of creative writing in writing-across-the-curriculum (WAC) initiatives, Alexandria Peary offers evidence for its value as an interdisciplinary pedagogy.[13] Our own local research revealed that many internship supervisors and recent alumni of the program value the skills learned in creative writing workshops, including the ability to seek out and make effective use of criticism—a requirement for any writer working as part of a professional team. Finally, during a 2014 academic-program review, our external reviewers suggested that we require that all professional writing majors take at least one introductory, multigenre creative writing workshop and that all specialists in creative writing take at least one professional writing course. They reasoned that both kinds of skills and pedagogies were important for a broad understanding of writing. In designing the new curriculum for the major, based on this program review, we identified key skills that we believe the creative writing course both fosters and reinforces: storytelling, shaping of voice, comfort with uncertainty, crafting high-level sentences, focus on details and brevity, understanding of genre, and teamwork through peer review.

Storytelling is perhaps the most important skill fostered in creative writing, one needed by professional writers, from journalists to marketing copywriters. Rhetoric has traditionally noted the role of language in shaping our realities. Richard Vatz points out that writers shape reality by directing readers' attention, by granting "salience"[14] to some elements of reality and ignoring others. Professional writers pay attention to the power of language in shaping reality, in shaping the identity of the writer, and enacting the writer's social relationship with the audience. Positioning one's audience ("invoking audience" in Ede and Lunsford's terms[15]) and presenting one's self effectively are as important in professional storytelling as in fiction writing. Questions of what details to state baldly, what to suggest, what point-of-view to write from are decisions made by storytellers in creative writing workshops, but they are clearly also decisions that must be made by our professional writers when they take jobs as communications directors or social-media managers. Consider the following example of a job posted on LinkedIn by Lowe's Companies, Inc., for a "senior storyteller": "Lowe's Senior Storyteller is responsible for creating a cohesive and coordinated set of strategic narratives around Customer Experience Design. ... The Senior Storyteller will work collaboratively ... to understand key communication needs, audiences, and storylines that drive the design work forward" (posting September 18, 2015). Any professional writers applying for that position would have been well served by taking a fiction workshop that helps students learn the "fundamentals of compelling storytelling"[16] and trains students in the effective use of narrative arcs and selection of salient details. Moreover, Janelle Adsit points to the connection between the ways selves are crafted and presented in creative nonfiction and in social media.[17] As our students take jobs in which they translate the ideas or goals of an organization into a cohesive media voice, this training in character creation will serve them well. Creative writing's attention to creating stories, characters, and worlds—as well as its focus on sentence crafting—can benefit professional writers. At St. Edward's, all writing majors take a series of three courses on crafting sentences. Students study English grammar as a linguist would, to understand how the phrases and clauses of their native or acquired language work; afterward, they look at how various choices of language affect style and meaning. Creative writing workshops build on that foundation. Perhaps nowhere is revision more expected and attention to sentence-level choices more acute than in poetry and fiction workshops. Our professional writers can learn a great deal from practicing this kind of attention to the detail of language choices and their effects on the text and its audience.

In the mandatory course Introduction to Creative Writing, as well as in creative writing electives, students often focus on the craft of syntax as a key tool of meaning. In poetry units, students examine MacArthur Fellow Ellen Bryant Voigt's idea of syntactical structure as "the purposeful order in which materials are released to the reader."[18] Students practice changing the length, layout, and order of syntax to see how the way in which information unfolds to the reader determines the reader's experience of both emotion and meaning in a poem. They begin to understand how syntax governs pacing, dramatic impact, the awakening of connotations, and thus, resonance. This requires them to understand the audience experience from the perspective of craft and allows majors to see how grammar and syntax apply to invention (in every sense of the word). The creative writing workshop completes the grammar cycle in which students move from rule to craft, from craft to art.

This very particular focus on how language creates meaning will be especially helpful for students who pursue careers that include writing in short forms. Whether they become advertising executives who write commercials or they manage a Twitter account for a non-profit or a newspaper, these students will better understand how to use brevity for maximum impact. Brief forms such as slogans, jingles, and catch phrases often show awareness of dual meanings, attention to the tension between connotation and denotation, and a kind of curiosity about how language is employed. The kind of deep attention to syntactical detail that renders a fictional world real or gives a poetic image resonance is the same detail that will create a winning campaign for non-profit donors or make a politician's speech memorable. In all these spaces, the power of the order in which information is released to the reader gives our majors an advanced way to think about the function and craft of language.

The workshop model common to creative writing classes also offers an extended study in peer review. Peer review often is key to the work of any writing class, but we spend less time in and on peer review than we do on other parts of teaching writing. Creative writing workshops flip the classroom in a way, requiring the teacher and all students, rather than smaller groups of peers, to participate. Workshop sessions let students see a larger number of peers working through ideas and methods of communication. They also allow the professor to give targeted feedback not only about the piece at hand but also about the way students are discussing the piece. This space offers a unique opportunity to assess and develop student voices both as writers and as readers. Students learn to craft accurate, useful descriptions of both what a piece of writing is doing and what their reaction is to that text. For most students, this makes them more effective when they later go into classes (or jobs) that employ peer review in short bursts, on specific tasks, or in service of particular goals.

In the workshops, students practice teamwork. They must be attentive not just to the document but also to the social dynamics of the room. They face real-world problems in presenting their evaluations of a text well: If they offer unqualified praise or only praise, they might build social cohesion, but the author will have little information with which to understand the text or begin revision. If workshop participants criticize work too vaguely or vehemently, they might shut down the possibilities the writer inherently perceives in the piece but hasn't yet realized. If we are to have students who create functional, congenial teams but who still effectively problem-solve and expect excellence from all team members, they must learn to navigate this dynamic.

Additionally, we have found that employers appreciate that creative writing students are accustomed to hearing multiple critiques of their work and view such criticism as constructive; writers who have experienced creative writing workshops seem less likely to take criticism personally on the job, a valuable skill for all writers, but especially for those early in their careers. It is possible this stems from the ways in which creative writing makes the author more vulnerable. In other writing classes, a student might be able to hide behind the assignment (e.g., "I had to write this biographical essay, so that's why I'm talking about my childhood"), but in creative classes, all students know that everything in a document is a choice made by the author. Creative work is also often read as being autobiographical, even when it's not. The idea that the writer is deeply identified with the piece—an assumption not necessarily made for more academic or professional documents—makes the dilemma of how to critique a text connected to an author more salient. Students understand they are in negotiation with both text and person. In this way, workshops also help students practice the interpersonal and intrapersonal skills that are vital to teamwork.

This team effort of the workshops demonstrates to students the need to develop empathy—as does the creation of the art itself and the reader's experience of it. As a reader, the act of placing oneself in another's shoes creates empathy for another's world experience. Many writers and readers of fiction discuss the way this art form can be a vehicle for opening the self up to other points of view or orientations to the world. President Obama recently said while speaking with novelist Marilynne Robinson,

> When I think about how I understand my role as citizen, setting aside being president … the most important stuff I've learned I think I've learned from

novels. It has to do with empathy. It has to do with being comfortable with the notion that the world is complicated and full of grays, but there's still truth there to be found, and that you have to strive for that and work for that. And the notion that it's possible to connect with some[one] else even though they're very different from you.[19]

One could argue that this need for creating empathy would be equally well served in literature classes. However, in a workshop, the reader actually is practicing empathy in two directions: first, with characters or people in the piece; second, with the author as he/she makes creative decisions and works to hone the craft of the piece. Allying this living empathy with the empathy created by a text deepens the experience. Whether students practice creative nonfiction or fiction, they must create characters who have resonance for readers and who lead the audience through a world they do not know. As a writer, crafting a world well requires a kind of empathy for a reader: What will they understand? Where will they be lost? This prepares professional and technical writers as they learn to write for an audience and to conduct studies to understand users' needs and how their work can respond to those needs.

At its heart, part of empathy comes from becoming comfortable with the unknown. Creative writing workshops give fledgling storytellers' hands-on training in negotiating uncertainty. In many writing classes, it is possible to build a rubric for what a final draft of a document such as an academic essay or memo should do and to apply that rubric to an early draft. In creative workshops, however, often the student and professor are figuring out concurrently what success for a particular piece will be. One poem may require a focus on image to succeed, while another may eschew image for linguistic music. While a good poem must use craft techniques, until that first draft is produced, neither the poet nor the workshop leader knows which technique will be most valuable to its completion. This makes it almost impossible to have a single rubric or a comprehensive guide for either writers or workshop participants. Thus students must learn to be comfortable negotiating drafts and revision without absolute guideposts.

While creative courses examine standard components of craft (for instance, in poetry: line breaks, musicality, and structure), inevitably students will have to do their own searching to figure out why a piece moves them or does not. This often requires students to perform deeper analysis of the text and become better readers of structure and craft. It is this skill—the ability to investigate in meaningful ways, even without guideposts—that makes our students the kind of employees who will be able to respond to the next generation of genres. This training in nimble thinking will also help students be the kind of people who can switch careers (and thus written genres) easily, using the tools they learn in all core classes to apply to a new range of problems and audiences. While professional writing programs often teach a rhetorical perspective on the study of "how various disciplines and activities use language for particular purposes,"[20] in creative writing workshops purposes can be infinite, governed not programmatically by audience but rather by what the piece itself needs or dictates. Literature must be invented anew in each work, and in order to evaluate a piece, a student must become skilled at seeing it in the realm of previous production but also as an *in situ* thing. In these ways, creative writing workshops may prompt students to ask harder questions and become more nimble problem-solvers.

This is especially useful as students enter the workplace, where audience parameters are sometimes more nuanced, contradictory, or absent than in academic situations. Working to create an audience, instead of just responding to one, is vital in fields such as publicity and advertising, where one is drawing on what already exists, but essentially seeking to create the next experience, the next zeitgeist. While our students must have knowledge and developed skills, to be truly successful they must recognize that what is already known cannot always determine what needs to be produced. The most successful professionals in these positions have to take a leap into the unknown. The comfort with innovation will be key to our students' ability to move up through organizations over the course of their careers.

Writers able to work collaboratively and creatively, writers who pay careful attention to their sentence craft and to the readers of their texts, writers who can deal flexibly and thoughtfully with uncertainty and with new worlds—these are the kinds of writers who will succeed as professional communicators. Professional writers need to feel comfortable with a variety of professional genres, and they must be able to think analytically about the elements of communication. They also need to see their craft as a creative one. Rather than seeing their writing as a recording of facts, professional writers need to see themselves as storytellers, bearing responsibility for the realities they construct. Doing so can make them more attentive to their craft but also more responsible for what they write. This is the kind of consciousness that can help professional writers, as Delli

Carpini noted, "to go beyond the imitation of already-finished professional discourses, and to examine the social constructions placed upon them by their occupational roles."[21]

The rhetoric courses in the program at St. Edward's emphasize the ethical and practical responsibilities of the rhetor/writer, but students benefit as well from the skills and habits of mind emphasized in creative writing workshops. We predict that our writers will succeed better in the long run if they bring to their work a professional's knowledge of how language can work, a rhetor's ethical understanding of audience and situation, and an artist's tools. We hope that emphasizing these foundational skills will allow our students to approach a variety of professional writing situations flexibly and creatively over the course of their careers.

NOTES

1. "Framework for Success in Postsecondary Writing." Council of Writing Program Administrators, the National Council of Teachers of English, and the National Writing Project, accessed August 2016, http://wpacouncil.org/framework.
2. Thomas P. Miller, *The Formation of College English: Rhetoric and Belles Lettres in the British Cultural Provinces* (Pittsburgh: University of Pittsburgh Press, 1997), 285.
3. Christian Weisser and Laurie Grobman, "Undergraduate Writing Majors and the Rhetoric of Professionalism," *Composition Studies* 40 (2012): 39.
4. Deborah Balzhiser and Susan H. McLeod, "The Undergraduate Writing Major: What Is It? What Should It Be?" *College Composition and Communication* 61 (2010): 418.
5. Candace Spigelman and Laurie Grobman, "Why We Chose Rhetoric: Necessity, Ethics, and the (Re)Making of a Professional Writing Program," *Journal of Business and Technical Communication* 20 (2006): 55.
6. Dominic Delli Carpini, "Re-Writing the Humanities: The Writing Major's Effect on Undergraduate Studies in English Departments," *Composition Studies* 35 (2007): 16.
7. Kristie S. Fleckenstein and Kathleen Blake Yancey, "A Matter of Design: Context and Available Resources in the Development of a New English Major at Florida State University," in *Writing Majors: Eighteen Program Profiles*, ed. Greg A. Gibberson, Jim Nugent, and Lori Ostergaard (Logan: Utah State UP, 2015), 175.
8. Greg A. Gibberson, Jim Nugent, and Lori Ostergaard, eds, *Writing Majors: Eighteen Program Profiles* (Logan: Utah State UP, 2015).
9. Spigelman and Grobman, "Why We Chose Rhetoric," 58.

10. Weisser and Grobman, "Undergraduate Writing Majors," 39–59.
11. Douglas Hesse, "The Place of Creative Writing in Composition Studies," *College Composition and Communication* 62 (2010), 31–52.
12. Mark Runco calls creativity "the ultimate economic resource." Mark Runco, "Creativity," *Annual Review of Psychology* 55 (2004): 658–677.
13. Alexandria Peary, "The Pedagogy of Creative Writing across the Curriculum," in *Creative Writing Pedagogies for the Twenty-First Century*, eds. Alexandria Peary and Tom C. Hunley (Carbondale: Southern Illinois University Press, 2015), 344.
14. Richard E. Vatz, "The Myth of the Rhetorical Situation," *Philosophy & Rhetoric* 6 (1973): 157.
15. Lisa Ede and Andrea Lunsford, "Audience Addressed/Audience Invoked: The Role of Audience in Composition Theory and Pedagogy," *College Composition and Communication* 35 (1984): 160.
16. Michael Dean Clark, "The Marketable Creative: Using Technology and Broader Notions of Skill in the Fiction Course," in *Creative Writing in the Digital Age*, eds. Michael Dean Clark, Trent Hergenrader, and Joseph Rein (London: Bloomsbury Publishing, 2015): 64.
17. Janelle Adsit, "Giving an Account of Oneself: Teaching Identity Construction and Authorship in Creative Nonfiction and Social Media," in *Creative Writing in the Digital Age*, eds. Michael Dean Clark, Trent Hergenrader, and Joseph Rein (London: Bloomsbury Publishing, 2015):106.
18. Ellen Bryant Voigt, *The Flexible Lyric* (Athens: University of Georgia Press, 1999), 124.
19. Barack Obama and Marilynne Robinson, "President Obama & Marilynne Robinson: A Conversation—II," *New York Review of Books*, November 19, 2015.
20. John Perron, Mary Rist, and Drew Loewe, "From Emphasis to Fourth-Largest Major: Learning from the Past, Present, and Future of the Writing Major at St. Edward's University," in *Writing Majors: Eighteen Program Profiles*, eds. Greg A. Gibberson, Jim Nugent, and Lori Ostergaard (Logan: Utah State UP, 2015): 208.
21. Delli Carpini, "Re-Writing the Humanities," 17.

CHAPTER 11

Theater and the Law: The Cross-Disciplinary Integration of Theory and Practice in the Theatrical Arts and the Art of Advocacy

Kevin S. Marshall, Sean Dillon, Michael O'Connor, and Placido Gomez

INTRODUCTION

This chapter reveals the "cross-informing" relevancies of the humanities and the art of legal advocacy. In particular, we discuss and demonstrate how both the theatrical arts and the art of advocacy provide robust, reciprocal insights for each other.

It has been stated that the humanities involve:

the study of how people process and document the human experience. Since humans have been able, we have used philosophy, literature, religion, art, music, history and language to understand and record our world. These modes of expression have become some of the subjects that traditionally fall

K. S. Marshall (✉) • S. Dillon • P. Gomez • M. O'Connor
University of La Verne, La Verne, CA, USA

© The Author(s) 2018
N. H. Hensel (ed.), *Exploring, Experiencing, and Envisioning Integration in US Arts Education*, The Arts in Higher Education, https://doi.org/10.1007/978-3-319-71051-8_11

under the humanities umbrella. Knowledge of these records of human experience gives us the opportunity to feel a sense of connection to those who have come before us, as well as to our contemporaries.[1]

Similarly, and relatedly, the law involves the study of how people/society process and document the human experience when confronted with and engaged in conflict. And without doubt, the processing of such confrontation and conflict is necessarily influenced by philosophy, literature, religion, music, history, and language relevant to the circumstances. It is in this regard that the law is distinctively human.

Karl Nickerson Llewellyn, legal scholar, professor, and commentator, observed that the law is:

> [a]bout the fact that our society is honeycombed with disputes. Disputes actual and potential; disputes to be settled and disputes to be prevented; both appealing to law, both making up the business of the law. ... The doing of something about disputes, this doing of it reasonably, is the business of the law. And the people who have the doing in charge, whether they be judges or sheriffs or clerks or jailers or lawyers, are officials of the law. *And what these officials do about disputes is, to my mind, the law itself.*[2]

It is within the context of these very disputes that the human experience manifests as drama, tragedy, victory, and defeat. Interestingly, Peter Brook, an award-winning English theater and film director, observed that "[d]rama is exposure; it is confrontation; it is contradiction and it leads to analysis, construction, recognition and eventually to an awakening of understanding."[3] And thus, as one generally reflects on the disciplines of law and theater, one is quick to see their cross-informing relevancies to each other.

The practice of law intimately involves and explores the complexities of the human experience as it manifests within unlimited social spaces, dimensions, and contexts. The law is concerned with how people process and document the human experience. It is charged with revealing truths from among ambiguous or even conflicting historical narratives filtered through personal, emotional, or cultural biases. It critically explores, assesses, and addresses human interaction, conflict, and tragedy in a highly conventional environment, on a jurisprudential stage with prescribed spatial relationships articulated by legal and evidentiary rules of process. It is the quintessential space in which the humanities become real, where theory and practice merge, and where the human condition comes to terms with itself.

Similarly, the theatrical arts intimately involve and explore the complexities of the human experience. They, too, critically explore, assess, and address human interaction, conflict, and tragedy within prescribed spatial dimensions articulated by the physical design of the stage, as well as by the procedural and literary rules and conventions of the theatrical arts. The theater has long been an instrument for communicating, expressing, and critically exploring complex social and ideal constructs such as love, remorse, empathy, guilt, innocence, and justice (to name a few). And from the perspective of the law, trial attorneys are typically charged with the duty to critically present such complex and humane constructs to various jurisdictional agents and participants charged with the responsibility of determining the truth as revealed by multiple actors and their narratives. Both disciplines have centuries of experiential lessons to share with the other. And it is this chapter's objective to celebrate and explore the inter-disciplinary relevancy of these two fields.

Here we (1) identify the fundamental cross-informing relevancy of law and theater, especially with regard to communicating facts and influencing perceptions with regard to human constructs, actions, and events; (2) describe the theatrical dimensions (and constraints) of the courtroom as a stage for exploring the human condition within the context of conflict and tragedy; (3) discuss and demonstrate the reciprocating value-added to both arts and their respective actors and litigators through cross-disciplinary study and application; (4) provide an illustrative, robust conclusion that the integration of the theater arts and the law provides a high-quality undergraduate and graduate educational experience that prepares both populations for adaptability in their careers and engaged citizenship; and (5) share a proposed integrated course framework that crosses the disciplines of both the theater arts and the law, as well as undergraduate and graduate populations and experiences.

THE COURTROOM AS STAGE

All trials—from the most mundane civil dispute between bad neighbors to the impeachment of a president on the floor of the US Senate are theatrical in nature. This recognition of the relationship between legal trials and the dramatic arts neither impugns the former nor taints the latter. Rather, this relationship robustly demonstrates the value each creates for the other in terms of advancing their pursuit of revealing and articulating the human experience to their respective audiences.

From the time of the Ancient Greeks through the present, the common bonds between these disciplines have been recognized and explored. For example, Aristotle recognized, pursued, and explored these common bonds, and ultimately (and profoundly) influenced both the art of legal advocacy and dramatic presentations on the stage and in the courtroom. Aristotle's *Rhetoric*, perhaps more than any other work, has shaped the manner in which lawyers think about persuasion.[4] *Ethos, Pathos,* and *Logos* provide the basic elements of any theory of persuasion and are familiar concepts to most practicing litigators.[5]

Equally important to trial lawyers, however, are concepts derived from Aristotle's *Poetics*, a seminal work on drama. "Plot" was described by Aristotle as "the structure of incidents," and is a familiar problem faced not only by playwrights but also by any lawyer preparing to tell a client's story at trial.[6] How can one tell a story effectively from a series of incidents described in witness statements, medical reports, and pieces of physical evidence? The manner in which those incidents are structured—the plot of the trial—may determine the outcome of the case. Providing unity of plot or structuring a coherent story from a series of often disjointed incidents is one of the main tasks allocated to the trial lawyer. "Character" and "thought," described by Aristotle as "the two natural causes from which actions spring," are attributes of those who must communicate that story, while "diction" is the actual telling of the story.[7] These elements of drama, written about tragedies in approximately 350 B.C. are familiar to anyone who has had a basic trial-advocacy class. However, the last element and the one rated least by Aristotle—"spectacle"—has a somewhat different meaning and an often greater importance in trials than it has in the theater.

Trials as spectacles have played an important role throughout history. Whether we look historically at the trials of Socrates, Joan of Arc, and Sir Thomas More or in more modern times to Nuremberg, the Chicago Seven, and the impeachment of President William Jefferson Clinton, the public spectacle was an essential component of those trials.[8] In such trials, there are numerous audiences for whom the trial is played. The jury (or judge) is always the most direct audience and the one for whom the drama is performed. But there are other audiences watching and judging the trial performances. In the grand spectacles previously mentioned, the audiences are myriad and the messages sought to be conveyed may be equally diverse.[9] But all trials have elements of spectacle, particularly those in a legal system like ours that guarantees the right to a public trial.

The right to a "speedy and public trial" is itself a statement that we as a society value the spectacle of a trial.[10] Trials, therefore, are a routine performance of our basic principles, demonstrated in public, freely available for all to see.[11] However, members of the public are far more likely to witness a trial on television or in the movies than they are to attend one of the public trials performing a real-life drama. Consequently, opinions concerning the justice system(s) in the United States are often derived from media dramas.[12] With the advent of televising court proceedings, however, the public has greater access to witness actual courtroom trials. This development over the past two decades has created new audiences for whom the drama is performed and has necessarily affected the manner in which trials are conducted.

Perhaps no trial was more clearly affected by the public spectacle of live television than the murder trial of O.J. Simpson.[13] The trial was broadcasted live for 133 days, and on the day that the verdict was read in open court, more than 90 percent of all the people watching television in the country were watching the trial.[14] The O.J. Simpson trial provided the country with a great spectacle and an important window into attitudes about race and justice in the United States.[15] The case also caused a widespread evaluation about the handling of forensic evidence.[16] However, the case demonstrated that lawyers, witnesses, and even judges can be affected by the fact that a (much) larger audience is watching them. Immediately following the trial, the California Supreme Court adopted new ethics rules governing what lawyers could say to the media outside the courtroom.[17]

The Simpson case is a cautionary tale about the potential consequences of a real-life courtroom drama combining with media hungry for any unseemly or salacious story. Without parameters governing the behavior of all parties, the spectacle of a trial can overwhelm many of the participants. The case also demonstrates the lasting effects of theatrical trials that capture the public's imagination. Most cases, however, involve a much more modest and sober use of dramatic elements in the attempt to persuade and achieve justice.

From a trial lawyer's perspective, it is folly to ignore the dramatic arts' relevance and potential for informing and providing insight with respect to comprehending the many legal spaces in which the human experience is probed, assessed, and judged. And given the very consequential nature of the jurisprudential stage with respect to life, liberty, and the pursuit of happiness, it seems most prudent for the legal advocate to invite and access the many insights of the dramatic arts. Moreover, it also seems most prudent for dramatic artists to welcome such an invitation since the courtroom provides a rich environment for the dramatic arts to bring theory to practice.

THEATRICAL PERSPECTIVES, INSIGHTS, AND CROSS-INFORMING RELEVANCIES

In order to begin an analysis of the ways in which the theory and practice of theater might inform the practice of law, it may be helpful to employ a critical framework often used in dramatic analysis in order to identify various aspects of drama that may be considered in the analysis of a theatrical text or production. In his *Poetics* (c. 335 B.C.E.), Aristotle identifies six essential parts of tragedy (i.e., plot, thought, character, music, spectacle, and diction), and a modern interpretation of these elements may offer an organized way in which to consider the various aspects of drama and how they may relate to legal proceedings.

The Relevance of Plot

The first element of the drama, plot, describes the structural elements of the dramatic narrative. Plot, it is important to keep in mind, is not the same thing as the story, but rather a carefully structured series of events that take place exclusively within the text or performance of the play. That is to say, plot involves selectivity and the imposition of a structure. Events outside the scope of the plot may make up a greater and more encompassing story of which the plot is a part. With respect to tragedy, Aristotle refers to plot as the "first and most important thing."[18]

An attorney, then, in presenting a case, has a responsibility to present a plot rather than a story, and to reveal a structure that is plausible and satisfying to the courtroom audience. Within the plot, some critical structural elements include (1) the inciting incident, (2) the resulting action, (3) the climax, and (4) the resolution. These structural elements represent a series of events in an understandable, causal relationship to one another, and satisfy the expectations of how a plot unfolds.

The Structural Elements of Plot

The inciting incident is the event or condition that may upset the delicate balance of the *status quo* and set events in motion. This may be related to the motives, intentions, and goals of the participants in the drama. In presenting any narrative that represents a theory of a case, the attorney may be required to offer an image of an undisturbed state that is driven into a state of action by an inciting incident.

The resulting action involves an aspect of complication; that is, the events and characters' actions become more entangled, and it is not until the plot reaches its conclusion that these complications are unraveled. In relating the action, both playwright and attorney must describe a causal sequence of events that lead logically, inevitably, and believably to the climax. "Of all plots and actions the episodic are the worst," says Aristotle, "in which the episodes or acts succeed one another without probable or necessary sequence."[19] The climax, of course, is the decisive moment in the drama, "the turning point to good or bad fortune."[20]

The Theme of the Plot/Case

Thought, sometimes called theme, in Aristotelian terms, is more about meaning than about events. An attorney presenting a case has the task of not only presenting a sequence of events or plot, but also giving context and meaning to those events and moving along the listener intellectually or emotionally. Thought encompasses "proof and refutation; the excitation of the feelings, such as pity, fear, anger, and the like; the suggestion of importance or its opposite."[21] Just as it is an indispensable element of drama, the courtroom's manifestation of thought, that is to say argument, is at the foundation of presenting a case.

Revealing the True Character of the Players

A character, in Aristotelian terms, is the agent of action and should be presented as true to life, true to type, and consistent. An attorney must build an image of a character just as a playwright would, and provide evidence that characteristic tendencies and consistencies are present and reliable. Even in representing unsympathetic people before the court, the attorney must present them in a favorable light without misrepresenting their nature. Aristotle's advice to the playwright is good legal advice as well: "while reproducing the distinctive form of the original, make a likeness which is true to life and yet more beautiful. So too the poet, in representing men who are irascible or indolent, or have other defects of character, should preserve the type and yet ennoble it."[22]

Diction, Rhetoric, Pace, and Sound

Aristotle refers to the importance of diction and music as the "medium of imitation," that is, the means by which the drama is conveyed. Diction is simply the "expression of the meaning in words,"[23] the rhetorical power and careful crafting of language is perhaps the highest expression of the skill of both the theater artist and the attorney in the courtroom, including the choices of words and the style of the spoken communication. In a modern context, and for analytical purposes, we may construe Aristotle's definition of "music" more broadly to include all of the aural components. There may be no common place for song in the context of the courtroom, but as a means of conveying content, sound is indispensable.

Spectacle

Finally, spectacle is the visual component of the drama, which Aristotle deemed the least important of the six elements, primarily because it was least connected to the work of the poet, and a superficial, though pleasing, expression of the technician rather than the poet.[24] We cannot dismiss spectacle as unimportant in the context of the courtroom, however, as the visual components may be subtly and artfully manipulated to be a powerful and persuasive part of the case being presented.

Director's Role

While there is great value in considering these elements of drama, the role of director is critical in harmonizing all of these elements in the creation and production of a theatrical presentation. It is the tools and techniques of the theatrical director that allow him or her to see the ways in which the elements are creatively and effectively employed in an effort to control the narrative. Aristotle knew nothing of the modern director's role, but an understanding of the methods of contemporary theater artists is of significant relevance and value to a trial advocate/litigator charged with orchestrating a cohesive and persuasive case.

Analysis

When a director engages with dramatic material, the first task at hand is analysis. Analysis is a step that requires strict objectivity in a careful consideration of the text to see what is indisputably present. The process of analysis is not a time to be swayed by one's own desires or expectations, nor is it a time to look for support for a particular theory or perception. In theater, the director has a duty to discover what is empirically true before devising any tactics or ideal perspectives. Likewise, an attorney has a duty to discover the objective truth to the extent possible and as supported by factual evidence.

Interpretation

Only when analysis is complete does the director move to the step of interpretation. Interpretation is the process of deciding what is meaningful about what is discovered in the analytical process. A director analyzes to digest what is in the text. Once digested, then he or she interprets for the purpose of assigning meaning. It is through interpretation that the subjective mind of the director is engaged to develop a perspective that is both supported by analysis and expresses a persuasive and compelling point of view. Likewise, the interpretive skills of the attorney are employed to determine the meaning of what has been discovered and to build a theory of the case. Through interpretation, the director becomes the advocate of a set of ideas, just as the attorney is an advocate for a client.

Conceptualization

The next step for the theatrical director is conceptualization. Developing a concept is envisioning the way in which important ideas are communicated. How does one present the theatrical interpretation to the audience in the most compelling way? A director must consider the audience, be true to the text, and present the distilled essence of the material, emphasizing and magnifying what is most important in communicating a particular point of view, while minimizing that which is unimportant, contradictory, or distracting. The concept includes the expression of style, the creative utilization of resources, and the distillation of a set of ideas that may be easily communicated to the production team.

Once a concept is created, the help of the entire creative team must be enlisted in order to give the concept its fullest expression. This concept represents the transformation of a play into a production and is what makes the work of the director powerful and unique. For the attorney, the formation of a concept derives from a careful analysis of the facts, an interpretive process about what information is most important to convey, and the strategy, that is, the conceptualization of exactly how the case is to be presented to convey the desired information in the most powerful way.

Realization

The next step, of course, is to actually realize that concept. This, for the director, involves leading the collaborative efforts of the entire team, the preparation, and ultimately the performance. The design and technology, as well as the performances, must be brought together to communicate the concept in the most unequivocal way possible. The concise and clear communication of the concept to all involved makes it possible to quickly resolve the thousands of decisions that need to be made in the process of the production. Cohesiveness is of paramount value. Each part of the production should agree with every other part in terms of the story it is telling, the point of view it is taking, and the style in which it is presented. For the attorney, too, consistency and cohesiveness are essential to a compelling case.

For the director, the most critical part of the realization process is rehearsal, where the director, the guardian of the creative vision for the production, must orchestrate the contribution of the collaborators toward a harmonious work of theater. It is at this stage that the realities of production collide with the ideal world of the director's vision, and conflicts must be reconciled, compromises made, and unexpected developments resolved. The attorney does not have the advantage of having a script to work from, nor does the attorney expect to have authority over the other participants. In fact, the attorney does not even have the expectation of being the only one presenting a carefully composed scenario, but rather must compete to have his or her ideas prevail over others. Imagine a director forced to share the stage with a competing director's contrary vision!

Staging

Perhaps the most time-consuming task in the rehearsal process for the director is staging. At that point, the director leads the actors into meaningful arrangements and movements. Composition is important here, as the director works in three dimensions to create a sculptural arrangement on the stage that conveys meaning beyond what is found in the text. Composition leads the eyes of the audience, creates a set of relationships of people and objects in space, conveys meaning, and tells a story.

Theater is not merely a three-dimensional medium, however. The dimension of time must also be considered in the director's craft, and movement is a critical expressive tool. This may entail the movement of actors, scenery, lighting, or any other visual element. The nature of this movement tells a story, reveals aspects of character, and creates a kinetic image for the audience that may be informative or persuasive. The director must also manage the time in which the theatrical production unfolds the rhythms and tempos of the performance, and the duration of the performance, which must not exceed the audience's capacity to appreciate it.

The litigator may not exert nearly as much control over the composition and movement in the courtroom as the director does in the theater. However, the litigator, as director, must nonetheless concern himself or herself with these four dimensions. In the highly conventionalized environment of the courtroom, the constraints of position and movement in the physical space are considerable. The attorney cannot freely create a visual image to support a position or a creative vision.

However, composition and movement in the courtroom, while restricted, can still be a powerful tool in shaping the impression of the courtroom's "audience" and conveying important and subtle sub-textual meaning. It is in the smaller expressions of movement that the attorney may exert the most control. The rhythms and tempos established by speech and movement may be deliberately crafted to form an impression on an audience, and the posture, gestures, inflections, and facial expressions of the courtroom's "characters," while small in comparison to large movements on the stage, may nevertheless be persuasive. They may even be a primary channel of communication, through which the observer derives more meaning from the non-verbal behavior than they may from the text.

Staging and Zoning

Another important element of staging for the director is the association of areas of the stage with particular ideas or characters, sometimes referred to as zoning. Zoning is a form of territorial connection, in which the audience may be influenced, for example, to make a familial association among characters who occupy a particular space or to have assumptions about good or bad character related to certain spaces. Certainly in the courtroom, such associations are already made as a matter of convention. The judge is associated with the bench, the jury with the jury box, the prosecution team with the prosecutor's table, and so on. While attorneys may have little influence over the zoning that is well established in the courtroom, they may still communicate meaningful associations with the careful and deliberate use of the space that they do have under their control.

Improvisational Realities in the Courtroom

For the theatrical director, the beginning of public performances may be the conclusion of her or his work. Once a production opens, the director's responsibilities are assumed by the stage manager, whose job is to maintain the standards of the performance and "keep the show in hand," or see to it that performances and technical cues remain as they were agreed upon at the conclusion of rehearsals. For an attorney, the work is just beginning. In many ways, the "performances" in the courtroom are more akin to improvisational acting than they are to a well-rehearsed traditional stage production. In either case, a performer must read the reactions of the audience and respond accordingly. While adhering closely to the text and rehearsed actions, an actor must still make fine re-calibrations during the performance in order to accommodate the particular audience, to adjust timing for audience laughter, to slow or accelerate as required. An improvisational actor must be able to react to the unexpected, to justify circumstances when some moment has gone awry, and to never, never break character.

"Cross-Informing" Insights

It is apropos in this chapter to reflect on the famous words of Jaques to Duke Senior in Shakespeare's play *As You Like it*:

All the world's a stage,
And all the men and women merely players;
They have their exits and their entrances;
And one man in his time plays many parts,
His acts being seven ages. At first, the infant,
Mewling and puking in the nurse's arms.

Then the whining school boy, with his satchel
And shining morning face, creeping like snail
Unwillingly to school. And then the lover,
Sighing like furnace, with a woeful ballad

Even in the cannon's mouth. And then the justice,
In fair round belly with good capon lin'd
With severe eyes and beard of formal cut,
Full of wise saws and modern instances;
And so he plays his part. The sixth age shifts
Into the lean and slippered pantaloons,
With spectacles on nose and pouch on side;
His youthful hose, well saved, a world too wide
For his shrunk shank, and his big manly voice.[25]

And this is particularly true in the courtroom, where all the participants (judge, jury, the lawyers, plaintiff(s), defendant(s), witnesses, the press, court reporter, bailiff, and even the spectators) are players in a real-life drama, with serious consequences implicating one's right to pursue life, liberty, and happiness. They all have their exits and their entrances.

And each provides audience to the other. And many play many parts, from antagonist to protagonist, from actor to director, from stage manager to media technician, and from custom designer to screen play writer. And the courtroom cast of participants often includes the dynamic integration of many individuals of many different ages, backgrounds, and degrees of comprehension and understanding. The premise of this chapter is essentially grounded on the acknowledgment of this Shakespearean observation of yesteryear. It was true then, and it is true now, especially within the context of public and judicial process. By integrating these two fields of study, their reciprocal and cross-informing value is revealed to both law student and theater student.

The law student is invited on a value-added journey of exploration into the power of intentionalized verbal and non-verbal communications and artistry. This is of critical importance to the law student in that he or she will be better prepared to assess in real-time the drama that is revealing itself in any court proceeding. Such real-time assessment is of significant value in terms of making adjustments to a trial lawyer's presentation of his or her client's case as the lawyer seeks to reveal the reality of the drama under analysis. A better understanding of the dramatic arts ultimately empowers the law student with supplemental tools and competencies relevant to his or her meaningful and zealous pursuit of the client's reality, which is under public analysis and ultimately subject to public judgment and sanction.

Similarly, the theater student is invited on a value-added journey of exploration focusing on the power of the discipline as it relates to the high-stakes drama of the courtroom stage. This is of critical importance to the theater student in that he or she will undoubtedly experience the relevance and importance of articulating and presenting narratives that have real-life consequences. It is of also great importance because it provides a real-life context in which to study the human experience under stress within one of its most dramatic of realms—the realm of life, liberty, and conflict. And it is within this context that the theater student is likely to experience the revelation that his or her work has serious and important sociological implications in revealing and assessing the human experience.

Theater and the Courtroom: A Course Framework

At the University of La Verne, the authors have collaborated to design a two-credit course drawing on the ways in which theater and the law can inform each other. The objective of the course is to guide law students focusing on advocacy and undergraduates studying theater arts through a participatory, collaborative journey exploring two related forms of communication—courtroom advocacy and theater. Both theater and courtroom advocacy are complex forms of communication, rich with history as described above. As the outline below for the course demonstrates, the similarities of the two forms are driven by similar purposes.

After a brief consideration of the "cross-informing" and reciprocal relationships between drama and courtroom advocacy, the course encourages a more profound analysis of the links. It provides a foundational exposure for students to Shakespeare and Greek tragedy, and then quickly moves to the identification, exploration, and application of major themes, practices, and skills relevant to both the law student and the theater student (e.g., the predominance of text in courtroom advocacy and how drama influences the law's pursuit of justice.) The design of the course also provides several opportunities for both types of students to experience the challenges and rewards of applying their disciplinary knowledge within the other's practice space and areas.

The course is not only designed for cross-disciplinary exploration in terms of content but also designed for a cross-population of students interested in both theater and law. By encouraging a collaborative journey across the disciplines of law and the theater arts, as well as across undergraduate and graduate populations, this course creates value-added learning opportunities regarding the power of the interdisciplinary exploration of the humanities and the professions. The course unfolds using both the university theater's stage and its law school's moot courtroom, as a constant reminder of the importance of contextual opportunities and constraints in using narrative while in search of human experience and truth.

A Proposed Course Outline[26]

Class 1. Introduction
The introductory class exposes students to the relationship between the courtroom and dramatic theater. Professor Ball's article discusses "judicial proceedings as theater requiring live performance" and presents similarities and distinctions between the two considering space, audience, and format.

Assignment(s): Milner S. Ball, *The Play's the Thing: An Unscientific Reflection on Courts Under the Rubric of Theater*, 28 STANFORD LAW REVIEW 81 (1975).

Class 2. The Foundation: Tragedy
The second and third classes introduce students to classic theater that presents Greek and Shakespearian drama linked to legal advocacy.

Assignment(s): Aeschylus, *The Oresteia*.

Class 3. The Foundation: Comedy
Students will read and discuss *Measure for Measure*, Shakespeare's comedy containing multiple themes including justice, mercy, and mortality.

Assignment(s): William Shakespeare, *Measure for Measure*; Subha Mukherji, "Locations of Law: Spaces, People, Play," *in Law and Representation in Early Modern England* (Cambridge 2006).

Class 4. The Importance of a Theme
Students will discuss the role of a theme in performance and advocacy.

Assignment(s): Reverend Martin Luther King, Jr., "I Have a Dream" speech.

Class 5. The Courtroom as Performance
The fifth class features the first of four film screenings and discussions. Students will view and discuss Otto Preminger's classic piece about a lawyer faced with convincing a jury of his client's innocence when the evidence seems to indicate guilt.

Film screening and discussion: *Anatomy of a Murder*, Otto Preminger director (1959).

Class 6. Text versus Performance

The sixth class discusses the law's traditional elevation of text over performance and asks students to "challenge the monopoly" of legal text in American jurisprudence. The class includes exercises, common in the drama curriculum, designed to highlight performance.

Assignment(s): Bernard J. Hibbitts, "De-scribing Law: Performance in the Constitution of Legality," http:/law.pitt.edu/archive/hibbitts/ describe.htm and his "Making Motions: The Embodiment of Law in Gesture," *Journal of Contemporary Legal Issues*, 51:6 (1991).

Classes 7 and 8. The Spaces

Classes 7 and 8 focus students on the courtroom and the stage as distinctive spaces, designed with a mission and specific purposes. Students will visit several courtrooms and stages.

Assignment(s): Norman W. Spaulding, "The Enclosure of Justice: Courthouse Architecture, Due Process, and the Dead Metaphor of Trial," *Yale Journal of Law and Humanities* (2012), Volume 24, No. 1, Laurie L. Levenson, "Courtroom Demeanor: The Theater of the Courtroom," *Minnesota Law Review*, 92 (1997–1998).

Class 9. Organizing the Presentation

Focusing on organizing the presentation of a story, students will consider Boucicault's controversial play depicting life in the South before the Civil War.

Assignment(s): Dion Boucicault, *The Octoroon* (1859); William Archer, *Play-Making: A Manual of Craftsmanship*, (Dover Publications 1912).

Class 10. The Courtroom as Performance

Film screening and discussion: *Judgment at Nuremberg*, Stanley Kramer director (1961).

Classes 11 and 12. In Pursuit of Justice

Classes 11 and 12 present the role of drama in the legal system's quest for justice. Students read Richard Harbinger's work presenting the adversary trial as a play within a play and arguing that effective trial lawyers combine several individual vignettes into a "single dramatic texture." Anne Bogart's work introduces students to seven major areas, violence being one, that serve as a potential partner and a potential obstacle to producing art. Low-Beer focuses on the role of judgment in both drama and adversarial trials.

Assignment(s): Richard Harbinger, "Trial by Drama," 55 *Judicature* 122 (1971–1972); Anne Bogart, "Violence," from *A Director Prepares* (Routledge 2001); F.H. Low-Beer, "Judgment as Social Function," from *Questions of Judgment: Determining What's Right* (Prometheus Books 1995). David Bodenhamer, *Fair Trial: Rights of the Accused in American History*, Oxford University Press, 1992.

Class 13. The Courtroom as a Stage
Students will view and discuss *The Crucible*, Arthur Miller's classic play about the hysteria surrounding the witch-hunts and trials in seventeenth-century Salem, Massachusetts. His presentation of the destructive power of socially sanctioned violence is timeless.

Film screening and discussion: *The Crucible*, Arthur Miller, Nicholas Hytner director (1996).

Class 14. The Audience: The Judge
Class 14 challenges students to focus on the decision maker, considering the work of Bertolt Brecht examining what happens when law conflicts with justice and questioning right and wrong in complex situations.

Assignment(s): Bertolt Brecht, *The Caucasian Chalk Circle*; Bertolt Brecht, *He Who Says Yes/He Who Says No,* in *The Measures Taken and Other Lehrstucke* (Arcade 2001).

Class 15. The Audience: The Jury
The final class considers the jury, as students view and discuss the classic movie *Twelve Angry Men* and consider Rand's drama *Night of January 16th*. Rand's drama was inspired by the death of a wealthy businessman. The setting for the play is a courtroom during the murder trial. A unique aspect of the play is that members of the audience serve as jurors; thus, the conclusion of the play depends on the audience.

Assignment(s): Ayn Rand, *Night of January* 16th (Penguin 1961).

Film screening: *Twelve Angry Men*, screenplay by Reginald Rose, Sidney Lumet director (1957).

SUMMARY

This chapter demonstrates that theater and advocacy pursue parallel visions. Both process and document the human experience using similar tools. Litigation is theater; the courtroom a stage. Both embrace plot, players, rhetoric, pace, and sound. Both have a director who influences analysis, interpretation, conceptualization, and realization. Both are stage dramas. Law students and theater students are participants on similar journeys. This chapter has laid a foundation for the convergence of these two treks.

NOTES

1. "What Are the Humanities?" Stanford Humanities Center, accessed July 28, 2016, http://shc.stanford.edu/what-are-the-humanities.
2. Karl Nickerson Llewellyn, *The Bramble Bush: Some Lectures on Law and Its Study* (New York, 1930), reprinted in *Karl Nickerson Llewellyn on Legal Realism* (Birmingham: Legal Classics Library, 1986), 2.
3. "Peter Brook Quotes," *AZ Quotes*, accessed July 28, 2016, http://www.azquotes.com/quote/781082. Peter Brook is "an English theatre and film director who has been based in France since the early 1970s. He has won multiple Tony and Emmy Awards, a Laurence Olivier Award, the Praemium Imperiale, and the Prix Italia," *Wikipedia*, s.v. "Peter Brook," last modified June 18, 2016, https://en.wikipedia.org/wiki/Peter_Brook.
4. Michael Frost, "Ethos, Pathos and Legal Audience," *Dickinson Law Review* 99 (Fall 1994): 86–87.
5. Ibid., at 86. Aristotle, among other ancients such as Cicero, recognized that the presentation of a legal case would often be made toward an "audience" that was neither legally trained nor particularly inclined toward justice. Krista C. McCormack, "Ethos, Pathos and Logos: The Benefits of Aristotelian Rhetoric," *Washington University Jurisprudence Review* 7, no. 1 (2014): 132–133.
6. Aristotle, *Poetics*, part 6, ed. S. H. Butcher, *The Internet Classics Archive*, accessed July 15, 2016, http://classics.mit.edu/Aristotle/poetics.1.1.html.
7. Aristotle, *Poetics*, part 6. Clarence Darrow, one of America's most famous trial lawyers, placed a high premium on the lawyer's ability to make the jury accept or like the defendant's character. Darrow is reported to have said, "Jurymen seldom convict a person they like, or acquit one that they dislike. The main work of a trial lawyer is to make a jury like his client, or, at least to feel sympathy for him; facts regarding the crime are relatively unimportant." Laurie L. Levenson, "Courtroom Demeanor: The Theater of the Courtroom," *Minnesota Law Review* 92 (2008): 575.

8. For a good discussion of the role of spectacle in political trials, see Ronald P. Sokol, "The Political Trial: Courtroom as Stage, History as Critic," *New Literary History* 2, no. 3 (1971): 495–516.

9. While governments seek to convey messages in highly publicized "show trials," the defense lawyers can use the spotlight directed on such trials for their own ends. Abbie Hoffman, one of the Chicago Seven, tried for conspiracy following the 1968 Democratic National Convention, famously described the defendants' disruption of proceedings as "an example of guerrilla theater." Pnina Lahav, "Theater in the Courtroom the Chicago Conspiracy Trial," *Law and Literature* 16, no. 3 (2004): 381, 386.

10. "In all criminal prosecutions, the accused shall enjoy the right to a speedy and public trial, by an impartial jury." US Constitution, Amendment VI.

11. Some of what is demonstrated, however, is not particularly flattering about our society. "Research suggests that people viewed as facially unattractive are more likely to be perceived as criminal than are facially attractive persons," David L. Wiley, "Beauty and the Beast: Physical Appearance Discrimination in American Criminal Trials," *St. Mary's Law Journal* 27 (1995): 211–212.

12. Christine Alice Corcos, "Legal Fictions: Irony, Storytelling, Truth, and Justice in the Modern Courtroom Drama," *University of Arkansas at Little Rock Law Review* 25 (2003): 507–508.

13. The 1995 prosecution of O.J. Simpson for the deaths of his wife and her friend, the live-streamed trial has become an Emmy Award-nominated television series. See Emily Yahr, "Complete List of Emmy Nominations 2016: 'Game of Thrones' and 'People v. O. J. Simpson' Lead the Pack," *Washington Post*, July 14, 2016, accessed August 9, 2016, https://www.washingtonpost.com/news/arts-and-entertainment/wp/2016/07/14/emmy-nominations-2016-complete-coverage/.

14. See, for example, the website Famous American Trials: The O. J. Simpson Trial, 1995 (University of Missouri–Kansas City), accessed August 9, 2016, http://law2.umkc.edu/faculty/projects/ftrials/Simpson/simpson.htm.

15. For a discussion about the impact of the O.J. Simpson trial ten years after the verdict, see "The O. J. Verdict: The Trial's Significance and Lasting Impact," *Frontline*, October 4, 2005, accessed August 9, 2016, http://www.pbs.org/wgbh/pages/frontline/oj/view/.

16. Ibid.

17. See Stephen Labaton, "Lessons of Simpson Case Are Reshaping the Law," *New York Times*, October 6, 1995, http://www.nytimes.com/1995/10/06/us/lessons-of-simpson-case-are-reshaping-the-law.html.

18. Aristotle, *Poetics*, chap. 7.

19. Aristotle, *Poetics*, chap. 9.

20. Aristotle, *Poetics*, chap. 18.
21. Aristotle, *Poetics*, chap. 19.
22. Aristotle, *Poetics*, chap. 15.
23. Aristotle, *Poetics*, chap. 6.
24. Aristotle, *Poetics*, chap. 6.
25. William Shakespeare, *As You Like It*, act 2, sc. 7, lines 139–166, accessed July 28, 2016, https://www.poets.org/poetsorg/poem/you-it-act-ii-scene-vii-all-worlds-stage.
26. This course outline draws from many experiences and analogous courses. Courses on law and the theater that provided specific and unique inspiration include those presented by the National Association of Criminal Defense Lawyers; by professors Mark Stevens and Stephanie Stevens at St. Mary's University School of Law; and by Professor Braislav Jakovljevic at Stanford University.

CHAPTER 12

Music in the Academy: Process, Product, and the Cultivation of Humanity

Linda C. Ferguson

THE EPISTEMOLOGY OF ATTENTION

In her book *The Body of God*, theologian Sallie McFague proposes an organic model for conceiving of God and, in doing so, reconciles the spiritual and material worlds. She employs "attention epistemology," which also describes the way many musicians approach their work and the way many artists live their lives. Attention epistemology is, according to McFague, "listening, paying attention to another, the other, in itself, for itself." It is "the kind of knowledge that comes from paying close attention to something other than oneself."[1] It is thus the opposite of measuring everything one encounters in terms of usefulness to oneself. It makes a distinction between asking "What does this mean to me?" and asking "What does this *mean*?"

An attention epistemology, according to McFague, "assumes the *intrinsic* value of anything, everything, that is not the self. ... An attention epistemology is central to embodied knowing and doing, for it takes with utmost seriousness the differences that separate all beings."[2] McFague finds this idea at work in Genesis, when God surveyed material creation and saw "that it was good." She finds it in Aristotle and Aquinas, in sermons of Jonathan Edwards, and in the writing of feminists whose

L. C. Ferguson (✉)
Valparaiso University, Valparaiso, IN, USA

© The Author(s) 2018
N. H. Hensel (ed.), *Exploring, Experiencing, and Envisioning Integration in US Arts Education*, The Arts in Higher Education,
https://doi.org/10.1007/978-3-319-71051-8_12

175

"knowing focuses on *embodied differences*."[3] This chapter proposes that it is also found in the work of artists, and specifically in the work of musical artists, both composers and performers.

It is in the attention to what is *out there* that the musician's work begins. What sounds are disturbing the air? Which have potential for expressing my idea? It is by attending to what is *out there*, as the work emerges, that the musician's craft is practiced, asking what the work in progress sounds like, whether it shapes the idea or feeling that needs forming. And again, it is in attention to what is *out there*, the idea now embodied in the sound of the music, that the listener gains access to the idea.

This chapter also considers the distinctive place for music in the academy, particularly in the comprehensive university, and by extension, in the life of an informed and humane community. Understanding musical works and music making requires recognition that process and product are distinct, and that performance and composition each involve both process and product. A musical work can be understood simultaneously as a theoretical, abstract creation (as evidenced in a musical score), and as a particularized, concrete creation (as perceived in a given performance of a composition). Thus, musical study can serve as a point of intersection between liberal and professional study, and as a potential model for integrating them. Representative historical and recent events can offer academic musicians and teachers of musicians a broad range of possibilities for considering the role of music in the life of citizens.

PROCESS AND PRODUCT IN MUSIC

Embodiment, to continue using McFague's language, of ideas, feelings, and experiences is the essential action of the artist. The art-maker objectifies the subjective experience—putting it outside of the self in a material form—an *other*—so that it can be perceived by others (and recognized as "an other" by the artist as well). The process of formalizing in matter what previously "was without form" is practiced variously by musicians as composing, performing, improvising, conducting, realizing, and—in the case of preparing recordings—producing. In any of these musical processes, the outcome (the product) is not merely symptomatic expression of self but rather a deliberate presentation of an inner knowledge made outer—made other—in order that the idea can be perceived and known by others. The product—whether composition, performance, improvisation, or production—is distinct from process and distinct also from the self whose experience it expresses. (With some exceptions admitted, it is useful to follow Susanne K. Langer's assertion that expressive forms in art are *symbols*, not *symptoms*—evidence of what we know of feelings, and not unmediated feelings themselves.)[4]

To establish the essential terms of music making, consider the communicative transaction in which a musician engages in the process of creating a musical work and a listener engages in a process of perceiving it. If the musician is a *composer* and the musical work is a notated one as in the Western fine art tradition, a material product known as a "score" employs printed notation or other directions for performing the work. That document provides evidence that the work exists and what its terms are, but it is not the expressive sonorous form itself. If the creator-musician is a *performer*, then the process of creating results in a product that is not the composition, but rather a particularized sonorous realization of it: a performance. Performance constitutes its own artistic category, distinct from composition.

Although performing is an activity and a process, it is a process that creates a product separate from process and thus is separate from the performer: Something is embodied other than the performer, and that something is the performance. It is true that occasionally performers are more full of themselves than of the music. It is also true that stage histrionics, deliberate or accidental, can emphasize the performer's self at the expense of the embodied idea. For example, Franz Liszt, who invented the performance genre of the solo piano recital in the mid-nineteenth century, is reported to have feigned passing out midway through a piece so that he could be miraculously revived to complete it, thus boosting his already high audience ratings. Even without extreme attempts on the part of the performer, an audience may through respect, admiration, or awe confuse the self of the excellent performer with the artwork, thus equating "the dancer with the dance."

In performances that successfully offer an "other" worthy of attention, the performer temporarily embodies something beyond the self—an idea, a form, an experience known and expressed by the self but not limited by it. If the act and outcome of performance are only processes, only activities, then the focus of attention is indeed on the self of the performer. But if performance creates a product, a dynamic object, as Langer has called it, an object that is not self-serving (or at least not *merely* self-serving), then performance becomes not just an activity but a creation of something beyond the self, embodied and evidenced in the self but not equated with it. In this created, embodied "other" named "performance," we have the object to which the listener attends.

Of course, the environment in which the listening takes place matters greatly in determining how much or little is actually communicated. Many complicating factors, scenarios, and exceptions can be developed to accommodate improvisation, electronically produced compositions, and oral musical traditions. These complications lie beyond the scope of this chapter, although they are not excluded from the essential claim. It is safe to generalize that the correspondence between idea, embodiment, and perception is dependent on an interplay of contrasting forces. For the artist, it is the interplay between the assertion of control over the matter of the work, and an allowance for spontaneity. For the listener, this is paralleled in the interplay between predictability and surprise as the musical work unfolds in time, leading the listener to ask, "Does the next sound go where I think it will go or does it go elsewhere?" and "What is my reaction to the affirmation or surprise I heard?"

This interplay between control and spontaneity in the creative process, and between predictability and surprise in the perceptual process resides in the work itself, whether considering the work to be a composition or a performance. The nature of this interplay results in qualities sometimes known as "classic" and "romantic." These traditionally opposed aesthetic ideals are generally familiar: The classic tendency favors control, calculation, order, and balance, while the romantic tendency favors freedom, spontaneity, and imbalance. The classic celebrates logic and an impulse to universalize, while the romantic celebrates drama and an impulse to individualize.

Dialogue between classic and romantic tendencies has generated the works Western culture recognizes and understands as meaningful. Traditionally the pairings noted in each element of the transaction (control/spontaneity; predictability/surprise; classic/romantic) have worked interactively with each other in various and fluid relationships. In the modernism of the early to mid-twentieth century, however, the pairs were pushed to extremes, making the contradictory parts mutually exclusive rather than dialogic. In twentieth-century modernism, works of such diverse composers as Arnold Schoenberg (representing highly controlled structures) and John Cage (representing extreme spontaneity) resulted in similar outcomes: alienation between composer and listener at the point of the work. In some cases, the work was subsumed by process—either in practice, as in the chance works of Cage, or in theory, as in some 12-tone serialism. And sometimes the traditional outcomes were reversed: music resulting from highly controlled systems (such as the stochastic works of Iannis Xenakis, based on mathematical probabilities) resulted in an extremely unpredictable, bewildering experience for most listeners. At the same time, works generated from uncontrolled spontaneity (such as Cage's *4'33"*), in which the creator relinquished control over the product to invite attention to randomness, frequently were experienced by listeners as predictable and boring. These cases are extreme, but were instructive in demonstrating ideas without necessarily embodying them. Cage's ultimate message, after all, was that we need to pay better attention. But the classical-music canon consists primarily of works and performance practices that have approached process as a dialogue between contrasting tendencies. Intersections and interactions between opposing tendencies have generated more enduring works than have extreme applications.

At the Intersection of Liberal and Professional Learning

R. Eugene Rice, a distinguished leader in American higher education, has plotted various kinds of scholarly work on two intersecting axes—an X-axis with active practice and reflective observation at its poles, and a Y-axis with contrasting approaches to knowing, ranging from the concrete to the abstract. Dynamic and productive scholarship resides in many locations along the axes, in the balances and interactions between action and reflection, between the abstract and the concrete. Advances in knowledge take place in the quadrants rather than at the poles.[5] This roughly parallels the earlier observation about the most enduring and valued musical works being those in which an interplay of tendencies exists in dialogue.

If music, as an expressive enterprise and as a field of study, is to be taken seriously in the academic setting, it cannot reside only on the periphery of recreational options, however worthy an activity it may be. There is no lack of a skill base that can be taught and learned; there is no lack of repertoire and historical, critical, and theoretical underpinnings for approaching the repertoires and practices of the past and present. What sometimes *is* lacking is recognition of the distinctive ways in which the study of music embodies the tensions inherent in attempts to integrate liberal and professional learning.

Comprehensive institutions specifically aspire to mediate and resolve the inherent tensions between these two educational models. Professional programs prepare students to make a living; liberal education prepares students to have a life. We reject the idea that these should be mutually exclusive categories. But what does "liberal education" mean for music programs attempting to serve both liberal and professional aims? A time-honored definition might be cited from Book 8 of the *Politics* of Aristotle, offering a distinction between liberal and illiberal pursuits, dependent on its purpose or end.[6] For Aristotle, the musical enterprise is illiberal when it produces wages for the professional or when it offers mere relaxation and amusement for the amateur. It is *liberal*, he says, when it contributes "to the enjoyment of leisure and mental cultivation." It is *liberal* when its end is neither profit nor mere pleasure, but when its end is "the good." That is, it is liberal when it invites recognition, in McFague's terms, of the intrinsic value of "other than the self."

Much removed by time and cultural circumstance, Aristotle is helpful in reminding us to distinguish between means and ends. What distinguishes a liberal arts approach to music? For the liberal arts professor, technical and performance studies are undertaken as a *means* to the understanding of music. The means is practical music making (taking piano lessons, for example, or singing in a choir) and the end is *understanding*. For the professional music teacher, on the other hand, skill in performance is usually the objective. In professional study, the *means* to this end involve a deliberate set of actions that may include analysis, contextual insight, productive practice, and interpretive exploration. In professional programs, "understanding music" is the means to an end, such as mastery of a repertoire for public performance.

Understanding music, most musicians agree, requires some measure of participation in its making and some mastery of its techniques. Liberal arts music curricula typically include these technical and practical studies as the necessary *means* to the desired *end* of understanding music. Professional music curricula owe it to their students to require some accomplishment in those competencies that prepare for life in the world: ability to understand, to articulate, to make connections, to interact, and to advocate.

With each decision and creative solution, musicians and teachers of musicians must be clear about means and ends. Students' success in relating their music studies to their other studies, to their personal experiences, to their campus lives, and to their professional expectations are assisted (or impeded) by their teachers' attempts to help them negotiate (or resist) what may seem to be conflicting purposes. Music as an academic discipline is unusually well positioned among the fields to model this kind of resolution: the poles of the abstract and the concrete are understood and integrated by every musician who has given serious thought to the relationship between the notated score of a composition and a single realization of that score in performance. The poles of the active and the reflective are similarly integrated in the work of every music student who simultaneously trains to perform and to listen. Music departments, whether offering liberal or professional programs or both, can model this integration in course and curriculum design and in daily teaching.

Music as taught and practiced by professionals in contemporary America is assumed to be more than a commodity of diversion. How do the curricula that prepare professionals ensure a significant role for music in society? What if the basis for understanding is short-circuited by an overly applied technical curriculum? What if the emphasis on active practice prevents critical reflective observation? What if the concrete certainties of technical accomplishment in performance prevent the performer from understanding the composition performed as something more transcendent than any one performance of it?

BRIDGING THE GAP

In the mid-twentieth century, as the gap between classical musicians and the general public widened, Leonard Bernstein led the New York Philharmonic in an outreach project that continues to inspire and inform. Shortly after he assumed the directorship of the Philharmonic, Bernstein's series of *Young People's Concerts* were broadcast live on CBS television in primetime. Between 1958 and 1972, 53 thematic lecture-demonstration-concerts made classical music widely available, also providing energetic interdisciplinary commentary and inviting audiences young and old to consider some of the very questions that get at the essence of musical works and their meanings. While Bernstein's "performances" as both teacher and conductor might be faulted for hyperbole, drama, and occasional over-simplification of complex ideas, as a consummate professional musician, he bridged the gap between word and tone. He employed the best methods of liberal education while utilizing the broadest possible means at the time of mass distribution.

Bernstein's six Norton Lectures at Harvard in 1973–1974, under the collective title *The Unanswered Question*, discussed a wide range of musical works and procedures from the perspective of linguistic theory, arguing that the best way to know a thing is in the context of a different discipline. Like the CBS broadcasts, these lectures have continued educating through mass distribution in print and recorded media. While outcomes beyond anecdotal are unlikely to be measurable, the Bernstein concerts and lectures set a new standard for how musicians and teachers of musicians might connect with a larger community.

Professional academically trained composers of the next generation have more recently sought to connect expertise and artistry with larger communities, if not on primetime network television. Composer Libby Larsen, for example, believes that "to compose is to learn all of the various instruments of a culture, and what they represent emotionally, culturally, and psychologically."[7] She means musical instruments of course, but she also means "instruments" in a more generic sense: the various mechanisms of sound making and of expression employed "out there," each expression potentially valuable and worthy of attention.

Composer John Corigliano's prefatory remarks at a Chicago Symphony Orchestra performance of his Symphony No. 1 in 1990 expressed an urgent need for composers to *make a difference*. And he was speaking about making a difference by means of a musical composition rather than peripherally through contributed services, sponsoring benefit concerts, or publicly espousing political or social positions. Corigliano had previously resisted what he saw as the self- indulgence of the traditional symphonic form until he found it served an idea from his life and the life of his time. This symphony (sometimes called the AIDS Symphony) was premiered in 1990 and was performed by more than a hundred major orchestras over the next decade—a remarkable success for a contemporary orchestral composer. His 1991 sequel, *Of Rage and Remembrance,* was, in the composer's program note, a "reimagining of [the symphony's first] movement as a ritual for community chorus. ... Its audience is not really the audience for choral music; its audience is the community blighted by AIDS."[8] Together the symphony and the choral work articulated and dignified a private grief through public address.

A decade later, composer John Adams commemorated the victims of September 11 in *On the Transmigration of Souls,* an extended work for chorus and orchestra commissioned by the New York Philharmonic, which the composer described as a communal "memory space" rather than a requiem or memorial. His title intends not only "the transition from living to dead, but also the change that takes place within the souls of those that stay behind, of those who suffer pain and loss and then themselves come away from that experience transformed."[9] The work's key elements include a reading of names, a prepared recording of ambient sounds of the city, and the singing of fragments selected from messages posted by families of those missing at Ground Zero. In an interview at the time of the work's premiere, on the first anniversary of the attacks, Adams noted that "what I discovered about the language of these messages was that it was invariably of the most simple and direct kind ... in the plainest words imaginable."[10] These contemporary American composers, and others similarly attuned, strive to embody integration, to work in the quadrants and not at the poles.

"GIVING OUT AN EXPERIENCE"

Musicians and teachers of musicians working in academic communities today can draw on historical evidence of music's role in societal experience. Mid-nineteenth-century America is particularly rich in resources for understanding the social role of music in times of strife. The flourishing culture of parlor music, sheet music, and the proliferation of the manufacture and distribution of instruments for amateur use in America coincided with the Civil War. The needs of military and political operations, joined with the demands of citizens seeking inspiration, solace, hope, and occasional respite on the battlefront and on the home front were met by an abundance of new and retro-fitted songs. Irwin Silber has linked this set of conditions to the hastening of an American musical culture reflecting its diverse roots. Further, he finds in the fact of its performability, that popular printed sheet music of the Civil War era offers a direct experiential connection with the past, distinct from other cultural artifacts and historical documentation.[11] He urges that this body of songs be understood not merely as "amusing or sentimental artifacts of an earlier time but ... a source of new insights into the lives of those who preceded us in the American saga."[12] Barry Schwartz has noted in particular how the mythologizing of Lincoln through popular expressions, including songs, established a "memory" useful in cultural coping at the time of World War I, through the Great Depression, and during World War II.[13]

The American public has typically found in the music of common culture a natural and efficient means of organizing emotional communal response to crisis and grief. Writing autobiographical notes in the 1930s, Charles Ives recalled the response of New Yorkers on May 8, 1915, on hearing news of the sinking of the Lusitania:

Everybody who came into the office, whether they spoke about the disaster or not, showed a realization of seriously experiencing something. ... Leaving the office and going uptown about 6 o'clock, I took the Third Avenue "L" at the Hanover Square Station ... a hand-organ, or hurdy gurdy was playing on a street below. Some workmen sitting on the side of the tracks began to whistle the tune, and others began to sing or hum the refrain. A workman with a shovel over his shoulder came on the platform and joined in the chorus, and the next man, a Wall Street banker with white spats and a cane, joined in it, and finally it seemed to me that everybody was singing this tune, and they didn't seem to be singing for fun, but as a natural outlet for what their feelings had been going through all day long. There was a feeling of dignity through all this. The hand-organ man seemed to sense this and wheeled the organ nearer the platform and kept it up fortissimo (and the chorus sounded out as though every man in New York must be joining in it). Then the first train came and everybody crowded in, and the song eventually died out, but the effect on the crowd still showed. Almost nobody talked—the people acted as though they might be coming out of a church service. ... Now what was the tune? ... It was nothing but "In the Sweet Bye and Bye." It wasn't a tune written to be sold, or written by a professor of music—but by a man who was but giving out an experience.[14]

Later that year, Ives composed "From Hanover Square North," which became the third movement of his Orchestral Set No. 2, affirming that this solace was real, that it was not mere diversion, that it was shared, and that it was about something beyond the self.

Martha Bayles commented on responses of artists, entertainers, and the American people shortly after September 11, 2001, in an essay in *The Chronicle of Higher Education*. She noted: "Sentimentality is a favorite dish of the American palate, and there's not much we snobs can do about it. The good news is that the worst snobs, the ones most inclined to sneer, have been forced to admit that cultivated taste is not the most important human virtue. The graves of true heroes are sometimes adorned with plastic flowers."[15] Alex Ross of *The New Yorker* concurred in his column of October 8, 2001: "when we are all in the grip of the same emotion ... a familiar tune billows above us, and we are carried along by it ... and only the most familiar, worn-out tune will do. When one part of the crowd is devoted to Jay-Z and another part to John Zorn, the common ground becomes 'God Bless America.'"[16]

And so an unassuming popular song can seem to capture exclusive rights to an event or an idea. "God Bless America" was never conceived as a ritual anthem. It was a Tin Pan Alley-style pop song composed in 1918 by a Russian immigrant named Israel Baline, later known as Irving Berlin. It was intended for, but ultimately not used in, a benefit variety-show revue for and about soldiers, which raised $80,000 for the war effort. Twenty years later, Berlin sensed he could articulate the current patriotic climate in the country and score a big hit at the same time; he revisited the unused song, updated and revised the text, and provided a major hit for singer Kate Smith in 1938. It eventually won him a Congressional Gold Medal in 1954. And while the public may elevate a Tin Pan Alley show tune to the status of anthem, tunes from the cultivated tradition occasionally find their way into more popular contexts, as in the many incarnations of Beethoven's Ninth Symphony's choral "Ode to Joy," or in Paul Simon's "American Tune" from Watergate days, based on the central chorale tune of Bach's *Saint Matthew Passion*.

CULTIVATING HUMANITY

Musicians in the academy are well advised to follow Martha C. Nussbaum's vision of liberal learning in the post-modern age, as expressed in *Cultivating Humanity: A Classical Defense of Reform in Liberal Education*. For Nussbaum, liberal learning is a dynamic process, interactive with contemporary life as it is lived in culture, in the market place, and in the professions, as well as in the academy. Nussbaum establishes in her first three chapters, the primary value set of liberal education: (1) skill in critical examination; (2) preparation for world citizenship; and (3) cultivation of the "narrative imagination." This last value is particularly dependent upon education in the arts, since the arts, she says, "cultivate capacities of judgment and sensitivity that can and should be expressed in the choices a citizen makes."[17]

How do music educators make specific application of these core values? First, "skill in critical examination" in music study includes achieving competence in technical mastery, analysis, historical and contextual knowledge, and valid interpretive choices. Second, "preparation for world citizenship" challenges the music student (and professor) to consider and articulate "the why" as well as "the how," to connect with the world, to engage with issues as well as activities, to develop a sense of artistic and ethical responsibility. And third, "cultivation of the narrative imagination" prepares the music student for higher-level problem solving and judgment. It requires the musician to have something meaningful to say and an ability to perceive, to empathize, and to express musically that which is worth expressing. It invites exploration of perspectives and meanings beyond one's own personal experience. It admits cultural diversity and much more, achieved through McFague's epistemology of attention to "otherness." Nussbaum's core values permit us and challenge us to go beyond the technical and the cultivated to consider music that typically has not been part of the fine arts tradition, nor part of the classical professional training. And the music of common culture becomes part of our study, not because it is common, but because it embodies ideas and "others" worthy of our attention.

While the study and performance of music of past times can offer insights into the circumstances of life in those times, today's teacher of historical music must help students link what is known of the past with what concerns them in the present. Current events, when considered as a collective supplemental resource, can help them do this. For the professional music student, reports of new findings by scholars of, or about, music and musicians of the past provide immediate connection to the field. And for all students, issues raised by music-related news whether artistic, sociological, economic, political, or scientific, offer occasions for discussions of the whys of music: the meanings, the implications, the controversies, and the moral dilemmas. The use of song to express solidarity in protest has a long and distinguished history in labor, civil rights, anti-war, and environmental movements. And certainly a composer such as Frederic Rzewski can intentionally express clear political agendas in complex concert works such as his monumental 1975 variation set for piano solo, "The People United Will Never Be Defeated," with a Chilean protest song as its theme. Occasionally a more ideologically ambiguous work can generate protests at the point of performance, with political concerns rather than musical ones in contention. Indeed the Metropolitan Opera's 2014 offering of John Adams's *The Death of Klinghofer*, dramatizing the 1985 terrorist hijacking of the *Achille Lauro* cruise ship and the subsequent execution of an elderly American Jew, generated much notice and active street protest, some of which extended into the opera house.[18] Although the work, dating from 1991, had been performed elsewhere on numerous occasions, the prominence of its Metropolitan Opera debut, heightened national alertness to terrorism, and the current sensitivities of partisans on both sides of its story (including some members of Mr. Klinghofer's family) generated new levels of public concern. Notable in this was the lack of any direct knowledge of or attention to the musical work itself on the part of the partisans.

Associations with music employed as means of terror and torture also have a history, as reviewed by *The New Yorker's* music critic Alex Ross.[19] His survey covers events and writing on the subject beginning with the US military's deliberate use of aggressive music intended to hasten the surrender of Manuel Noriega, dictator of Panama, in 1989 and forward to the present day. He concludes with the observation: "To admit that music can become an instrument of evil is to take it seriously as a form of human expression," reflecting a position on music also made in ancient times by Greek philosophers and early Christian fathers. To struggle with the question of whether musical works, practices, and events can or must carry ethical weight is implied in Nussbaum's second core value: preparation for world citizenship.

"Each Now Is the Time"

In "2 Pages, 122 Words on Music and Dance," John Cage expressed an artist's version of McFeague's attention epistemology: "To obtain the value of a sound, a movement, measure from zero. (Pay attention to what it is, just as it is.)." He concluded, "Each now is the time, the space. Are eyes open? Ears?"[20] In 2015 the Metropolitan Museum of Art commissioned composer and environmental activist John Luther Adams to prepare "Soundwalk 9:09." The work, which premiered in March 2016, includes a prepared set of sounds of the city, selected and ordered by the composer from recorded samples collected by volunteers walking between the museum on Fifth Avenue and the new satellite museum location, the Met Breuer, on Madison Avenue. It is, the composer says, "an invitation to listen more deeply to the music of the city." The recorded portion of the work is delivered via mobile devices, to be heard as the museum visitor walks between the buildings. The route, however, is not prescribed although the time frame is fixed. The composer, mediating between the controlled and the spontaneous, suggests that "the ideal listening balance between the 'live' and recorded sounds is one in which you aren't always certain whether a sound you're hearing is coming from your ear buds, your imagination, or from the streets around you."[21]

The variety of strategies and efforts to help students navigate their sonic environments all really come down to a single mandate: *Pay attention to what is out there, as it is happening. Think about it, its value and meaning, and relate yourself and your experience to it if you can.* Exercises in "everyday life" listening provide a starting point both for discussions of what is and is not music and for cultivation of an aesthetic attention and development of what Nussbaum called the narrative imagination. Similarly, exploring current events related to music and musicians reported in mainstream media can generate the beginnings of serious conversation. A student in an undergraduate class on eighteenth-century music history produced a reflective essay on the problem of finding a suitable balance, in twenty-first-century productions of eighteenth-century operas, between innovation and relevance on the one side, and historical intent and context on the other. Another student focused on perceived "political insensitivity" in modern contexts when performing historical works with "problematic representations and language" regarding race, ethnicity, and gender. A related essay treated the co-opting of standard repertory works for new political agendas. And yet another discussed the living and changing nature of our understanding of historical music, citing a scholar's recent discovery of some manuscripts by Buxtehude and Reinken known to have influenced J. S. Bach.

Students in one memorable introductory general-education music class became fascinated with an Associated Press account of the Philharmonic Orchestra in Marshall, Missouri, a town of 12,000 claiming to be the smallest in the country to support a classical orchestra.[22] Some students expressed admiration for the "band tax" that had been assessed to Marshall residents since 1934. They wondered whether this might help the orchestras and opera companies they had been reading about that were struggling in larger cities. This led to discussion of the advantages and disadvantages of public support for classical-music organizations. The Marshall Philharmonic story revealed that standard assumptions that high-culture concerts would be located in urban venues and attract the elite were flawed. To the students, a classical-music community in the heart of hog farming country was an attractive idea, signaling an inclusivity they had not previously imagined.

Music serves best in the academic setting when it generates dialogue between liberal and professional approaches to teaching and learning. The liberal arts teach us that music matters, in complex ways not limited to the ways in which the classical quadrivium justified it. Not all the music worth noticing is from the Western concert tradition and sometimes the music that matters may not have been covered in the professional course of study. In making music, the processes of creating and of perceiving are themselves dynamic interactions: between spontaneity and control, between predictability and surprise. The product embodies these dialogues, perhaps under the rubrics of classical and romantic styles or in completely different terms of everyday life. The special role of music in the academic community, and in the community beyond that, is to remind us and model for us the interplay between the spiritual and the material, between the active and the reflective, between the cultivated and the vernacular, and between the self and the other.

Notes

1. Sallie McFague, *The Body of God; An Ecological Theology* (Minneapolis: Fortress Press, 1993), 49.
2. Ibid., 49–50.
3. Ibid., 52.
4. Susanne K. Langer, *Problems of Art* (New York: Charles Scribner's Sons, 1957), 25–26. See also: Susanne K. Langer, *Feeling and Form* (New York: Charles Scribner's Sons, 1953), 369ff.
5. R. Eugene Rice, "Making a Place for the New American Scholar" (Preliminary Draft prepared for discussion, AAHE Conference on Faculty Roles & Rewards, Atlanta GA, January 1996), photocopy, 15.
6. Aristotle, *The Politics,* trans H. Rackham (Cambridge, MA: Harvard University Press, 1944), vol 21, 8.1337–1340.
7. Libby Larsen, "Music, Musicians, and the Art of Listening: Seven Truths about Music in the 21st Century," *Pan Pipes* (Spring 2001): 8.
8. "Of Rage and Remembrance (1991) Program note," John Corigliano's official website, 2008–2014, accessed June 20, 2016, http://www.john-corigliano.com/index.php?p=item2&item=81.
9. "Interview with John Adams," originally posted on New York Philharmonic website September 2002, on John Adams's official website 2016, accessed June 27, 2016, www.earbox.com/on-the-transmigration-of-souls.
10. Ibid.
11. Irwin Silber, ed., Introduction to *Songs of the Civil War* (New York: Dover, 1995; repr., New York: Columbia University Press), 3–4. Many other collections of Civil War era popular music are also easily accessible for student performers and listeners, including Richard Crawford's *The Civil War Songbook* (New York: Dover, 1977), which includes complete facsimiles of 37 sheet musics.
12. Silber, "Preface to the Dover Edition."
13. See Barry Schwartz, "Memory as a Cultural System: Abraham Lincoln in World War I," *International Journal of Sociology and Social Policy 17.6* (1997): 22–58.

14. Charles Ives, *Memos*, ed. John Kirkpatrick (New York: W. W. Norton, 1972), 92–93.
15. Martha Bayles, "Closing the Curtain on 'Perverse Modernism,'" *The Chronicle of Higher Education*, October 26, 2001: B14.
16. Alex Ross, "Requiems," *The New Yorker*, October 8, 2001, accessed June 27, 2016, http://www.newyorker.com/magazine/2001/10/08/requiems.
17. Martha C. Nussbaum, *Cultivating Humanity: A Classical Defense of Reform in Liberal Education* (Cambridge MA: Harvard University Press, 1997), 86.
18. Michael Cooper, "Protests Greet Metropolitan Opera's Premiere of 'Klinghofer'" *New York Times*, October 20, 2014, accessed July 1, 2016, http://www.nytimes.com/2014/10/21/arts/music/metropolitan-opera-forges-ahead-on-klinghoffer-in-spite-of-protests.html?_r=0.
19. Alex Ross, "The Sound of Hate; When Does Music Become Torture?" *The New Yorker*, July 4, 2016, 65–69.
20. John Cage, "2 Pages, 122 Words on Music and Dance," in *Silence* (Middletown CT: Wesleyan University Press, 1961), 96–97.
21. "Soundwalk 9:09, To the Listener: a note from John Luther Adams," accessed July 5, 2016, http://www.metmuseum.org/events/programs/met-live-arts/soundwalk.
22. Alan Scher Zagier, "Small-town Symphony Thrives in Missouri Musical Mecca," *Southeast Missourian*, May 21, 2006, accessed June 30, 2016, http://www.semissourian.com/story/1153552.html.

CHAPTER 13

Gospel Music: Cultural Artifact or Cross-Cultural Opportunity?

Adriane Thompson-Bradshaw and Margaret Cullen

One of the challenges for university educators in a diverse American society is facilitating the interaction of people with varied identities and backgrounds within the context of an academic community. So important is this effort that the US Department of Education and its Office for Civil Rights provide periodic guidance to colleges and universities about their expectations that schools will create environments supportive of all participants. Contemporary campuses include those with various gender identifications; Americans of multiple ethnic origins, such as Native American, African American, Asian American, Native Hawaiian, Pacific Islanders, and Euro or other ethnically white Americans; and adherents to all global religious and spiritual affiliations, as well as non-American international students. College administrators, faculty, and staff seek ways to prepare students for living in and contributing to diverse communities, both on campus and, after graduation, in the larger society.

Mentoring students to live well in heterogeneous milieus has become especially important in the second decade of the new century because of the proliferation of concerns regarding diversity within the larger society that ultimately influences campus life. Student-affairs deans from small private institutions in Ohio who met in 2016 dealt with this topic. Their discussion

A. Thompson-Bradshaw (✉) • M. Cullen
Ohio Northern University, Ada, OH, USA

© The Author(s) 2018   191
N. H. Hensel (ed.), *Exploring, Experiencing, and Envisioning
Integration in US Arts Education*, The Arts in Higher Education,
https://doi.org/10.1007/978-3-319-71051-8_13

touched on pressing issues such as the safety needs of under-represented students, and specific movements, such as Black Lives Matter versus All Lives Matter versus Blue Lives Matter, as well as populist discontents expressed by many citizens, including students, about a spectrum of controversial social issues. An example of the broader issues regarding social diversity that can influence a university is the turmoil at the University of Missouri in the fall of 2015. The administration there faced accusations of being slow to respond to racial tensions on campus, and after outraged students demonstrated in the full light of media attention, the chancellor resigned in response to those pressures. Similar and related protests spread to several colleges and universities across the nation. The focus of this chapter, Ohio Northern University (ONU), a small private institution of 3100 predominately white students in rural northwest Ohio, typically does not witness demonstrations or other strong, open conflicts about diversity. Nonetheless, administrators, faculty, and staff realize that sensitivity to potential conflicts is essential, both for them and for their students. ONU's commitment to supporting awareness and acceptance of diversity on campus is bolstered by its membership in the National Association of Colleges and Universities (NAC&U), an organization that promotes personal and social responsibility within a liberal arts emphasis, including the cultivation of intercultural knowledge and competence.

For almost 30 years (1987–present) the Ohio Northern University Gospel Ensemble has been devoted to the art of performing African American gospel music while also fostering a safe and supportive space for complex cross-cultural experimentation. During its first years, the intercultural aspects of the enterprise involved a black director and singers interacting with mostly white audiences at ONU and in the region. Over time, though, shifts in the interests of black students; the increased acceptance of ethnic mixing, especially by young people; the mainstream appeal and popularity of gospel music, as well as the general international disbursement of gospel performance, both musically and sociologically, combined to alter the demographics. By 2014, when director Adriane Thompson-Bradshaw, currently ONU's vice president for student affairs and dean of students, completed a research project documenting the ensemble's history, many of its members were white (or of other non–African American ethnicities). These changes have broadened participants' and audiences' perspectives from conventional black/white categories to complex cultural configurations that provide opportunities to preserve a musical heritage that Thompson-Bradshaw asserts to be "central to the mission of the Ensemble,"[1] while experimenting with ethnic identities and cultural formation within a supportive campus arts organization.

BEGINNINGS

When Thompson-Bradshaw, a young African American woman fresh out of graduate school, arrived at ONU, both she and the African American students there felt the need, in her words, for the formation of a small gospel choir to "express spirituality in a way not practiced on campus or in the Ada community."[2] As she and many of the students were familiar with gospel music from shared backgrounds, their expressive needs found fulfillment in this gathering, which became for many a place of African American spiritual grounding and a supportive university community. As Thompson-Bradshaw states, in the early years the solidarity of this association provided students with both "authentic communication with God through their music," and "a refuge from what felt at times like a strange land."[3] Thompson-Bradshaw and the singers created a strong sense of companionship in their shared music and prospered in the endeavor.

The experience of the original students corresponds to the observations of scholar Horace Boyer, who notes, "Gospel music is the unifying element of Black students all over the campuses of the United States. Gospel choirs began on college campuses to provide some continuity between the black church and the academic life, but students found that they liked it and wanted to perpetuate its existence."[4] Thompson-Bradshaw's research, including personal communication with the founding African American participants, affirms Boyer's observation. For example, one student commented that "coming out to Ada and to Ohio Northern, that was eye opening. I was terrified. I was scared to death coming out there. I had no idea how I would be welcomed or not."[5] Another celebrated the fact that in the homogeneous camaraderie, "We could pray, we could praise, we could laugh and that just kind of lifted our spirits." The student added, "For me it helped. ... You need something that's kinda like home away from home. It was hard to come to Ada."[6] That singer's sense of feeling at home with a small, all-black choir echoes the comments of many others from that original cohort and reinforces Boyer's observations.

Further, the ensemble's founding in 1987 was a scant 20 years after the passage of federal civil rights legislation and the resultant movement toward integration of American higher education. In the late 1980s, gospel music was generationally close to the epic black struggles for human and legal rights. Although the original students may not have explicitly articulated the power of that connection, most likely the feeling of "home" they describe included a feeling of being grounded in a history of empowerment encoded even in the most seemingly spiritual lyrics. Thompson-Bradshaw, as the leader, was keenly aware of the link between the ensemble's music and African American history. In her research project, she asserts that "music in the African American tradition is a product of a rich and problematized history."[7] As a member of a slightly earlier generation of African Americans than her students, she functioned as a vital link for them to the past she had inherited from her elders in traditional black culture.

Many gospel scholars share Thompson-Bradshaw's perspective regarding the important relations between gospel music and the African American past. For example, Melva Wilson Costen describes the music as being "both a genre (song form) and a style of performance, embodying the soulful expressions of the history of black people in and out of bondage and looking with joy to the future."[8] Another scholar, Gerardo Marti, affirms Costen's views, saying that "Gospel music is perceived to be an independent stream of music that most preserves, captures, and characterizes the black experience."[9] T.V. Reed specifically ties gospel to the liberation movements of the 1950s and 1960s. He asserts that "the forms of culture most central to the civil rights movement were undoubtedly music and religion,"[10] and celebrates the "liberating musicology" that fused liberationist praxis with the "tradition of African American song."[11]

Clearly, at the inception of the ONU ensemble, the art of gospel music provided an empowering space for African American students on a largely white rural campus to connect with their cultural and historical "home" identities, while also communicating their collective presence to the university and its locality. This significance is reinforced by research of scholar Terrell L. Strayhorn at the much larger Ohio State University (OSU), located in the state's capital, Columbus. He conducted interviews with 21 African American undergraduates involved in the OSU gospel choir and found themes similar to those documented by Thompson-Bradshaw in her surveys. He notes that black gospel participants benefited from "establishing a sense of belonging, developing ethnic identity, and nurturing resilience."[12] Thus African American students at both a small, rural private university and a flagship urban institution found strong grounding in an arts organization founded on music from their shared heritage.

UNINTENDED DIVERSIFICATION

From 1987 to 1994, ONU's ensemble maintained its original identity as African Americans sharing the gospel music that had developed the United States since the 1930s. Neither the director, Thompson-Bradshaw, nor the participants, excluded people of other ethnicities—nor did they seek them out. However, undergraduates from ethnically white backgrounds began to embrace the ensemble, which was part of the general outreach programs of the United Methodist-affiliated chapel at ONU. The chapel did not highlight ethnic identifications in its presentations of music or improvisational drama, nor in its faith-related events under the direction of the white campus pastor. In addition, of course, the chapel reinforced the diversity initiatives of the larger university. Further, Thompson-Bradshaw, an administrator at ONU as well as the ensemble's musical director, shared and promoted common multicultural objectives with her chapel colleagues.

Given this background, in 1994 when the first white student approached Thompson-Bradshaw with the desire to participate, she was immediately welcomed into a fellowship that had been exclusively African American for its initial seven years. The acceptance of this pioneer in diversity was so inclusive and genuine that she says that "it never crossed my mind that I would be the only white student and it didn't bother me at all. ... It wasn't something that was an issue."[13] Once the boundary of ethnic identity opened, the participation of white students increased, augmented by some international students and an occasional white faculty member. In the 2012–2013 academic year, for example, African Americans were the minority contingent. Of the 17 active people that year, 4 were African American; 1 was biracial African American and white; 10 were white Americans; and 2 were international students from Africa and the Middle East.[14]

One of the factors that attracts white students to gospel music is their perception that its expression has a special quality of authenticity often lacking in other types of spiritual music. Gerardo Marti comments that those outside of African American communities often note the "'soulfulness' in singing gospel and this makes worship for blacks a unique area of envy and privilege in the United States."[15] Marti interviewed people from various backgrounds and found that there was an almost universal acceptance of the idea that the symbols of "true worship" involve black people singing gospel music and engaging in uninhibited praise.[16] Overwhelmingly, people who were interviewed spoke of how central gospel music was to "black worship" and that most "perceived 'black worship' to be superior."[17] Marti links this idea with the history of slavery, saying that "because blacks are the only group to have experienced slavery in the United States, they are believed to have a deep connection to suffering and therefore a deeper connection to the mercy and grace of God in comparison with other groups."[18] Although those at ONU outside of the African American community might not consciously accept Marti's explanation of their attraction to gospel music, many do appear to be drawn to a depth of human life expressed in this genre.

One white member of the ensemble, for instance, says that she always just "loved gospel music. It was just in my soul."[19] Another white participant recalls African American colleagues who encouraged their white counterparts to explore the reality of the inner soul of the music. She writes that there were "some people in the Ensemble, of color, ... definitely encouraged some of the Whiter members to find their soul. ... I grew up in a small town that was very Caucasian, so I had not had a lot of exposure before college to African American people in general, and it was a really cool experience."[20] This attraction by white people to the deeper resources of African American gospel is not limited to ONU or even to the United States. For example, African American researcher E. Patrick Johnson, in his book *Appropriating Blackness*, explores the development of the Café of the Gate of Salvation Gospel Choir in Australia, which is composed mostly of atheists who are attracted to perceived soulful qualities of the genre. Johnson says that "a lot of [gospel] songs are a metaphor for the freedom that people are longing for" and that "gospel is a universal language that transcends difference."[21] Clearly, something about the nature of humanity encoded in the gospel genre attracts those outside of the African American world.

The ensemble's ethnic diversification transpired during a time of great change in the genre of gospel music. Those alterations find their roots in the civil rights movement itself. One of the great black leaders of the 1960s, Dr. Martin Luther King Jr., advocated for expression of multicultural spirituality. He asserted, "I was convinced that worship at its best is a social experience with people of all levels of life coming together to realize their oneness and unity under God."[22] Spurred by beliefs such as King's and openings for crossover to mainstream success, gospel writers and performers expanded the scope and appeal of the art, both in general performance and in church services. This transformation of the musical heritage itself no doubt contributed to the changes in the ethnic backgrounds of ensemble members at ONU. Also, as noted previously, these singers were primed to be inclusive by their participation in general chapel programming and by the commitment of ONU administrator Thompson-Bradshaw to a culturally open campus.

The alterations in African American musical traditions witnessed by Thompson-Bradshaw over several decades are not surprising historically. Angela M. S. Nelson traces the development of this music since 1900, demonstrating that creators and performers of it have continuously innovated. The ascendancy of classical gospel music in the 1930s was pioneered by Thomas Dorsey, who wrote over 1000 songs. Before that, in the early twentieth century, the black tradition included hymns that combined popular tunes with spiritual blues and jazz harmonies with piano accompaniment and congregational singing as well as male quartets following the example of late-nineteenth-century jubilee singers.[23] Nelson notes that since the late 1960s, African American-inspired gospel music has merged with a variety of cross cultural forms, often inspired by urban influences.[24] Furthermore, Deborah Smith Pollard comments that beginning in the 1970s, African American churches began to incorporate the emerging praise and worship music (also known as contemporary Christian music) to enliven congregations' engagement, especially among the young, as did white churches in the same era.[25] Given this background in gospel music, potential ensemble members—black, white, and other ethnicities—had been exposed to border-crossing gospel and related music by the time the first white student joined the previously homogeneous troupe in 1994. So the ethnic changes in the group mesh historically with the transformations of the musical genre itself.

African American members of the ONU ensemble have expressed their clear understanding of the increased complexity of gospel and related music over the past few decades. One comments that "it's more than Black people listening to Mary Mary, Hezekiah or Richard Smallwood. It's a much wider focus."[26] Another comments more fully, saying that the "African American tradition has changed so [much]. Now, if you're still singing those same songs really you should get with Israel or you should be singing something else like Donnie McClurkin or something different. I would be disappointed if the same songs were being sung now that were sung then."[27] Further, artists such as Israel Houghton actively push the ethnic boundaries of inclusion in gospel tradition; Houghton calls his movement the Sound of New Breed Worship.[28] This popular innovator is an African American who was raised in a white family and attended a

Hispanic church.[29] As a multicultural gospel artist, Houghton says that many youth are "not listening to older versions of gospel stuff; they're listening to the new stuff, which is not that cultural."[30] His assertion in his song "I Hear the Sound" resonates with many young gospel enthusiasts: "It isn't a black thing. It's isn't a white thing. It ain't a colored thing."[31] Clearly, the universe of gospel creativity has transformed since Thompson-Bradshaw began her all-African American ensemble.

Some established figures in gospel music openly approve of the ethnic inclusivity that newcomers like Houghton promote. Gospel legend Bishop Rance Allen (who supports and has performed with the ONU ensemble) founded the Rance Allen Group and has spearheaded gospel crossover innovation for four decades. As Angela W. K. McNeil reports, Allen and associates were "the first modern gospel group to take secular sounds and performance practices and recast them with religious lyrics," a strategy that launched a cascade of cross-cultural musical trends in gospel.[32] Another veteran gospel artist, Chris Byrd, the musical director for the Rance Allen Group who has also participated in performances with the ensemble, affirms cross-cultural gospel music. He says, "I always try to make music that is … unique to where it will capture everyone's attention no matter what race they are. When you think about music that we hear in the world, like pop music, a lot of pop music … goes beyond race, 'cause everybody loves it. So, I think it's important … that we try to make our sound more broad so that we can capture everybody's attention and make it appeal to everybody."[33] So inclusive has this genre become that Martha Munizzi became the first white artist to win a Stellar Award, honoring black gospel music, not once but twice—in 2005 and 2006.[34] Given this changing context and the direct support of luminaries such as Allen and Byrd for the ONU's ensemble's eclectic identity, it is no surprise that student participants have found a safe place for cross-cultural dialogue as they broaden their individual perspectives on ethnicity through practicing the art of gospel music.

LIVING IN INTERSTICES

No doubt the multicultural benefits gained by those in the ensemble and the campus community as a whole have been considerable over the decades of the organization's history. However, intercultural interaction in America and on the ONU campus is never complete but is an ongoing, vital, and sometimes challenging process. The cultural critic Homi Bhabha highlights "interstices," those spaces where "the intersubjective and collective experiences of ... community interest, or cultural value are negotiated."[35] These negotiations form an important part of a university education but are not simple matters, as witnessed by the events and issues mentioned earlier. The concerns of African American students manifested at the University of Missouri, for example, are not unique, nor are ethnic tensions easily resolved even on a relatively quiet campus such as that of ONU.

Although the diversification of the ensemble has been peaceful, that process has not been without complexities as it moved through ethnic interstices. During Thompson-Bradshaw's 2014 research project, several originators of the then all-black enterprise expressed reservations about the ethnic evolution. Said one, "It's questionable for me. When there's an all-white ensemble or very few of us [African Americans], it's a distraction. I'm more focused on 'what are they really doing up there?' When you see other colors worshipping, it doesn't seem real sometimes."[36] Another wrestled with the tension between ethnic inclusiveness and cultural distinctiveness: "I'm not saying it should have been segregated, but it was just something that was ours. ... It's not right to be selfish, but at the same time ... when you start diluting it, it takes away the effect of what it meant to some of the others ... something that got them through. There's certain things that are culturally just for us that we can relate to."[37] Critic Obery M. Hendricks Jr. articulates the shortcomings of eclectic performance of contemporary gospel music that these students may be attempting to express. Hendricks sees the present-day ethnically diverse gospel movement as a diminishment of black historical memory. He asserts, "Gospel music has gained the world, but it has lost the prophetic heart of black sacred music."[38] The students' comments about diversity introducing distractions, a sense of inauthenticity, or a cultural dilution resonate with Obery's concerns that the greater mass appeal and performance of gospel has dispersed its value as authentic liberationist culture.

In her research on the ensemble, Thompson-Bradshaw herself questions the cultural outcomes of what has become a prized campus presence with a long history. She has "struggled throughout the years with the notion of authenticity and being true to the heritage of the music."[39] She cites critic Pearl Williams-Jones's warning in 1975 that anticipates the students' and Obery's more contemporary cautions. Williams-Jones writes that she hopes that "the acceptability, respectability and universal receptivity to gospel music will not eventually bring a 'kiss of death' and route to the dilution of this art form. It is imperative that black gospel maintain its strong self-identity."[40] Thompson-Bradshaw notes that the "journey of African Americans is such an integral part of the development of black gospel music that I believed that being intentional about preserving that connection was important."[41] Over the decades at ONU, however, that preservation has evolved into multicultural negotiations involving multiple and changing variables in the group's ethnic composition and the diversification of the gospel genre, as Thompson-Bradshaw has sought to validate an authentic tradition that is also relevant on a twenty-first-century campus.

The voicing of concern about the current direction of gospel music is in dialogue with other voices that characterize new waves of gospel participation as an opportunity for cross-cultural benefits. Some believe that just as Thomas Dorsey changed the nature of African American spiritual music in the 1930s, artists such as Israel Houghton may be leading the way to new intercultural renditions of it. One ensemble member highlighted the sense of discovery he felt because of diversification: "Coming from an all-Black church ... then going to Gospel Ensemble and seeing a lot of White members, it was like an experience ... like man everybody's singing and blending and sounding good together, so it was cool."[42] A member of the 2013 cohort (whose ethnicity was not specified) highlighted how the diversity benefits the music: "The racial mix of the Ensemble has helped spread the music and exposed it to people of other races that did not know about this kind of music. If we have one Hispanic or Caucasian singing in the group, it will attract people from those races to come experience it."[43] Recent African American students in the ensemble still echo the sense of belonging expressed by those who founded the organization. One woman who sang from 2011 to 2013 said "I love gospel music and I enjoy singing. Being away from home I thought joining the Gospel Ensemble would be the closest thing to the gospel music I listen to when I am home. ... From the first day of rehearsal I knew that this was perfect and exactly what I needed."[44] These voices emphasize the positive potential for a more ethnically diverse gospel tradition.

Along the same lines, a recent African American alumnus who has been a praise and worship leader in several churches, both black and white, stresses the connection between gospel and contemporary praise and worship music. He says, "I primarily do praise and worship music, but I throw in gospel because it's all connected to the same source. Without gospel music there would be no praise and worship music, especially in the black church."[45] A counter argument to Obery's concerns about maintaining the authenticity of black sacred music is articulated by Bishop Andrew Merritt, founder of a church in Detroit, who sponsored a mass event called One in Worship in an area stadium. He asserts that diversity "is a reflection of the core of Christ, out of one blood made He all nations. ... Arabs will participate, Greek, French, Hispanics. But no cultural names, no denomination will get in the way of what people are coming here to do, and that is to worship as one body."[46] Clearly, the difference between Merritt's and Obery's articulation of African American sacred music is wide; however, both are part of the ongoing, necessary negotiations about the authenticity of a historically significant spiritual art form.

Living fully in the cultural interstices created by 30 years of gospel music under Thompson-Bradshaw's guidance, the students in ONU's ensemble have learned to embrace rather than to avoid complex cultural dialogues, even those including sensitive issues of ethnic identity. Critic Victor Turner's insights into "liminality" apply to the ensemble; he describes liminality as the dynamic space between established structures and situations offering the opportunity for "invention, discovery, creativity and reflection."[47] Thompson-Bradshaw and her musical cohorts have participated actively in mining the riches of liminal spaces by doing what D. Soyini Madison advocates for effective dialogic performance—bringing many different voices into the conversation without subduing or quieting any of them.[48] In welcoming diverse ethnic voices to gospel music, the ensemble demonstrates how gospel music can contribute to building community, provide emotional support and even encourage spiritual transformation through the open process that Madison advocates. That multicultural dialogic legacy has equipped a succession of participants, and those influenced by them, to be better prepared after graduation to negotiate the ever-changing diversity of the world.

This unique preparation equips alumni of the program to feel more confident about encountering other diverse cultural situations and be more empathetic to those who are different from them. One of the earlier African American ensemble members, who has been on the staff of an Ohio university for over a decade, says that the diversity of the ensemble was "eye opening for both, when we finally starting having more Caucasian members."[49] He came to realize that in a diverse shared artistic activity, people from different backgrounds could actually "have the same experiences ... feel the same type of things I'm feeling,"[50] a realization that has served him well in his university career. In a similar way, the first white member of the group says that her ensemble experience "changed my life in so many ways." She says that "looking back on that time in my life, it truly was one of the richest memories in my life. I think about it a lot and I treasure the friendships and life lessons I learned."[51] What is more, this woman has transferred the lived intercultural knowledge and interaction that was part of her education at ONU to the next generation—her two sons. She says, "My boys are very much like me; they know no stranger and they could care less what someone looks like."[52] The empowerment of these two alumni for intercultural engagement is echoed in the post-graduation lives of many others.

The 30-year legacy of the Ohio Northern University Gospel Ensemble demonstrates the value of the innovative use of music in the liberal arts education to prepare students for cultural adaptability in their careers and engagement with their larger communities. The group became an authentic safe space for participants, one that did not isolate members from others who are different, but rather creatively joined them in an ethnically diverse collective. In this inclusive arts environment, difference is openly acknowledged, and the resulting cultural shifts engendered by exploration of diversity are processed within a supportive context. Opportunities such as those provided by the ensemble augment the value of the education ONU provides and affirm the power of creative liberal arts to foster an education that will last for a lifetime in an ever-more diverse world.

NOTES

1. Adriane L. Thompson-Bradshaw, "The Impact of Race on Perceptions of Authenticity in the Delivery and Reception of African American Gospel Music," (Ph.D. dissertation, Bowling Green State University, 2014), 8, http://rave.ohiolink.edu/etdc/view?acc_num=bgsu1395429657.
2. Thompson-Bradshaw, "Impact of Race on Perceptions," 9.
3. Ibid., 13.
4. Jerma A. Jackson, *Singing in My Soul: Black Gospel Music in a Secular Age* (Chapel Hill: The University of North Carolina Press, 2004), 134.
5. Thompson-Bradshaw, "Impact of Race on Perceptions," 41–42.
6. Ibid., 41.
7. Ibid., 9.
8. Melva Wilson Costen, *In Spirit and in Truth: The Music of African American Worship* (Louisville: Westminster John Knox Press, 2004), 76.
9. Gerardo Marti, *Worship Across the Racial Divide: Religious Music and the Multiracial Congregation* (New York: Oxford University Press, 2012), 53.

10. T.V. Reed, *The Art of Protest: Culture and Activism from the Civil Rights Movement to the Streets of Seattle* (Minneapolis: University of Minnesota Press, 2005), 2.
11. Reed, *The Art of Protest*, 13.
12. Terrell Strayhorn, "Singing in a Foreign Land: An Exploratory Study of Gospel Choir Participation Among African American Undergraduates at a Predominantly White Institution," *Journal of College Student Development* 52, no. 2 (2011): 137.
13. Thompson-Bradshaw, "Impact of Race on Perceptions," 44–45.
14. Ibid., 15.
15. Marti, *Worship Across the Racial Divide*, 55.
16. Ibid., 53.
17. Ibid., 52.
18. Ibid., 62.
19. Thompson-Bradshaw, "Impact of Race on Perceptions," 46.
20. Ibid., 48.
21. E. Patrick Johnson, *Appropriating Blackness: Performance and the Politics of Authenticity* (Durham, NC: Duke University Press, 2003), 180.
22. Marti, *Worship Across the Racial Divide*, 3.
23. Angela M. S. Nelson, "Why We Sing: The Role and Meaning of Gospel in African American Popular Culture," in *The Triumph of the Soul: Cultural and Psychological Aspects of African American Music*, eds. Ferdinand Jones and Arthur C. Jones (Westport, CT: Greenwood/Praeger, 2001), 99.
24. Nelson, "Why We Sing," 104.
25. Deborah Smith Pollard, *When the Church Becomes Your Party* (Detroit: Wayne State University Press, 2008), 24.
26. Thompson-Bradshaw, "Impact of Race on Perceptions," 52.
27. Ibid., 101.
28. Pollard, *When the Church Becomes*, 36.
29. Ibid.
30. Ibid.
31. Ibid.
32. Angela W. K. McNeil, *Encyclopedia of American Gospel Music.* (New York: Routledge, 2005), 8.
33. Thompson-Bradshaw, "Impact of Race on Perceptions," 132.
34. Pollard, *When the Church Becomes*, 33.
35. Homi K. Bhabha, *The Location of Culture* (New York: Routledge, 1994), 2.
36. Thompson-Bradshaw, "Impact of Race on Perceptions," 51.
37. Ibid.
38. Obery M. Hendricks Jr., *The Universe Bends Toward Justice: Radical Reflections on the Bible, the Church, and the Body Politic* (Maryknoll: Orbis Books, 2011), 3.

39. Thompson-Bradshaw, "Impact of Race on Perceptions," 18.
40. Pearl Williams-Jones, "Afro-American Gospel Music: A Crystallization of the Black Aesthetic," *Ethnomusicology* 19 no. 3 (1975): 384.
41. Thompson-Bradshaw, "Impact of Race on Perceptions," 10.
42. Ibid., 45.
43. Ibid., 56.
44. Ibid., 42.
45. Ibid., 95.
46. Pollard, *When the Church Becomes*, 35.
47. D. Soyini Madison, *Critical Ethnography: Methods, Ethics, and Performance* (Los Angeles: Sage Publications, 2012), 170.
48. Madison, *Critical Ethnography*, 186.
49. Thompson-Bradshaw, "Impact of Race on Perceptions," 45.
50. Ibid.
51. Heather Davey, e-mail message to Thompson-Bradshaw, October 23, 2016.
52. Ibid.

CHAPTER 14

Affecting Campus Climate: Fine and Performing-Arts Community Outcomes

Sarah Jarmer Scott and Samantha Siegel

INTRODUCTION

For two decades Wagner College has been at the forefront of engaged learning through the liberal arts and the national conversation about civic responsibility and democratic values in higher education. Specifically, Wagner has implemented strategies called for by the Association of American Colleges and Universities' National Task Force, a body charged with more deeply integrating civic and democratic learning in education. The call for action initiated by the task force in its *Crucible Moment* study asked that colleges prepare students *with knowledge and for action,* so that students may approach their civic work with greater understanding of global and cultural contexts.[1] It is through the involvement of students directly with the community that the value of civic engagement can be lived as well as learned. As discussed by Wagner faculty,[2] the New American Colleges and Universities (NAC&U, a consortium of which Wagner is a member) and others,[3] students, parents, and prospective employers are calling on undergraduate educators to provide opportunities for both excellence in critical thinking and real-life experiences. Wagner has been involved in a number of studies to improve its own deep-seated mission of

S. J. Scott (✉) • S. Siegel
Wagner College, Staten Island, NY, USA

© The Author(s) 2018
N. H. Hensel (ed.), *Exploring, Experiencing, and Envisioning Integration in US Arts Education,* The Arts in Higher Education,
https://doi.org/10.1007/978-3-319-71051-8_14

205

fostering democratic learning. The dovetailing of national conversations about embedded civic learning and our curricular planning and change at Wagner have resulted in several administrative and pedagogical shifts at the college, including two projects undertaken as a result of the creation of the Port Richmond Partnership (PRP).

THE PORT RICHMOND PARTNERSHIP

The PRP was established in 2009 through a memorandum of understanding committing Wagner to engage in civic work in Port Richmond, an area of Staten Island near the college where socioeconomic and community relations were under significant stress. Faculty and administrators at Wagner had become increasingly aware that the energies devoted to community-based learning and service over the previous decade had resulted in improved lives for both local communities and the college community. Considered to be the cornerstone of the civic engagement curriculum, nearly 40 percent of Wagner faculty members engage with Port Richmond through community-based research, the arrangement of a lecture featuring a local community leader or organization, course-required field placements, or field trips. Wagner has become an anchoring institution and, as such, has worked to overcome some of the common pitfalls of community-engaged work, specifically through arts-based projects.[4]

One of the most important components of successful community–campus partnerships is project planning based on the needs of the communities.[5] At the establishment of the PRP, four key types of initiatives existed: in the areas of education, economic development, health, and immigration (a fifth initiative, the arts, was added in 2013 as a result of one of the projects discussed below). At the outset of the partnership, the general goal was to lift up an economically distressed community considered to be the historic cradle of Staten Island. In the fall of 2011, a local Staten Island foundation gave funding to Marga Incorporated, a New York-based consulting group focused on strengthening community partnerships with anchoring institutions such as colleges and/or hospitals, so that it could review the first two years of PRP's work and develop a strategic plan for the next phases of the PRP. The assessment suggested there was a growing desire among a cross-disciplinary group of faculty to focus more intentionally on the arts. This resulted in extensive participation and a strategic plan for institutional support of public art projects such as *Mariposas Amarillas* (Yellow Butterflies) and the Sound of Port Richmond. The report found that community stakeholders felt the PRP was having a positive impact on the community, provided meaningful experiences for students while simultaneously aiding the community, and eased the workload of organizations by providing capable interns and volunteers.[6]

Arts programs through the PRP were designed to bring together traditionally segregated groups to work and be empowered together, with true reciprocity.[7] Our work is continually evolving as we strive to attain more integrated and proactive communication and aim for, in the words of the national advocacy organization Imagining America (IA), "excellence as a socially negotiated experience of creativity and agency."[8] Interdisciplinary courses through Wagner's First-Year Program and Learning Communities[9] are often the most powerful and involved examples of community and course collaboration because both Wagner students and faculty deeply engage in preparation and training for these experiences.

The best community-based courses are interdisciplinary in nature, have a long-term vision of success, view the community partner as a co-facilitator of knowledge, and collaborate with the Center for Leadership and Community Engagement (CLCE) at Wagner to provide support for multiple programs.[10] This chapter looks at how one classroom-based project and another center-based project worked with the PRP to encourage deeper relationships between the Port Richmond and Wagner communities, and to discover specifically how arts-based programs could encourage change in the hearts and minds of people in both communities regarding the importance of deepening their relationships and making changes for the social good.[11]

The *Mariposas Amarillas* (Yellow Butterflies) Project and Sounds of Port Richmond (SoPR) both sought to introduce Wagner students to a local needy community with the hopes of helping lift up and unite the community through visual and interactive art projects. *Mariposas* was a work of public art in which Wagner students worked for three years to design and implement community workshops based on the iconographic themes of the art such as immigration, cultural heritage, diversity, and landscape. SoPR was a community theater project in which Wagner students helped the community design and perform a theatrical production centered on community issues.

MARIPOSAS AMARILLAS

During the winter of 2013, the PRP committed itself to generating a list of needs from its community partners. One need was development of a series of beautification projects across the community. Three partners in the PRP (El Centro del Immigrante, Project Urbanista, and Wagner) were successful in receiving a Department of Transportation (DOT) grant for public art in 2014 using local graphic designer Lina Montoya. One of the grant's goals was to install a work of public art on DOT property. The mural, ultimately installed on a chain link fence and measuring more than 20 feet high and 200 feet wide, depicts the New York City skyline through blue plastic clips and thousands of yellow vinyl butterflies flying across the skyline. The iconography, developed by Montoya, was intended to express ideas related to collective community identity and the impacts of migration and immigration in urban environments.

In addition to beautifying a high traffic, semi-industrial area of Port Richmond, the goals of the project were both to involve students and members of the local community in the installation and to educate the local community about the value of public art. One of the authors, Professor Sarah J. Scott, led the planning for Wagner and focused the attention of students in both the First-Year Learning Community and in museum studies on the project.

Interdisciplinary work was a highlight of this project. Scholarship on immigrant artists suggests that visual art provides means for communication and integration between immigrant and local communities as artists use artistic expression as a means to share their own culture, establish economic stability, and provide educational outlets.[12] *Mariposas* has drawn inspiration from multiple immigrant artists in Port Richmond. It has been shown through public art projects that murals have been particularly successful in harnessing public memory so that communities can capture their pasts for future generations. By capturing ideas and history through art and sharing this art publicly, communities become stronger.[13] Museum and art education is a third discipline informing the work of *Mariposas*. The utilization of creative and exciting strategies to bring arts education to a more diverse public frees art and art history from the ivory tower, making it relevant to all.[14]

Public art is a fantastic tool for teaching outside the classroom. Not only does public art beautify spaces and encourage community members to reflect on their own neighborhoods, but it also can be used as a springboard for discussions about history, science, math, and art.[15] *Mariposas* became an agent to stimulate discussions about individual identity, community identity, and family heritage. By using works of public art as inspiration for such discussions, it was easier for participants of different backgrounds to come together around visual iconography and connect through their common experiences with such imagery (survey data suggest that this was one of the most successful aspects of the project). Students learned about symbolism and other abstract concepts, and they asked questions about how symbols are related to their community's past, present, and future.[16] In other words, art can make it easier to talk about community problems. It is through the use of art outside the classroom that such breakthroughs are possible.

Public art has increased agency if the local community is involved with the creation of a work of art from the planning stages—when history and symbolism are collectively created—all the way through to the execution and installation of the art.[17] Montoya's drive to do that resulted in the creation of the installation on Richmond Terrace, a heavily trafficked industrial area of Port Richmond, and Professor Scott relied heavily on the students' reactions and involvement with this installation for their subsequent creation of new works in their classrooms and around their community. Scott worked closely with Project Urbanista, Lina Montoya, and Public School 20 to develop an outreach program that would involve both local Port Richmond schools and Wagner students. The program took the form of a series of workshops on migration, immigration, and community identity, held for third- and fourth-grade students at P.S. 20. The workshops included a walking tour in Port Richmond to view the *Mariposas* mural as well as other works of public art and an in-class exercise in which the elementary students created their own small butterflies, decorated with images they felt expressed ideas of their own identity. The butterflies then were all pasted onto a large world map based on the countries of origin of students' families. A second in-class exercise gave the students the chance to create their own family tree, using small butterflies for names of each family member.

Education through the arts, to achieve the results discussed above, specifically warrants community involvement originating from community-identified needs.[18] Although the PRP is an example of such a success, visual and performing art projects, as products that are intended for the public sector, necessitate the close cooperation of community groups. By working with the P.S. 20 community, we have learned that teachers' involvement, discussions about family heritage, and addressing the diversity of students are essential.[19] Bilingual education and needs-based and dignity-based rights of the students were all part of the planning process for the *Mariposas* workshops.

Finally, the elementary students took a trip to the local Staten Island Museum to take part in workshops in the galleries. These workshops included gallery activities in which students interacted with exhibits relevant to the themes of the mural: metamorphosis of Cicadas, migration of the Lenape Indians, and the history of transportation in and around Staten Island and the city boroughs. All workshop activities were designed and led by students from Wagner's First-Year Learning Community, under the direction of Scott and museum educators. Students from both P.S. 20 and Wagner reported a deeper understanding of diversity in their own communities as well between communities through their exposure to public art. Cooperation among Port Richmond, Wagner, and the museum has followed in the model of other cooperative museum efforts that resulted in furthering programming and engagement among all participants.[20] By drawing on the expertise of museum educators, Wagner students were able to more deeply integrate the topics of public art with the museum trips. Integrating the *Mariposas* mural and other works of public art in Port Richmond with the collections at the Staten Island Museum has allowed the college and the museum to engage in further conversations about broadening the audience for the museum and about future collaborations. Such successes are similar to those shown in other museum/ higher education/community partnerships.[21]

During these 2014 workshops, Scott worked with Montoya and the Wagner community to develop a longer-term program that would link Port Richmond and Wagner through art. It was concluded that the college could benefit from the installation of a work of community-installed public art just as Port Richmond had. Therefore, it was planned that in the fall of 2015 a related artwork would be installed on Wagner's campus. Workshops similar to those held in 2014 were conducted, with walking tours and in-class activities focusing this time on themes of neighborhood and landscape. The Staten Island Museum tours also focused on the theme of landscape, as the museum had recently installed a new exhibit on local landscape art. The 2015 program culminated in the installation of a new *Mariposas Amarillas* public art project on the east side of Wagner's Horrmann Library. Third- and fourth-graders from P.S. 20 came to the campus to take part in workshops about community, diversity, and neighborhood, and worked on the installation of a temporary mural featuring butterfly iconography.

Using visual arts as tool has been shown to be particularly successful in strengthening communities, furthering cultural understanding, and developing students' abilities for collaboration and innovative thinking.[22]

The visual arts have been shown to be a successful discipline for encouraging young students to more consciously think about values in their community.[23] Exposing young students to their local art museums too has been a successful way to encourage creative and critical thinking, and studies suggest that the earlier students are exposed to museums, the more apt they are to continue to use them as learning outlets.[24] The *Mariposas* project has physically and actively engaged students, using both public art and museum objects in the curriculum. Perhaps most importantly, public art in a community setting is most successful when it is participatory.[25] Taking art to the street, literally, has been a current trend in art education and has resulted in hugely successful projects across the country.[26] Using public art as a means for constructing the necessary scaffolding of understanding around communities of difference has been successful in multiple contexts.[27] It was with the workshops developed in 2015, and the cooperation around the on-campus *Mariposas* installation and experience, that the project finally got the community and campus humming. By making and creating art both in Port Richmond and in the campus community, two very different, distinct communities came to engage with and appreciate each other more deeply, while also recognizing the need to do so more often.

The community–campus relationship around public art that developed though *Mariposas* deepened through two additional nascent projects. When Scott's museum-studies class was assisting in the installation of the campus *Mariposas* mural, the students were also working on an exhibit on local artists working in Port Richmond. The research conducted for the exhibit is currently being used in a new grant project to develop an interactive website and Internet-based map of public art in the Port Richmond and the North Shore areas of Staten Island. In addition, Wagner is committed to developing more arts-based curricula focused on public art and, therefore, is developing new courses and surveying potential sites for public art installations.

One of Wagner's missions is to encourage and promote civically minded living for their students. *Mariposas* was created in service to this mission. It was particularly hoped by project administrators that the students involved would come to understand that education and learning is not a transmission-based process.[28] Although the Wagner students were older than the elementary students, they were not necessarily the teachers. Active learning comes from the participants, not just the teachers, and so we, the Wagner faculty, wanted our students to see that the role teachers play is not as traditional as they might have thought. Wagner students learned to bring new ideas to children from diverse backgrounds. They also learned about how public art can help them learn more about the people they live with. It allowed them to interact with people they might not have otherwise met. Wagner faculty, staff, administration, and other students now have a greater awareness of how public art can bring communities together. They also have a greater knowledge of Port Richmond children. Ultimately, we believe we have changed the prevailing thought of many participants in the project regarding the power and agency inherent in public art.

SOUNDS OF PORT RICHMOND

The SoPR community theater project was born in the winter of 2013 during a brainstorming conversation in Wagner College's main dining hall. Stephen Preskill, Distinguished Professor of Civic Engagement and Leadership, and Samantha Siegel, director of the CLCE, hosted Kevin Bott, associate director of the national advocacy organization IA, for an annual visit to discuss the future of collaborative projects. Traditionally, collaborations between Wagner College and IA existed as relationships between individual faculty members and the organization. Each year several professors from multiple disciplines, including history, sociology, political science, and art history, normally attend IA's national conference as a way to connect with like-minded colleagues passionate about the possibilities of art, democratic engagement, and community-based learning. However, in the case of Wagner, rarely did these relationships result in anything beyond fostering a robust professional network. Such a network developed between Stephen Preskill, Samantha Siegel, and Kevin Bott during the 2012 national conference. At that time, Bott asked a simple question: "How can we infuse public art into the Port Richmond Partnership?" Before the trio shared their final cup of coffee, they had decided that Bott would return for two weeks to lead an intensive pilot program in the summer of 2013 to develop a community theater project.

In keeping with faculty interest and the findings of the Marga report, the CLCE had three goals for the community theater project. The first was to maintain a Wagner presence in Port Richmond despite the limitations of the academic calendar; the second was to engage more community members not associated with community organizations in Port Richmond; and the third was to gain a better understanding of the assets, needs, and challenges of community members.

Bott, Preskill, and Siegel collectively agreed that community theater has the power to transform communities by giving space for the stories of community members to be shared openly and authentically in a public setting. Project coordinators used the story-circle method to build community and draw stories from participants to create a script. The first project resulted in a ten-day workshop facilitated by Bott with logistics handled by Siegel through the CLCE in August 2013. The project was funded by a modest grant from the New York Council for the Humanities, Wagner College, and local non-profit organizations. Constant dialogue and collective community buy-in were critical to the success of the project.

The culminating performance was held in the basement of St. Phillip's Baptist Church, a community space for many neighborhood activities, during a monthly friendship dinner. The bilingual participatory performance titled *Sterling and Maria* cast approximately two dozen people and explored the historical racial tensions between the Mexican and African communities of Port Richmond. Audience members were encouraged at designated points to change or alter the script by sharing their ideas about a character or conflict facing the cast.

While the performance was powerful, the community members who participated remarked that the collective organizing, process facilitation, and the bonds developed by performing together were even more profound than the final product. When the participants became the curators of socially conscious public art, of stories beyond their own, the art became more than the theater piece. The profound experience was the sharing of personal stories and co-creation of the piece by cast members and less about perfecting the actual craft.[29] As in similar studies, community theater and social art were the vehicles through which a successful dialogue and communication was achieved in a unbiased, non-judgemental way across differences and boundaries.[30]

Wagner and IA's commitment to allowing the Port Richmond community to dictate the production and general process was critical to the success of the project.[31] This approach built leadership within Port Richmond and among students that might not have happened if the anchoring institutions had directed the community theater work; this belief is reflected in the mission of the institutions and the Marga findings.

Over the next year, Wagner and IA continued to build a large community of practice. During the following summer the SoPR partnered with the Faber Park Recreation Center and shifted its focus to youth empowerment. Bott did not facilitate each story circle; rather, community members emerged as facilitators to develop the performance piece. A series of short, expressive pieces came together around the theme "Art creates hope and community." Topics such as domestic violence, gun violence, hunger, and interracial dating were explored.

Again, while the performance drew nearly 100 people and the show was powerful, the true transformation came from the process of community members and Wagner students sharing stories and creating the performance. A leadership team subsequently emerged whose goal became the utilization of strategies learned through the summer program in various community settings throughout the year. In the midst of the summer rehearsals, the cast was notified that a Staten Island resident, Eric Garner, had been killed as a result of a police chokehold after he was apprehended for selling loose cigarettes. Garner's death shook Staten Island and compelled the leadership team to explore its role as a community theater group, as part of the national, city, and local conversation about police brutality and racial inequality that was dramatically affecting their own community. Local resident and actress Charnae Alexander, was named the first SoPR president. With the support of Wagner and the counsel of Bott, Charnae Alexander, a Wagner intern, and others led community theater classes at Faber Park through the spring of 2015. These classes continued to discuss police brutality and youth activism openly and honestly through theater games and exercises.

As the infrastructure of the SoPR grew stronger, for Wagner to justify its continuing fiscal contribution meant that more faculty and students needed to engage in the project in an intentional way related specifically to student learning. IA and the CLCE hosted a series of meetings to encourage faculty participation and input. The film department emerged as a leading partner because it could document the project, and footage is currently being edited for submission to film festivals.

The final summer of the SoPR was unlike the others. The police officer who was responsible for placing Eric Garner in a chokehold that resulted in his death was not indicted for murder. In December of 2014 the community was in a confused and angry uproar. The relationships between Staten Islanders and the police were strained despite efforts of the NYPD and City Hall. The Sound of Port Richmond Leadership Team changed course; members decided to create a play by collecting stories and interviewing Staten Islanders. For nearly five months the leadership team collected and recorded stories; in May 2015 they hosted auditions for the cast.

The goal was not to create a production with professional polish but rather, a powerful piece relying on the commitments and communicative power of the diverse cast of community residents. The cast studied other pieces of documentary-style theater such as the *Laramie Project* and *Fires in the Mirror: Crown Heights, Brooklyn and Other Identities* in order to understand the style of work they were seeking to produce. They continued the story-circle method, drawing from their own experiences surrounding racism, identity, and classism to create a piece honoring the story of Eric Garner and Staten Island. The final performance was held in the Staten Island Arts Cultural Lounge in the St. George Ferry Terminal. The group hosted three sold-out performances and earned widespread applause for successfully, thoughtfully, and respectfully sharing the untold stories of the island.

Through the SoPR, Sarah Friedland, a Wagner College film professor, worked with several students in creating a documentary about the production at the ferry terminal, which had been named *Every Time You See Me (ETYSM)*. She advised adjunct professor Jay Weichun and two students who assisted with filming rehearsals and performances and conducting interviews of cast members. Throughout the fall semester Friedland continued her oversight of the film's editing process and integrated the work into several courses. Friedland said: ETYSM was a unique experience where the greater community of Staten Island, including residents, students, and academics, came together to make space for conversations that are generally ignored in our society. Thoughtful dialogue around race, class, sexuality, gender, and police brutality led to a compelling collaborative process and artistic expression. For students of film production it was invaluable to be part of this project because it was an opportunity to represent filmically a diversity of voices and experiences that are not often depicted in mainstream media.

CONCLUSION

Both *Mariposas Amarillas* and the SoPR projects started out as creative/education-based endeavors to link communities with Wagner students. Initially, we wanted these groups to engage with each other in order to have mutually enjoyable learning and to break down the barriers of perceived cultural differences. Activities between groups occurred in and around Wagner's learning communities, which are classes that are part of Wagner's curriculum. During the three years of work, it became clear that much more was happening and that further work could be done in order to deepen the relationships between parties. Additionally, it became clear that it would be possible to integrate more formal, outcome-based programs to benefit both the community and the college. There was a great deal of positive anecdotal feedback from the teachers, administrators, and non-Wagner community members; there was palpable buzz about these programs on Wagner's campus. We suspected that these programs had resulted in real climate change on campus. The goal became the creation of more deeply embedded programs within the college. In order to design such programs moving forward and to determine how to structure such programs, a formal assessment was conducted to determine how to go about designing for the future.

The goal of the assessment was to determine the impact public art projects had on the campus and how participants view public art as a tool for social change/impact. A survey was conducted to ask if the campus community (staff, faculty, students, and community members) was more culturally aware and sensitive to issues of diversity as a result of the public art initiatives led by the PRP. The survey also sought to investigate whether the campus was more committed to increasing the number of socially conscious public art projects. Ultimately 68 percent of the survey respondents were Wagner College students, 16 percent were community members, and 16 percent were faculty or staff at Wagner. At the beginning of both public arts projects, 58 percent of participants believed that public art would positively impact communities; at the conclusion of the project 78 percent of participants believed that public art had positively impacted the Wagner and Port Richmond community. Further, 80 percent of participants expressed a desire to see more public art on campus, while 74 percent of participants indicated they felt more aware of diversity and social issues affecting the local community. There was a great deal of positive feedback during subsequent interviews with members of the community. We are very pleased to have effected such positive change in the campus climate, and look forward to continuing both projects with greater integrity, community involvement, and campus engagement.

The Wagner students have learned that Port Richmond inhabitants have very different backgrounds than they have. During an evening workshop at the college, they learned about the history of the area, the European colonization, importation of religions, the economic boom of the early twentieth century, the economic decline of the late twentieth century, and the influx of Latino and African immigrants in the last two decades. Knowing the recent history of the area, Wagner students were looking forward to helping to bring prosperity and improved community health to the area. They all had concerns, however, about the differences they might encounter. What they learned was that through the creative process of making art and theater, the differences they encountered were in fact a huge asset to a community needing to build pride and economic success.

Additionally, the engagement that the two media (art and theater) provided gave the Wagner community an entry point through which to immerse themselves. Two examples serve to illustrate this point. First, it was important for students and community members to discuss ideas about movements of and diversity in the population. Learning about new places, the history of one's family, even things like new cuisines and fashion, were not everyday conversations for young people. But through the *Mariposas* project, specifically though the creation of drawings and the repeated iconography of the butterfly, conversations around these themes naturally occurred as a result of group participation. The Wagner students learned about the assets inherent in the Port Richmond community, and they were able to then talk about them and enforce them with the school children. The Wagner students were overwhelmed by the openness and affection the Port Richmond students showed toward them. The Wagner students were shy and hesitant when first encountering the school children, but many reported feelings of increased self-worth and amazement at how engaged the school children became over the course of the project, and Wagner students were surprised at how much difference they thought they could make in the community. The students learned that by embracing a visual arts symbol as a theme, it was easier for them to find ways to bond with the children; students frequently remarked that the experience helped them to further understand themselves and each other, and that they were closer as a community. Responses such as the following were common in the survey results: "I learned that taking part in public art projects can connect people and make them feel more accepted within a community."

Second, with the SoPR project, Wagner College participants (students, faculty, and staff) developed a deeper sense of empathy for concerns that had ravaged the Port Richmond community for the past decade. They learned about the emotions and misunderstandings that had caused a rift in the community; by re-living and being physically present in the theater production, they could more intimately understand the community's experiences. Ultimately, it became clear through the productions that the diversity in the Port Richmond community, although it created points of conflict, also created experiences that brought the diverse groups together and made for a tighter community. And the Wagner participants understood this process through their own participation, as illustrated by comments such as the following: "I learned to also be more aware of how other cultures adapt and forms bonds based on their experiences," and "Participants can be challenged to embody or act as the 'other.' And since all are acting, as opposed to conversing about their positions or revealing their opinions on issues, people are sitting with the position and experience of the 'other,' longer and in a more powerful way."

Both projects helped Wagner students to think more concretely and creatively about their future professional directions. While working with the Port Richmond community, some students found themselves naturally acclimating to educational roles and forming bonds with children. Those students remarked that they are now thinking about pursuing education or guidance professions. Other students emerged as leaders of their own peer groups; some of these individuals then spoke about possibly pursuing careers in education or business management or administration. Other students saw and engaged with the organizational components of projects, designed the visual art packages, or developed the museum tours. These students remarked that they had discovered the behind-the-scenes activities essential to running museums or galleries and were thinking about pursuing museum careers.

Ultimately, students who took part in these two projects came away with a deeper awareness of the world around them. By looking, acting, and creating with others using stories beyond their own, they realized that the end product was not only a tangible object, but also the acquisition of *two* new identities: (1) knowing themselves better as more socially conscious citizens, and (2) knowing they have an important place in a community they never realized could be called their own.

NOTES

1. The National Task Force on Civic Learning and Democratic Engagement, *A Crucible Moment: College Learning and Democracy's Future* (Washington DC: Association of American Colleges and Universities, 2012).
2. Sarah Donovan, Lily McNair, and Samantha Siegel, "Work That Matters: Preparing Future Leaders from Vulnerable Communities," forthcoming.

3. William M. Sullivan, *The Power of Integrated Learning* (Stylus Publishing, 2016).
4. Rita Axelrod Hodges and Steve Dubb, *The Road Half Traveled: University Engagement at a Crossroads* (East Lansing, MI: Michigan State University Press, 2012). Anchor institutions can provide urban communities with a multitude of necessities and amenities that make life attractive and engaging, often serving as "engines of urban renaissance." Eugénie L. Birch et al., *Arts and Culture Institutions as Urban Anchors; Livingston Case Studies in Urban Development* (Philadelphia, PA: Penn Institute for Urban Research University of Pennsylvania, 2014). Eduardo J. Padrón, "Miami Dade College and the Engaging Power of the Arts," *Journal of Higher Education Outreach and Engagement* 17, no. 3 (January 1, 2013): 69–84.
5. Steve Dubb and Ted Howard, *Linking Colleges to Communities: Engaging the University for Community Development* (College Park, MD: The Democracy Collaborative at the University of Maryland, 2007).
6. David J. Maurrasse "The Wagner College Port Richmond Partnership" (New York: Marga Incorporated, 2013). At the time of the Marga survey members of the education subcommittee identified the creation of a High School Leadership Academy that supported the growth of students' leadership, emotional, and scholastic improvement as the ultimate goal. Presently, the Port Richmond Partnership Leadership Academy is perhaps Wagner's best example of true civic engagement and community impact. To date the program has raised nearly $1.3 million and involves 6 faculty members, 7 Wagner administrators, 9 student interns, an advisory group of 12 community members, 2 Port Richmond High School teachers, 3 Port Richmond High School guidance counselors, major donors, and private foundations. The program is the result of years of collaborations and serves as the example of what is possible when resources are aligned in a mutually beneficial and thoughtful way.
7. Donna J. Cherry and Jon Shefner, "Addressing Barriers to University-Community Collaboration: Organizing by the Experts or Organizing the Experts?" *Journal of Community Practice* 12, no. 3/4 (2004): 219–233.
8. Cynthia Koch, "Making Value Visible: Excellence in Campus-Community Partnerships in the Arts, Humanities, and Design," Imagining America, 2005.
9. Jeannette Kindred and Claudia Petrescu, "Expectations Versus Reality in a University-Community Partnership: A Case Study," *Voluntas: International Journal of Voluntary & Nonprofit Organizations* 26, no. 3 (June 2015): 823–845.
10. The Learning Community Model is composed of three course suites (First-Year, Intermediate, and Senior) and was developed to work specifically in league with Wagner's mission emphasizing scholarship, achievement, leadership, and citizenship anchored in the liberal arts.

11. Other examples of civic engagement include the Bonner Leaders Program, a national college access program that provides students with the financial opportunity, theoretical framework, and field experience to work in their local communities for 300 hours a year (above and beyond anything required by their academic programs) in exchange for a small scholarship. Presently, 58 students have made a four-year commitment to serve as a Wagner Bonner Leader, meaning that each year the Bonner program alone places highly trained students in community organizations for a minimum of 17,400 hours of community work totally funded by the college. Bonner placements are strategic in nature; students are aligned with lead partners of the Port Richmond Partnership, often playing the role of capacity builder in organizations that Wagner Professors are working with as well. In April 2016 Wagner hosted a summit at which leaders of community organizations and Wagner faculty and administrators exchanged ideas on how the partnership was working, and made plans for moving ahead with new projects. The summit participants focused specifically on what the local needs were, and worked to create projects that will assist with them.

12. Michael Birchall, "Socially Engaged Art in the 1990s and Beyond," *Oncurating.org* 25 (2015).

13. Paul DiMaggio and María Patricia Fernández-Kelly, *Art in the Lives of Immigrant Communities in the United States*, The Public Life of the Arts (New Brunswick, N.J.: Rutgers University Press, 2010).

14. Judith Baca, "La Memoria de Nuestra Tierra: Sites of Public Memory," *Foreseeable Futures* 8 (2015).

15. Janet Marstine, *New Museum Theory and Practice: An Introduction* (Malden, Mass.: Blackwell, 2006); Andrew McClellan, *Art and Its Publics: Museum Studies at the Millennium*, New Interventions in Art History (Malden, Mass.: Blackwell, 2003).

16. Carol Argiro, "Teaching With Public Art," *Art Education* 57, no. 4 (July 2004): 25–32. Art as a tool for education has been specifically useful in addressing questions of diversity and community development where such topics have been problematic in other contexts. Maria Lim, Eunjung Chang, and Borim Song, "Three Initiatives for Community-Based Art Education Practices," *Art Education* 66, no. 4 (July 1, 2013): 7–13.

17. Argiro.

18. Deanna Grant-Smith and Tony Matthews, "Cork as Canvas: Exploring Intersections of Citizenship and Collective Memory in the Shandon Big Wash Up Murals," *Community Development Journal* 50, no. 1 (January 2015): 138–152.

19. Katie Carlisle, "Arts Education Partnerships: Informing Policy through the Development of Culture and Creativity within a Collaborative Project Approach," *Arts Education Policy Review* 112, no. 3 (June 2011): 144–148.

20. Sharon Verner Chappell and Drew Chappell, "Building Social Inclusion through Critical Arts-Based Pedagogies in University Classroom Communities," *International Journal of Inclusive Education* 20, no. 3 (March 2016): 292–308.

21. Theodore M. Dillaway, "Co-Operation of the Public School System with the Pennsylvania Museum of Art, *"Bulletin of the Pennsylvania Museum* 27, no. 143 (1931): 15–20.

22. Amanda Gluibizzi, "'Artist as Activist': Promoting Collections, Outreach and Community Learning," *Art Libraries Journal* 34, no. 2 (April 2009): 31–34.

23. Carlisle, "Arts Education Partnerships."

24. Sheng Kuan Chung and Christy Ortiz, "Art Education in Action on the Street," *Art Education* 64, no. 3 (May 1, 2011): 46–52.

25. Sharon Shaffer, "Opening the Doors: Engaging Young Children in the Art Museum," *Art Education* 64, no. 6 (November 2011): 40–46.

26. Cynthia Nikitin, "Making Public Art Work," *Sculpture* 19, no. 3 (2000).

27. Chung and Ortiz, "Art Education in Action."

28. David M. Donahue, "Connecting Classrooms and Communities through Chicano Mural Art," *Multicultural Perspectives* 13, no. 2 (January 1, 2011): 70–78.

29. Brian C. Charest et al., "Turning Schools Inside Out: Connecting Schools and Communities through Public Arts and Literacies," *Journal of Language and Literacy Education* 10, no. 1 (March 1, 2014): 188–203.

30. Birchall, "Socially Engaged Art."

31. Holly Giffin, "When A School Becomes A Theatre Company: Plays At the Gold Hill School," *Stage Of The Art* 7 (1995).

CHAPTER 15

Conclusions

Nancy H. Hensel

Despite the wide variety of topics ranging from architecture to gospel music discussed in this collection of chapters, a common theme emerges. The authors believe that experiencing the arts is critical for the development of insight into the human condition, an expanded worldview, and knowledge that contributes to success in careers and life.

A 2013 report from the American Academy of Arts and Sciences, *The Heart of the Matter*, stated:

> As we strive to create a more civil public discourse, a more adaptable and creative workforce, and a more secure nation, the humanities and social sciences are the heart of the matter, the keeper of the republic—a source of national memory and civic vigor, cultural understanding and communication, individual fulfillment and the ideals we hold in common.[1]

Several Members of Congress requested the academy's report "to advance a dialogue on the importance of the humanities and social sciences to the future of our nation."[2] In this report the humanities are defined as including the arts. The key points of the report are that these disciplines:

N. H. Hensel (✉)
New American Colleges and Universities, Laguna Woods, CA, USA

© The Author(s) 2018
N. H. Hensel (ed.), *Exploring, Experiencing, and Envisioning Integration in US Arts Education*, The Arts in Higher Education,
https://doi.org/10.1007/978-3-319-71051-8_15

- educate Americans in the knowledge, skills, and understanding they will need to thrive in a twenty-first-century democracy;
- foster a society that is innovative, competitive, and strong;
- equip the nation for leadership in an interconnected world.[3]

The goal of the chapters included in this volume is to help advance a dialogue about the importance of the arts and liberal arts for our country. We believe that the inclusion of the arts in a student's undergraduate program, regardless of major, can better prepare a student for success in the student's chosen career and life. We also believe that the arts are critical to the creation of a compassionate, just, and equitable society. The chapters examined the role and impact of the liberal arts and arts in education through three dimensions: interdisciplinarity, development of professional skills, and arts in the community. These three dimensions are closely related to the key points articulated in *The Heart of the Matter.*

INTERDISCIPLINARITY

Jane Chu, Chairman of the National Endowment for the Arts, says that the arts "can illuminate possibilities in entirely different fields."[4] Certainly the complexity of the social, economic, and cultural problems confronting contemporary society could benefit from the illumination of possibilities from many disciplines. Nearly every chapter in this book includes interdisciplinarity as an important component of undergraduate education. Interdisciplinary courses help students to make connections and increase their understanding of the content. Montana State University, for example, has chosen to incorporate interdisciplinary courses into its general education requirements as a way to encourage creativity and innovation. Montana State based its program on a commonly held belief that the juxtaposition of two or more disciplines, such as music and architecture or music and economics, deepens the appreciation of both disciplines while also encouraging new ways of thinking about each discipline. Designing a building in response to a musical composition or composing a symphony after viewing an architectural masterpiece can stimulate the creative thinking of the musician and the architect. Even the design of a building that is energy efficient and strong enough to withstand a devastating tornado benefited from the perspectives of many disciplines beyond architecture, including art, business, communications, and nursing. Illustrating the benefits of cross-disciplinary work, a Drury University nursing student asked an architecture student about the livability of the proposed building, challenging the architect to think more deeply about who would live in the home. At the same time, the interchange of ideas increased the nursing student's understanding of workflow in a building, knowledge that may be useful in her future career. Theater and law faculty at the University of La Verne explored how the intersection of theater and law improves the courtroom presentations of trial lawyers and enhances the understanding of actors and directors of real-life experiences that are portrayed on the stage.

Steven Pane asks how the musical practices of interpretation and performance can inform the practices of reading and writing. As he follows a student learning to play a challenging Chopin piece, we see how the student is able to increase her understanding of both the music and a piece of literature she is studying by connecting the ways in which ideas are shaped through sound and word. By applying the methodology of one discipline to another, the learning process has deepened for the student, and she comes to a greater appreciation of the music and literature.

Valparaiso University developed a minor in cinema and media studies that combines the study of criticism and production, since faculty believe that knowledge of both better prepares the student for a profession in either aspect of the film industry. Mary Rist and Sasha West believe that professional writers benefit from taking a course in creative writing. The creative-writing course helps students to develop empathy for their subject, to feel more comfortable in taking risks with their writing, and to understand the emotional impact of their words by seeing themselves as storytellers.

When students have the opportunity to learn about major ideas, methodologies, and practice through interdisciplinary courses, they can develop a deeper understanding of their own discipline and will have a wider repertoire of strategies to use in their professional work.

Developing Professional Skills

In addition to expanding a student's way of thinking, the arts also develop more specific professional skills. The collection of chapters expands on the skills identified by employers in the Peter D. Hart survey.[5] Jennifer Blackmer, for example, looks at the relationship between the entrepreneurial mindset and the arts. Entrepreneurs are open to new opportunities, are flexible and adaptable, can think both critically and creatively, and are negotiators. Artists also need to see opportunities. The creation of a play, a poem, or a painting requires the artist to be flexible and adaptable as she or he encounters the inevitable obstacles of any creative endeavor. While artists think creatively, they also need to be able to look at their work critically. Sometimes the critical approach also necessitates negotiation in order to solve the creative problem. These are skills that are useful in any profession. Ilene D. Lieberman and Mara Parker look specifically at how developing skills through the arts contributes to education in the medical profession and could contribute to many additional professions. Artists and medical personnel need to understand human nature, find new ways of thinking about the unknown, and be comfortable with cultures other than their own. They also need to be comfortable with ambiguity and uncertainty. The arts develop these skills and the additional skills of listening or observing closely. The doctor needs to listen closely to her patients and be a careful observer of not only symptoms but also patient behavior. The ability to look closely or observe carefully, what Amy Herman calls visual intelligence, is an ability that is useful not only for doctors but also for policemen, social workers, teachers, and for many other professionals.[6] By paying close attention, one might ask questions about why a person behaves in a certain way, what a person may be feeling that can lead to a more sensitive and compassionate interaction with a patient or client. An understanding of and sensitivity to the human condition is perhaps the most important skill for professions that involve working with people and is a skill that can be effectively developed through the arts.

DEVELOPING COMMUNITY

The arts, as an expression of our culture and humanity, bring people together through shared experiences. Linda Ferguson discusses how music encourages us to listen closely and think beyond ourselves. She describes two particularly powerful compositions that responded to national events, the AIDS crisis and 9/11, that provided a way for people to share their grief with one another. Music, she suggests, can serve as a bridge between the various parts of our being—the spiritual and material, the active and reflective, the cultivated and vernacular, and self and the other. Adriane Thompson-Bradshaw and Margaret Cullen describe how gospel music served as a unifying element for the small group of black students on the predominately white Ohio Northern University campus. The gospel choir also became a cultural bridge when white students asked to join the choir. Bringing together black and white students led to complex discussions about ethnic identity that eventually contributed to an understanding that people from different backgrounds can have similar feelings about shared experiences. The arts also brought together Wagner College students and the largely working-class residents of Port Richmond to address cultural barriers and develop mutual understanding.

Jim Leach, former Member of Congress and former Chairman of the National Endowment for the Humanities, said that the arts and liberal arts are essential for citizenship.[7] He suggests that we need to understand our own communities, other cultures, and the creative process and that this is best done through studying the arts and liberal arts. The arts in particular stimulate the imagination and encourage people to think outside of the box, an ability that is needed for changes in our society and innovation in our economy. He further states, "The most meaningful discovery in a liberal arts education is that everything is related to everything else. Wisdom involves the tying together of threads of learning. The challenge is to discover and then correlate discoveries, the most important of which relate to perspective: values, methods of thinking and doing rather than facts."[8]

The essays included in this text support the idea that the arts help to develop creativity and innovation, a transformative worldview, insight into social problems and the human condition, and allow us to engage in the difficult dialogues of our time. When the National Endowment of the Arts and Humanities was created in 1965, the founding legislation stated:

- An advanced civilization must not limit its efforts to science and technology alone, but must give full value and support to the great branches of scholarly and cultural activity in order to achieve a better understanding of the past, a better analysis of the present and a better view of the future.
- Democracy demands wisdom and vision in its citizens. It must therefore foster and support a form of education, and access to the arts and the humanities, designed to make people of all backgrounds and wherever located masters of their technology and not its unthinking servants.
- The world leadership which has come to the United States cannot rest solely upon superior power, wealth, and technology, but must be solidly founded upon worldwide respect and admiration for the Nation's high qualities as a leader in the realm of ideas and of the spirit.

- Americans should receive in school, background and preparation in the arts and humanities to enable them to recognize and appreciate the aesthetic dimensions of our lives; the diversity of excellence that comprises our cultural heritage, and artistic and scholarly expression.
- It is vital to democracy to honor and preserve its multicultural artistic heritage as well as support new ideas, and therefore it is essential to provide financial assistance to its artists and the organizations that support their work.[9]

National, state, and education leaders who periodically call for public defunding or elimination of arts programs should be reminded of the benefits of arts and humanities programs so clearly articulated in the founding legislation for the National Endowment for the Humanities and National Endowment for the Arts.

Jim Leach called the humanities a national asset.[10] We believe that the arts and our liberal arts approach to undergraduate education are also national assets that contribute to our economy, democracy, and the continuing advancement of knowledge.

NOTES

1. American Academy of Arts and Sciences. *The Heart of the Matter,* (Cambridge, MA: American Academy of Arts and Sciences, 2013), 9.
2. Ibid.
3. Ibid.
4. Jane Chu, "The Beauty of the Ordinary," National Endowment for the Arts, accessed February 27, 2016.
5. Peter D. Hart, *How Should Colleges Prepare Students to Succeed in Today's Global Economy,* (Washington, D. C.: Peter D. Hart Research Associates, 2007).
6. Amy E. Herman, *Visual Intelligence: Sharpen Your Perception, Change Your Life,* (New York: Houghton Mifflin Harcourt), 2016.
7. Jim Leach, "Defending the Liberal Arts," speech at the American Council of Learned Societies, Washington, D.C., May 6, 2011.
8. Ibid., p. 3.
9. National Endowment of the Humanities, National Foundation on the Arts and the Humanities Act of 1965 (P.L. 89–209), accessed February 14, 2017, https://www.neh.gov/.../national-foundation-arts-and-humanities-act-1965-pl-89-209.
10. Leach, "Defending the Liberal Arts."

Index[1]

[1] Note: Page numbers followed by "n" refers to note

© The Author(s) 2018
N. H. Hensel (ed.), *Exploring, Experiencing, and Envisioning Integration in US Arts Education*, The Arts in Higher Education, https://doi.org/10.1007/978-3-319-71051-8

229